Voices of Aotearoa

'… Murray Gray, who has manned the ramparts of Going West for 20 years. His continued devotion to this festival has enriched and delighted thousands of readers and offered support and nourishment to hundreds of writers. To you Murray, with gratitude.'

Stephanie Johnson, 'Holding the Line', 2015

Voices of Aotearoa
25 years of Going West Oratory

Contents

PREFACE — **Robyn Mason** 07
INTRODUCTION — **Naomi McCleary** 10

1996	BERNARD MAKOARE, NGAHUIA TE AWEKOTUKU, ROBERT SULLIVAN Breathing Words 16	
1997	MAURICE SHADBOLT Getting a Word In 32	
1998	IAN WEDDE The Nation's Narratives 40	
1999	VINCENT O'SULLIVAN Fit to Print 58	
2000	DAME FIONA KIDMAN Friends and Lovers 72	
2001	MICHAEL KING Never Lost for Words 86	
2002	DAME MARILYN WARING Tracking the Vernacular 104	
2003	GEOFF PARK Wild New Zealand — Voices from the Landscape 118	
2004	DAME CHRISTINE COLE CATLEY Between the Lines: A tribute to Michael King 144	
2005	NIGEL COX Word of Mouth 156	
2006	PATRICIA GRACE The Truth about Stories 170	
2007	TONY SIMPSON Food for Thought 184	
2008	CHRIS PRICE Trouble with the Truth 202	
2009	TE RADAR By Buy Bye the Book 220	
2010	DAME ANNE SALMOND Right Word, Right Place, Right Time 236	
2011	ALLEN CURNOW Landfall in Unknown Seas 252	
2012	PETER WELLS Almost Always: Never Quite 258	
2013	CHARLOTTE GRIMSHAW In Conversation On Conversation 272	
2014	ROBERT SULLIVAN 'small islands of meaning' 288	
2015	STEPHANIE JOHNSON Holding the Line 302	

2016   MAUALAIVAO ALBERT WENDT **Writing from the Edge**   316

2017   ROD ORAM   **Between Here and There**   326

2018   PAULA MORRIS   **Spread the Word**   338

2019   ELIZABETH KNOX   **Cutting Through**   352

POSTSCRIPT — **James Littlewood**   368

THE SPEAKERS   371

SELECTED NOTES   378

ACKNOWLEDGEMENTS   382

PHOTOGRAPH CREDITS   383

Preface

These words from the first Going West Literary Festival programme in 1996 heralded the launch of a new event in the Auckland literary calendar:

> From the beginnings of time there has been sound in the forests of Tiriwa—the Waitakere Ranges. Inspired by the wonderment of nature, people began to spin their tales. Going West pays homage to those beginnings, and through the creative mind of the artist, we are shown a new future.

Going West was Auckland's first major literary festival, and it is the country's longest running. It also inspired two early festival stalwarts (with Going West's blessing and support) to found the internationally focused Auckland Readers and Writers Festival.

Going West continues its kaupapa of holding our writing and reading whānau close, of honouring our tangata and whenua, and hosting the festival at our place — West Auckland, the Waitakare Ranges, home to the creative spirit: to writers, musicians, architects, poets and potters.

Every year there is a festival theme that is addressed — directly, obliquely, or contrarily — by the keynote speaker and each appears here along with the year and the orator's name. The 1996 inaugural Going West address, by Bernard Makoare, Ngahuia te Awekotuku, and Robert Sullivan, was a celebration of taonga pūoro, and mōteatea, Māori prose and chant poems, and their influence on contemporary Māori writers as expressed through Robert and Ngahuia's poetry.

Our keynote orators read snippets from their own writing, and full poems and extracts by others: Charles Brasch, Arapera Blank, Sir Āpirana Ngata, James K. Baxter, Alistair Te Ariki Campbell and West Aucklander A.R.D. Fairburn all make an appearance in this anthology. In 2015 an unexpected poet gate-crashed the stage.

West Auckland summer resident Allen Curnow spoke at the festival as a poet, never as the keynote speaker, but keynote speakers quote him with abandon. The 2011 festival theme was the title of his classic work 'Landfall in Unknown Seas', and we have included it here in full.

All bar one of the edited addresses have been created in house by Going West — they are based on audio recordings made on the night. Our transcription typist, a Kiwi exiled in Australia, worked during lockdown to put voice into print. Then began the hard mahi of editing the transcripts, researching proper names, and checking quotes against sources — in most cases without accompanying author notes.

Our orators are entertaining, witty and interesting. Some display sweeping eclecticism, for example Geoff Park in 2003 on the theme 'Wild New Zealand', who based his address on his ground-breaking work, *Ngā Uruora: the groves of life: ecology and history in a New Zealand landscape*. This was the address most challenging to edit.

Sadly, Geoff Park died in 2009, but we felt his presence as we chased his quoted sources. This took us on a journey, in one instance as far as the University of Wisconsin, Madison to find the elusive 1807 poem 'The Mire Nymph' by Sir Joseph Banks. It had been quietly slipped into a work in the 1980s and had never surfaced again until Geoff retrieved it from obscurity. It was difficult to source as it had appeared under the pseudonymous authorship of Martin Mudlark Tide Waiter. As Geoff says, 'we have known and blamed and honoured [Banks] for many things, but not literature.' Ironically, given that Banks had promoted and made a fortune from the drainage of the ancient peat lands of his childhood, he sounds in this poem like a modern conservationist. Perhaps the man who reported that Aotearoa had 'swamps that might easily be drained' — think dairy farms where once were wetlands — was having second thoughts.

There is much to explore in *Voices of Aotearoa*: identity, (Dame Marilyn Waring, Robert Sullivan, Maualaivao Albert Wendt); the power of storytelling (Maurice Shadbolt, Patricia Grace); living a writer's life (Dame Fiona Kidman); why and how our writers write, (Dame Anne Salmond, Paula Morris); how we see the world and how others see us (Nigel Cox). There is humour, there is outrage, there are secrets revealed. Some of the oratory was prescient of global developments (Chris Price, Charlotte Grimshaw), and Rod Oram's 2017 address was described by *Metro* magazine as 'the opening night of the year'.

Stephanie Johnson in her 2015 oration 'Holding the Line' said, 'Going West is not just a book festival, it's a commons: a place where people can come together to encounter new ideas and ways of thinking; a place where revolutions, big and small can be fomented.'

Welcome to our commons.

Robyn Mason
Titirangi, April 2021

Murray Gray and Naomi McCleary

Introduction

It is a love story; well maybe more than one. It starts in the 1990s with a bookseller in an iconic Parnell bookshop. He harbours a life-long love affair with the writing and writers of Aotearoa, past and present, and has long dreamed of taking a steam train of book lovers from Auckland Central to Helensville and back with Maurice Gee on board to read, on Henderson Station, his classic description of the train ride from his novel *Going West*. It's a whim at this stage. Enter two more players: one (Sir) Bob Harvey, the newly minted mayor of Waitākere City, who is always up for a great idea; then the also freshly appointed arts coordinator for the city. Two conversations and the possibility of Going West is birthed.

1996 and the Going West Literary Festival roars into life, its first words in te reo; a day of literary conversations in an old warehouse at the Corban Estate and a train trip to Helensville with very eclectic word-based entertainment, lubricated with Westie wine and food. A steep learning curve — but right then two key components are born; generous hospitality and a programming style that is intelligent and quirky — indeed often unpredictable. In these early years programming is shared between Associate Professor Peter Simpson from the University of

Auckland and the aforementioned bookseller, Murray Gray. Murray continues for 20 years. When asked about his programming philosophy, he always replies, 'I programme what I love,' — end of story.

The reading public fell in love with Going West, now domiciled in Titirangi. They warmed to the relaxed and intimate atmosphere and the mix of established writers and emerging talent; the back-to-back programming that allowed one to stay for the weekend and be constantly surprised.

The writers loved it because they were the stars, not the support acts. They were welcomed with a pōwhiri and nurtured for the entire weekend; able to spend time with both their readers and fellow writers.

The steam train continued for nine years until double-tracking, weekend services and exorbitant costs killed it off. It is a story in its own right: a mad caper of food, wine and extraordinary moments of performance magic in heritage stop-offs. Think Glenn

Going West Books and Writers Festival, 1999. Beneath Michael King's umbrella stand Allen Curnow and Roma Potiki. Beside Allen Curnow is Elizabeth Knox and to her far left, Hone Tuwhare, with Vincent O'Sullivan behind (arms folded) and next to Bill Manhire. On the far right are Marilyn Duckworth and Maurice Shadbolt. Photograph by Marti Friedlander

Colquhoun and Serie Barford reading love poems to each other balanced on a luggage trolley on the Helensville Station platform. Think Little Chapel of Faith in the Oaks, and three Dalmatian babas breaking our hearts with songs of love and loss, while C.K. Stead reads from *Talking About O'Dwyer*. The chapel is tiny but the acoustics miraculous. And yes, think Maurice Gee standing on a box on the old Henderson Station. Tears were shed.

In 2006 the Going West Trust was formed to protect the festival in the event of political change or instability; a prescient decision if ever there was one given that the amalgamation of Auckland into a 'supercity' was not yet part of the conversation. Post-2010 the role that Waitākere Council had taken in funding and delivering Going West was now taken on by the Waitākere Ranges Local Board. Their engagement has been pivotal to the ongoing survival of the festival, as has been The Trusts Community Foundation. Westie pride and passion in play. That fierce localism has drawn a regional audience and national acknowledgement as evidenced by ongoing support from Creative New Zealand and Foundation North.

From 1997 Going West was a full weekend literary event and the ritual of inviting a notable writer to give a keynote address based on the festival theme was born. This collection, based on 24 years of fascinating and considered writings, holds a treasury of some of the most important voices in Aotearoa. Many of them are now not with us.

Everyone will have their favourites and to bring them together in this way tracks the ebb and flow of our culture in this past quarter century. My recall, unreliable as memories ever are, comes as snatched fragments when the extraordinary occurred. 1998: Ian Wedde delivers *The Nation's Narratives* and we stand transfixed by the weight and beauty of his words. Michael King is up there. He was a regular presenter and facilitator from the early years and was invited to give the keynote address in 2001. Four days before opening night 9/11 rocked the world and we were all paralysed with shock and horror. An email to Michael asking whether we should simply cancel the whole affair was met with a short but loving reply: 'Despite this devastating day, the show must go on — and culture and laughter and poetry and music are all the best forms of healing. I know it will still be a fabulous weekend.' In those four days he completely rewrote his address; a family memoir of forgiveness and reconciliation. The hall was packed. White-faced, we clung to each other. Other names float in a kaleidoscope of moments; the regal dignity of Albert Wendt, the astounding theatricality of Rod Oram, the Dames, Fiona Kidman and Anne Salmond, radiating power and wisdom, Stephanie Johnson camping it up, Peter Wells, Nigel Cox, both brilliant voices now stilled.

2014 and the keynote address was renamed The Sir Graeme Douglas Orator to honour the festival's most generous private benefactor. Sir Graeme loved Waitākere City and saw Going West as a marker of its innovation, creativity and generosity. Over our regular morning teas in the boardroom we talked books and business and laughed, as the years passed, at the vicissitudes of aging. A dear friend now sorely missed.

Here's another love story. In 1996 we were introduced to Davyd Hodge. 'He's a good sound man,' we were told and we booked him to simply amplify the voices from the stage. At the end of that first day he said, quite casually, 'I've recorded it all on broadcast quality tape.' In the mad rush of creating that first festival we barely registered it! Davyd is in love with recorded perfection. Year after year, first on tape, then CDs, now digital, he edited and cleaned and delivered Going West — literally every word of it. His work was partnered by one of Aotearoa's living treasures, Gil Hanly, who likewise became a fixture at every festival, her familiar face and her ever-ready camera recording each speaker in action. Occasionally Marti Friedlander would breeze in and boss writers into unforgettable line-ups. In later years Gil was supported by local photographer Liz March. Eventually this growing archive found a home and protection at Waitākere Central Library in Henderson. Although always available to interested and determined punters, there has been for years a dream to make it accessible to a wider audience. Strangely, Covid-19 has made it possible. There's not much good to come out of this pandemic, but forcing us to abandon any version of a live event in 2020 and tuning us to the online world has been a blessing. There sat 24 years of intelligent, warm, funny, sad, controversial voices, ripe for podcasting to the world. Put that with the generosity of Creative New Zealand and the Going West Podcast Platform was born.

The pandemic also created breathing room for this book to be born. It is fitting that this is a Westie affair, the fruit of a partnership between the Going West Trust and Oratia Media. Growing book sales and the burgeoning of independent bookshops gives us a sense of certainty. A book in the hand, and a beautiful one to boot, is an object to love.

The future stretches out fraught with excitement and anxiety. We have learned to dance with uncertainty; we have built a new and younger team of creatives who have stylishly crafted the ongoing podcast programme and are now turning their talents to commissioning new work. Live festivals will return over time but will tangle with new realities and unimaginable possibilities.

And yes, there was, and is, a love story.

Naomi McCleary

1996 BERNARD MAKOARE, NGAHUIA TE AWEKOTUKU, ROBERT SULLIVAN

Breathing Words

BERNARD MAKOARE

I would like you to do something for me before I begin. I would like you to try and get the sounds of the piano and the guitar, the radio even, the sounds of the automobile, the car, the motorbike, the chainsaw, the motor mowers that start up regularly on Saturday mornings in West Auckland — try and get those sounds out of your head. And I'm going to introduce you to the words of my ancestors. Some of these words are words of the environment; some of them are words and voices of animals, of birds; some of them are voices that we can feel and not hear. And that's the reason I'm not going to be speaking very much. I'm not even going to bother explaining to you the voices that you're going to hear. I'm going to leave that to your imagination. I'm going to leave it to your creativity as writers yourselves, and as people who enjoy creativity; I'm going to leave it up to your creativity to determine what you're about to hear. Morena tēnā koutou.

[This introduction was followed by a performance with taonga pūoro and karakia]

NGAHUIA TE AWEKOTUKU

E te tangata pū kōrero, tēnā koe. E mihi aroha ki a koe mō ēnei taonga tuku iho. Mō ēnei reo whakahirahira o rātou ko whetūrangitia. He taonga, he taonga. He taonga tuku iho. Nō reira, e te tangata, tēnā koe te tohunga. He mea tino whakamīharo tēnei mō mātou nei. He mihi whakawhetai, he mihi aroha ki a koe, tēnā koe. Taku tungāne, kia ora. Ki a koutou rā, tēnā nō koutou. Kia ora Adrian [Birkbeck] for your greetings this morning.

I'm finding it quite difficult to actually rise and perform after so moving and intense, and glorious a moment from Makoare. Bernard, tēnā koe. It takes us right back, certainly many generations, and indeed, in this area, many centuries to those first voices that echoed around these hills, that ventured from one coast to the other, that explored the harbours of this region. Voices that for some decades were lost, but that are now being heard again. The origins of Māori literature, I believe, are as much in our words as they are in our music, and both, to me, are inseparable. We will weave together for you a demonstration of that.

After the whaikōrero that my brother here presented to you this morning, you heard the chant I performed. Taku Rākau is a plaintive waiata tangi, or lamentation, composed almost 200 years ago by a Tūhoe woman whose name was Mihikitekapua. And those of you familiar with the writings and the research of Āpirana Ngata will have noticed that in the collections of mōteatea, or ancient Māori prose poems and chant poems — which Āpirana Ngata compiled and which were revised by Pei Te Hurinui Jones — most of the authors were, interestingly, and I think significantly, women. This is one aspect of ancient Māori performance art that is often not realised. Related to that too is the spontaneous and usually improvised — certainly in the rural communities and where Māori remains the mother tongue — karanga, or what I think has been mistranslated as the 'welcoming call', also performed by women. And I believe that in many ways the karanga itself is the genesis of much of our ancient literary tradition, which comes inevitably from spontaneity, from improvisation.

Going from there we come to the twentieth century, and of course the nineteenth and its many ugly realities and the loss or — I suppose that's far too strong a negative a word — the threat of the loss of te reo Māori. And of course, without a Māori language we cannot have in its truest form a Māori literature.

That is how I see the situation, although ironically almost all my published work has been in English. Today I will be sharing with you some of my works in English. Nevertheless, with Māori now being an official language and the ascension and comparative success of Te Taura Whiri i te Reo Māori, The Māori Language Commission, and of course the development and triumph of the Kōhanga Reo movement and the Kura Kaupapa Māori, or Māori language schools movement, we are seeing *again* the writing, the emergence, the development of a literature in the Māori language.

Nevertheless, I'm here today to read a few things to you in English, and I suppose to also posit a few further ideas: that much of our contemporary writing is social commentary, just as much of our contemporary art is social commentary and a response to the colonial process, which is ongoing. I was intrigued — for those of you who know Ralph Hotere's work — that when Makoare performed with the second pūrerehua, with the second bullroarer, the chant which he spoke is actually the text that Hotere uses a lot in many of his canvases. So there you have a rather exciting blending of a number of different Māori creative realities, which I think in many ways reflects the nature of our world.

Anyway, rather than go on, I'll read you something short. This is from a book published last year in response to the Mururoa, or Moruroa, atomic tests, *Below the Surface: words and images in protest at French testing on Moruroa*, edited by Ambury Hall and published by Random House. This actually happened. This is in many ways a social commentary and a sad story, and a true one:

Purotu
Her face, her large body there, in the Bureau de
Change, in the next queue.
Her face, glowing soft gold across well contoured
bone, enhanced by lips broad
and full. Beneath a straight yet modest nose.
Skewered upon her crown, blue black hair formed a
knot, drawn tight from her high unwrinkled forehead.
Her eyes met mine.
She watched me, openly staring.
And in those darkfringed oval depths, I knew.
She looked just like my auntie.
She knew, too. We laughed.
Giggling, weeping, shaking, we lunged for each other.
We lost our places in the queue. We didn't care.
Around us, clattering and flicking about their gallic
business in the Gare du Nord,
not unamused, the queues reformed.
'Est-ce que vous êtes Polynesienne?'
Straight white teeth flashed me a question.
'Ae, he Maori hoki ahau. No Aotearoa — la Nouvelle
Zélande.'
'Maori!' More tears fell. 'Maori!'
The bleak metallic stench lifted away;
the train noise faded.
Excited, we dashed off for a drink.
Purotu. Eleven years in Calais.
Son mari, un marin; her husband, a seaman. They met
in Pape'ete; he honoured her, she sighed. With
marriage. With four daughters and a son. With life in
France. Unlike her eldest sister. Purotu's reason for
being in Paris.
Her eldest sister's baby.

They both came to Paris, the baby, the sister. She was
looking after them. They both came, from Hiva Oa.
Only four days ago
For the baby.
'La leucémie.' (Leukemia)
She sniffed the pungent citrus of her waxed pink cup.
Curved ivory nails plucked at its rim;
She crushed the straw
'La leucémie. Et elle est très petite, la bébé, très petite'
My French was beginning to fail me; I tried Maori
again, reaching out across the plastic, ash-pocked
bench, reaching out across a thousand years of koiwi;
shared bones, common blood, warm as Pacific waters.
Where anger surged. And hopelessness.
He honoured her. With France.

'C'est la bombe, n'est-ce pas? Tera mahi kōhuru, mahi
kino, mahi taurekareka! Purotu, Purotu,
ka tangi au. Mo to mamae, mo to mamae.'
Mo to mamae. For your pain. I weep.

Our fingers touched, hands braided suddenly, together.
'Ae', she sighed. 'La bébé. He mamae, he mamae. Et
mon fils, aussi, et mon fils. Il y a huit ans. Eight years
ago. My son.'

It was then I noticed the skull smiling at me from beneath
her fine. brown skin. Purotu.

Kia ora koutou.

ROBERT SULLIVAN

Ngā mihi nui ki ngā mātanga Māori, tēnā kōrua. E ngā mana, e ngā reo, e hoa mā, tēnā koutou katoa.

Hi, I'm Robert Sullivan. I'd like to echo Ngahuia's comments about the pricelessness of our taonga, and hearing the voices of the past and of course now, the present. I'd also like to comment on Ngahuia's reference to *Ngā Mōteatea* by Sir Āpirana Ngata, Pei Te Hurinui Jones, and latterly Bruce Biggs. First of all acknowledging their work in gathering those poems together, but also acknowledging their influence on our contemporary Māori writers. In fact, I cannot think of a single Māori writer, and I include Alan Duff in this, who has not been influenced in some way by our traditions, our ways of seeing the world.

I'll start by reading a few poems. This poem is for a forthcoming book, it is called 'A Biography':

We held them to catch
this. The glass shelves
are spotlighted to catch
green curves, green layering
and prices – but I only want the singing.

The song is ancient. Flecks in the stones
show they're breeding, which
is important. But turn the lights out
and there is only singing. This
stone is one of the singers:

I watch the top waters
flow – catching the spare light
I lie here waiting
for you to hold me.

I am life and its shape,

shaped to you.
The song filling your heart,
Moving the blood of this stone.

Creatures flow in the space
around the stone, some control
the way they tumble. When
there is light the stone is here.
When there is no light the stone

is here. The presence of the stone
fills us, ribs our hearts as we tumble.
We have been tumbling a long time.
When we land, we land on other stone –
lining prison floors, reinforcing

citadels that launder
clothes and cheques.
But even in the gravel
that makes the grey stone,
there is greenstone.

What else keeps singing the song?
We hear it – yet there is nothing to see.
Our pounamu sings.
Even in the gravel there must be
flecks of pounamu.

We cannot leave, we came from here.
We cannot go back – this is our England.
We bring pounamu up from our rivers.
The greenstones on our chests
are the life of this land.

I try and write social commentary. In the early days when I first began writing I tried to mimic rap because that was the language of the streets back in the 'eighties. So, I'll read one of my street poems to give you an idea of what other things influence writing. Not just Māori writing, because we have our traditions, but new traditions; pop music and being part of an international community. This one's called 'Not the 1990 Poem'. Te Kēmara was a rangatira who voiced very strong objections to the Treaty:

Not the 1990 Poem
A slip of land subject to any peculiarity
the season throws, roughed by tongue and wool,
rock oysters, à la crap, this land's laureate
Is a stirrer, the reason behind old Te Kemara's fear:
'… low, small, a worm, a crawler, me down, the Governor up'.

If the Treaty were a person he or she'd be schizophrenic.
It has so many voices, and more critics! 'Wars in the North,
gumfields, forest's falling … Titewhai, Syd, Deidre — ha!
just like Koro-gate, all that airtime. Mongrel Mob
fights the power, Black power smacks their yellow guts
green, White Power slugs Homes and Philip Sherry, spit drips
from Winston in the wings, they're talking about a revolution
with one missing rocket launcher, no one can separate the lies
from the Blacks and the Whites. If only Electricorp

could pull the plug on all this Networks Blues,
these loaves and circuses. This city is an abuse.
Concrete medians, busty bridges, four-way off-ramps,
triple channel replays of benzine sunsets, A Kenworth
sixty-nines a Bambina, a tribal madman slashes
One Tree's obelisk,
(I wrote this five years ago when I predicted it)
everyone and everything must 'integrate':

look at the Games! the Whitbread fleet! that's entertainment.

Yet the pull of a fist or slitting your wrists
doesn't stack the dishes or fix the issues, does it,
 Catullus? Alright, that's all the hate you need to hear.
Straight up, our land speeds towards calamity.
Live well, people, we're all living in Roman time.

And I'd like to read 'Karakia', which I'll read again at the end with Bernard's accompaniment. 'Karakia for Bruce Stewart':

I touch Papatuanuku my earthmother
        give hands up to Ranginui
my skyfather
        then beat both wings of the heart
skull it down through the pelvis
to a rosewater bowl
filling with stones: chance/angst/loneliness/failure
dip hands in this sprinkle
                heads in clarity pass the speech of people on
blush and touch make love slowly (be careful)

we slide in a round of writhing
weeds that thrash a jive
expressed in a loud way (I'm out of my circle)
persevere beat your heart's wings
                        fly out to greet them

shout 'Hii!' (hee) to the ground
shout 'Haa!' to the sky
through veins people give and take
            fine as those crossing a petal
            floating on a bowl

> health to you brother (we hongi)
>   health to you sister (we kiss)
> splash your paddles
> breathe deeply drink up
> we've got a chant of unbroken
>   tone/s to toast!
> a meeting on respected grounds
> an open sound so pure it shakes the host

And I meant about drinking up, because of course, we're at a great spot for that.

So, kia ora.

NGAHUIA TE AWEKOTUKU

I work as an art historian, and for much of the last three years I've been researching and working with museums in North America, Europe and the British Isles. Currently we are planning a major exhibition of the Māori collections in the British Museum in London. And these poems, these two, are related to my work. It's called 'The Museum's Sequence', but I'll just read two today with Mokoare. Kia ora.

This is called, 'For LMS145, a bone flute at the British Museum':

[Poem is accompanied by Bernard Makoare on taonga pūoro]

> **For LMS 145, a bone flute at the British Museum**
> bone: resting lizard stretched
> along the grain : bone
> that once lamented and rejoiced
> that once sensed the blood's
> currents and rhythm : bone
> that once sang bold songs
> of triumph

that once lifted a warrior's arm
now
you are mute : bone
your silent eloquence
your dozing reptile
tell me more
than a million melodies
rising
above the water in the
fierce fluid moving night
bone : moe mai rā,
moe mai, moe mai.

Kia ora koutou. The next one is 'For one trophy from the Waikato war, now in an unnamed museum':

such a face; yours a
moulded perfection of
tilting eyes, nostrils fine and chiselled
lips; I wonder, I wonder
what did your sightless gaze
witness
that morning that day that night
when you were torn down because
your beauty, your magic
were recognised and claimed as
a prize of war
while close to the river she moved
on and the rarauwhe burned
steaming with new blood amid
the goads and shouts of obscene
triumph and destroying
they took you

bundled you into a scrim bag;
ripped you away from home. To
this, a bleak grey place where lonely
tissued by the layers of pulp and
plastic, your beauty your beauty
and our pain our pain
shine through.

Kia ora koutou.

ROBERT SULLIVAN
[Poem is accompanied by Bernard Makoare on taonga pūoro]

Maori are Children of God
Somewhere in the land's mind a taniwha
lifts his head and grins, a mountain
walks off with a female mountain,
a waiata is sung in honour of the above

Maori are children of God

a dead tohunga sees me and I see this
we are talking about the madness
that has taken the people by the sip
in aluminium pints quarts and handles

Maori are children of God

the sickness of the city the iwi's filtered
oration on streets with rap not speech
and the power of their history strong as Edison
or Einstein weaker than the matakite man

Maori are children of God

and soldiers and mercenaries and free people
and makers of villages and makers of waka
and breathers of spirit and air and growers
and laughers and artists and the solemn

who represented all these things
of war-peace-food-love-beauty-sleep-
river-ocean-wind-fatherdom-motherdom-
forest-man-woman and the numbered

and should not forget as they live
in this mixture of a time where they are
folded into a document that takes blackness
from dignity and spits/gifts some back.

The Maori are children of God.

1997 MAURICE SHADBOLT

Getting a Word in

I've often toyed with this thought: if I were to stick a pin in a randomly chosen page in any New Zealand telephone directory and come up with a name, I might, if the subject were willing and there are a few artefacts and documents to hand, come up with New Zealand's whole story. More than that, given good luck and an ample supply of shoe leather, I might even, following that one name in the telephone directory back into the past, come up with the story of the entire human race. Individuals we may be, but we carry the story of our species in our heads and our hearts.

Insignificant as we may seem as individuals, we trail huge histories, vivid dramas. Exploring those dramas to see what might be found there, what motives, is what I've been up to for the last 16 years. The business of fiction, it seems to me, is to transmute the particular to the general, to journey from the small picture to the large. Especially is this true of the historical novelist, whose business is to breathe life into the dead.

As a recent autobiographer, I've been reflecting on the nature of fiction and autobiography. After trying to make sense of my own life, largely by way of my ancestors, I now see that the reverse is also true. Where the novel moves boldly from the particular to the general, biography and autobiography move stealthily from the general, to the particular. Autobiography casts its net wide, catching up many people in its net, but finishes with one life. I hope, very briefly, to show you what I mean.

Let me look at fiction first. Some of you will have read my novel *Season of the Jew*, a novel which ostensibly deals with Te Kooti's war with colonists in the 1860s. A large subject then and a fairly fat book, as tales of human conflict usually are, and with a cast of at least a couple of thousand and a half dozen roaring battles. But this novel began small. It could not have begun smaller. It began in fact with one obscure life, one forgotten human being. It began with a patch of waste ground at the back door of the Wellington cottage where I lived for three years in the 1950s. That cottage sat hard up against a fragment of wall which was all that remained of the old Terrace Prison.

Soon after moving into the cottage, I became aware that the patch of waste ground had a history. It was where those executed in the prison yard had afterwards been buried. Another year or two on and I learned from a note in a Wellington newspaper that among those interred in that patch of waste ground was a young Māori named Hamiora Pere. He'd been hanged, of all things, for high treason. High treason, I ask myself. High treason? So far as I know he was, and is still, the only person to be hanged for high treason in New Zealand. There had to be a story there, I told myself. But it meant an historical novel, something I didn't feel qualified to undertake in the 1950s. I didn't pursue the thought further.

In 1981, more than 20 years later, I went down to Wellington to pick up the New Zealand Book Award for my novel, *The Lovelock Version*. That novel was my first and sometimes frivolous excursion into New Zealand's distinctive past. It suggested I could handle the nineteenth century after all. I was staying with the late Father Frank McKay, just around the corner from the Turnbull Library.

The morning after the award ceremony Frank asked me what I was going to do by way of celebration that day. 'Chase a dead Māori boy,' I said, bewildering poor Frank. 'That doesn't sound like celebration to me,' he said. I explained that I was looking for my next novel. I had no notion that the hunt for Hamiora Pere, casually begun that wintery Wellington morning, was going to take five years out of my life.

Colonial newspapers gave me the grisly facts of his trial and execution. But neither his name nor his end at a hangman's hand rated a mention in formal histories of New Zealand. I was all on my own. There was then no historian to help me out nor was there any help from oral history. I went up to Poverty Bay where Hamiora Pere had begun his march to the gallows and found none of his people, none of his tribe, remembered him at all. Mystification was general when I came up with his name. He no longer existed outside a few old and brittle sheets of newspaper. But I persisted. I saw the book I wanted to write as neat, tight, and dramatic and concerned largely with his trial and execution, on the ludicrous charge of high treason.

It appeared that he had indeed fought alongside Te Kooti's warriors, that he might, in a very minor way, have been party to the Poverty Bay Massacre, or Poverty Bay Incident as some call it now. More to the point, however, he had, like many young Māori, been conscripted unwillingly into Te Kooti's lethal band. He was, in short, the classic innocent of war and he was tried and hanged because someone had to be, because Te Kooti and his lieutenants had the good sense not to make themselves available. Because he was the only one around and someone, anyone, had to be hanged. To account for Hamiora Pere on that scaffold, I had to account for what and who had put him there. I had to account, for example, for the Poverty Bay Massacre. Then I found that to account for the Poverty Bay Massacre, I had to account for the battles and skirmishes which preceded the massacre. Indeed, I had to account for the Waikato War, five years earlier, a story in itself.

I had to account for Te Kooti, to account for the militiamen who hunted him down, to account for his Māori allies and enemies, to account for the religious conviction with which he had inspired his people. I had to account for his embracing the Old Testament rather than the New and what that meant.

All this then swung on one little life: the life of Hamiora Pere, whose bones had never been rattled in the century or more since his death, when he was interred in my Wellington backyard. There's more to it. As I researched and wrote, the story, not through design on my part, became more and more contemporary, with ringleted Rastas to the right, urban activists to the left. I seemed to be writing a cautionary tale, a parable for present day New Zealand. Recent events have underlined it.

So that was how *Season of the Jew* came into being. It began with one life, just one, which lit my way into New Zealand's past. One life which seeded something unexpectedly large. Those of you familiar with the novel may recall that the trial and execution of Hamiora Pere occupies something less than a tenth of the book. It was something less and something more than the novel I set out to write. The tragic tale of an individual that became a portrait of colonial New Zealand and with characters I had never foreseen. Nor when *Season of the Jew* was published, was that the end of my excursion into the nineteenth century.

Hamiora Pere led to Te Kooti. Te Kooti led to Titokowaru and his Yankee associate Kimble Bent in the Taranaki War. Titokowaru and Kimble Bent led me even further back into history, to the Ngāpuhi chiefs Hone Heke and Te Rua Kawiti and the battle for the Bay of Islands in 1845. One life led to another, each life led to a large picture, a very large picture, a trilogy of more than a thousand pages. Thanks to my one-time Wellington neighbour, Hamiora Pere, I continued to mine New Zealand's past.

So much for fiction then, in verse form or prose, which has been making our human existence luminous since the bards of Greece first sang the Iliad. Now for non-fiction.

Several years ago I began thinking about a memoir, of using up much of the material and many of the anecdotes which resided in the bottom drawer of my desk and seemed unlikely to find their way into fiction. The problem was winning a continuous narrative from this material.

There was another problem, a personal one. Most New Zealand autobiographies seem to be curdled gossip, telling us more than we might wish to know about the author's sedentary life. Certainly, far too much about dead and gone literary feuds and all too little about those times. My sixtieth birthday was approaching. If ever I was to write that memoir, to account for my times, it was now.

While still contemplating this, something entirely fortuitous pointed me in the right direction. At a family funeral early in 1989 I learned that my great grandfather, Benjamin Shadbolt, a bearded and top-hatted and entirely respectable and prosperous Canterbury squire, was not all he seemed, not the paragon that family legend had him to be. He was in fact a convicted and transported felon, one of the 160,000 convicts which Britain dumped in the Australian colonies in the eighteenth and nineteenth centuries.

My luckless ancestor, an English rural labourer and an unsuccessful thief, had survived the whips and chains of Norfolk Island, the floggings and solitary cells of Van Diemen's Land. I'd always known there was something eccentric about my family: the crankiness I explored in my first novel, *Among the Cinders* and more especially in the comic saga called *The Lovelock Version*. Now I knew what was behind that crankiness; research told me more. In the process I discovered that my great-grandfather was no isolated case. His story, I thought, could stand for the unremembered hundreds, perhaps thousands, of men and women who fled the horrors of convict Australia for New Zealand's more serene shores in the nineteenth century. They don't exist in the histories of New Zealand. They've never been acknowledged or numbered amongst our founding fathers. Their story has been lost, much as that of the Māori has. Many of these migrants were as industrious and successful as my ancestors. I had in fact stumbled on one of this country's best-known secrets. I now had a lead into my memoir, or autobiography if you like, the book I would later name *One of Ben's*.

A navigator of strange seas, I began mapping my great-grandfather's life, then the lives of his children, grandchildren, and great-grandchildren. In the process I managed, sometimes intentionally and sometimes unintentionally, to get a good deal said about New Zealand and its history. The cast was huge; the drama was great, and that is why, dear readers,

I don't get born until page 100 of this 300-page book. I had to get all those early lives out of the way before I found my own life. My life made no sense without theirs. It was certainly impoverished without theirs.

So, what have I established? Perhaps just this. In the fiction called *Season of the Jew* I began with one life, Hamiora Pere's, and finished with many. In the non-fictional *One of Ben's*, I began with many lives and finished with mine.

Celebrating forgotten lives, making them visible, remains my business in either form. It is the business of every writer. There is not a day of my life when I don't reflect on my great good fortune. For the characters who people my narratives, including Hamiora Pere and Benjamin Shadbolt, are more than just characters to me. They are, all of them, the lives of my life and my lifelong companions.

Thank you.

1998 IAN WEDDE

The Nation's Narratives

First of all, I really want to make it clear that I don't intend to take this lying down. I know perfectly well that Peter Simpson, my dear old friend, has jacked up the title of this talk, probably to try and flush me out of some of the thickets of the government's SRAs, or Strategic Result Areas, for national identity. Because I come from Wellington these days, presumably I'm thought to be able to answer these questions, so we'll see.

What are the SRAs? We might as well get this out of the way to begin with: Is there an official line? What is the heritage division up to? What's the Foresight Project's* attitude to national ID? Is the branding of New Zealand as the Silver Fern Nation evidence of a national unity conspiracy?

For those of you who aren't familiar with the phraseology of the SRAs, or the 'strategic result areas for the public sector', and for those who don't come from Wellington and aren't immunised against this bureaucratic speak, it all does sound rather sinister. I thought I might just quickly once-over-lightly this stuff; it is interesting. It is exceedingly interesting when you get under it.

The section on economic and social participation declares, 'Particular emphasis will be placed on developing policy frameworks and effective programmes which stimulate and affirm New Zealand's evolving identity and cultural heritage, contribute to building strong, self-reliant communities and encourage civic participation by all New Zealanders.'

Good?**

The Ministry of Cultural Affairs, which provides policy advice to government on the cultural sector, sets itself the goal of achieving the following: 'The encouragement of creative expression by and for New Zealanders', and 'The promotion of New Zealand's cultural identity both in New Zealand and overseas and improved management of New Zealand's cultural heritage'.

Again, sounds good?**

Given that 'the cultural sector' is pretty much another way of saying 'the human race', I have to begin by wondering what will happen when the rubber hits the road in respect of such high level statements as SRA policy. It is fairly clear that national agendas for unity do run fairly strongly, not too far under the surface, and that we might expect that some of the roads hit by the Treasury rubber will be pointing at something like a national unity programme.

I'll diverge here for a moment and indicate that this is not necessarily as bad as you might think, because a comparative example can be found at the moment in South Africa. To cut straight to what amounts to an interesting piece of gossip, you can now visit Robben Island as a tourist, if you have 60 bucks for the boat fare, and you will find yourself conducted further by a prior inmate. We can set that at one margin as a rather spectacular example of a national unity project, and be thankful that we're not quite there yet.

We should not be so naive as to be surprised or upset by this, but I think we have to address some of the issues that are implicit in Peter Simpson's title, not my title. But I welcome it wholeheartedly, 'the nation's narratives'. We have to accept some responsibility to discuss this in a non-paranoid and forthright way.

I began my engagement with the business of narratives and national identity as a poet and subsequently as a novelist about 35 years ago and, like most poets aged somewhere between 15 and 35, my first narratives were narratives of the self — or, to be honest, of myself — and the first identity I investigated was my own. I wasn't remotely interested in national identity, especially as I lived out of New Zealand during the early years of my writing, and didn't know I'd missed the place, which I associated with the war in Vietnam and with my metaphysics teacher at university in Auckland here, a Catholic who exhorted us to admire potatoes because when you put them in a dark place they sprout and 'reach for the light'. On both the political and the intellectual fronts, I didn't feel I had a great deal to miss.

I didn't know I'd missed the country of my birth until I came back in the early seventies and saw three things: short-sleeved shirts, freckles on forearms and punnets of strawberries. Equally compelling, now I think about it, was the coloured plastic bunting on used-car lots along the Great South Road. I suppose I could crank up a case for short sleeves, freckles, strawberries and used-car lots reconstituting a location for a sense of New Zealandness I'd not had since I was a kid, when it was probably the taste of Paine's ice cream in Blenheim, the smell of my father's farts and sandy woollen togs at Waikawa Bay that vectored my sense of knowing where I was.

But all such details, even though they're vivid enough, are really only the beginnings of primitive and sentimental taxonomies — a kind of biosystematics of identity given a slightly kitsch twist by one who, this many years later, never wants to hear ever again that a catalogue listing Buzzy Bee, Vegemite, school milk, the Four Square grocer, Gallipoli, the Plunket Society, Seagull outboard motors, number-eight wire and beer squirted out of hoses can tell me anything I need to know about identity. The nation's or mine; it doesn't really matter which.

I make no apology for this. And it wouldn't do me or anyone else any good if I did, now, repudiate the subjectivity of my first narrations of identity. I was, after all, trying to work out *how I was placed*. For me that's the key phrase, and it's a phrase that I use with my kids. ('How are you placed?' usually means, 'Have you got enough money? And if not, don't ask for some.') I'll try and come back to later to 'How are you placed?'

What does do me good, and I hope by extension does some good to the people I now address as a curator — and somewhat as a cultural bureaucrat rather than as a writer — is to embrace the subjectivity of most narrations of identity, including national identity, and to note with liberated pleasure that there does not exist any convincing taxonomy or typology of national identity, but that there do exist a great many stories about identity. And our need to tell these stories and to hear them is not diminishing, even though the Government's commitment to mainstream storytelling media, such as television and film is at the moment — one would have to say — diminishing.

So, what I have to say here is going to be peppered with stories, because that's the only way I know how to deal with the topic. And also, because it's really the only way I know how to get to grips with Peter Simpson's title's framing of the subject of this weekend.

In July this year, we had some fun in Wellington: we organised a symposium called *Culture Shocks*. In the course of this thoroughly enjoyable event, we talked about the *location of culture* and we tried to use the question, 'Where is culture?' to unlock a few investigations. The question was meant to prompt thoughts about culture and location in respect of history and memory, language and place, artefacts, media and architectures, politics and society, the economies of production and distribution and so on. The question, 'Where is culture?' was principally looking for some analysis and discussion of the relationship between public and private culture, a key question, I think; in particular, the whereabouts and the influence of official culture, which is iconic rather than personal, nationalist, rather than national, and concerned to converge at national *unity*, rather than diverge with national *unities*.

Clearly we have to look at foundational histories, both official and personal, if we're going to understand this. Foundational histories such as the whakapapa which leads from Te Kore down to Māui, to the discovery of Te Ika a Māui by Kupe, to the migrations known collectively as Te Hekenga

Waka. This is an official history, which gets personal when it comes down to hapū and whānau and to the sense of belonging that individuals have.

Because we are, collectively, one way or another, a nation of immigrants, our foundational histories all involve stories of voyaging and of encounter. This is as true of early Polynesian navigators as it is of Dutch immigrants in the 1950s, for example. Clearly these stories of encounter, in this context, are crucial. I think here we encounter what has to be one of the critical factors in any narrative of national identity: what Glenn Denning cautiously refers to as the commonsensical attributes of official history, are often, if not usually, contradicted — if not completely stuffed up — by other accounts, more personal ones.

For example, there's a story that we came across recently, doing some research at Te Papa into Dutch immigrant communities in New Zealand. Dutch immigration in New Zealand in the 1950s was officially framed as a story of proto-Britishness and successful assimilation. A parallel government policy can be found in the Hunn Report's assimilationist approach to Māori. A different version of this official successful assimilation line with respect to Dutch immigration was provided by the account of a woman we talked to, who happened to be travelling on a train that deposited a single Dutch man with a suitcase at each small station the length of the South Island.

It's a fabulous piece of poetry, and it will make you cry. One man stepping out in each little iconic spot, all alone. This extraordinarily poignant image is the product of an official policy of 'peppering', of separating Dutch immigrants from their natural communities. The anger this has caused is only now beginning to show up in the accounts of Joris de Bres and Redmer Yska, for example — irrespective of that other great national New Zealand myth of the successful, hard-working Dutch, which is not an untruth — but the anger has lain underneath that myth.

Anne Salmond has written about the way stories of encounter are likely to talk past each other. And for me, one of the key stories of encounter in the Pacific is that of Captain Samuel Wallis of HMS *Dolphin* arriving at Matavai in Tahiti in June 1767. It is one of my favourite stories.

I like Glenn Denning's account of this, which brings out the complexities and takes a few risks with the narrative, rather than Neil Rennie's, which places the Tahitian view of the encounter, 'beyond the scope of reliable ethnohistory'. I have some quite serious difficulties with that phrase, 'the scope of reliable ethnohistory'; it sounds like an oxymoron. Whether it's reliable ethnohistory or not, Denning's account tells us that the Tahitians' perception of the arrival of the *Dolphin* and Wallis' narrative of the encounter are both congruent and wildly different, in bizarre and surprising ways.

Wallis' account was framed by imperial narratives of discovery and of exchange between civilised and 'barbarous' peoples. For the Tahitians, the encounter was framed by cosmology and a cosmogony in which power was seasonally exchanged between divine and human realms. So, when HMS *Dolphin* came into Matavai Bay, it was perceived by the Tahitians as the rainbow craft of the divine Oro. Wallis didn't know that, any more than he knew that as a Tahitian god his timing was perfect: he'd sailed round the island in the right direction; the masts, sails and bunting of the ship were just what the Tahitians expected; and his imperial use of a flag was also highly appropriate. All these signs conveyed meanings to the Tahitians that Wallis did not intend. He certainly could not have known that Tahitian cosmology and the place of the divine in it were exceedingly secular, in comparison to a more absolute Western division between the sacred and the profane. Therefore, he could not have known that it was okay for the Tahitians to provoke their gods by pelting them with stones and by sexual taunting on the part of women, both of which actions Wallis interpreted in his own way.

We are luckier than both the Tahitians and Wallis because we now have, as Wallis and the Tahitians did not have in 1767, a meta-narrative of the encounter in Matavai Bay — a meta-narrative which is in itself the narrative of an encounter and has therefore become a foundational history. It has become a portal to national identity. The significant content of this meta-narrative is the eerily precise *misunderstanding* which occurred, and its consequences, almost immediately, for Tahitian politics, and for subsequent European encounters, including those of Cook, Bligh, and all the vast, immeasurable ensuing narrative of encounter: Beaglehole's of Cook's journals, as well as Marlon Brando of *Mutiny on the Bounty*, and all that comes with it.

We are not done with this and we never will be; we shall keep on doing it. It all begins with that peculiar mismatch that occurred with Wallis in 1767. That is where we kicked off.

We also learn that narratives of national identity are not just constructed, but continuously deconstructed and reconstructed — even the official-history versions of them suffer this. It seems to me incredibly important to recognise, especially in company such as this tonight, that the writing of revisionist history by the likes of Jamie Belich or Michael King or Anne Salmond is not just the appearance of meta-narrative informed by hitherto-unheard voices of those dispossessed of the control of narratives but, much more importantly, a continuous cycle of consumption and reinvestment of meaning and value by *audiences*. The huge factor of continuous public agency — the cycling-through and reinterpretation of historical narratives — is absolutely critical, and it's something I want to come back to later.

A few days ago Jamie Belich said yes, it was true that he had always believed that the writing of books was crucial to the health of culture and to the revision of official culture, but that he'd never really understood how little an historian could do in the milieu of books until the showing of the television series *The New Zealand Wars*. All at once he had realised that 95 percent of the target audience for that information had never before been reached. He was suffering some interesting shocks as a result and getting some extremely interesting correspondence, and reading some in the newspaper.

The cycling through of historical re-interpretation and of national narrative in a big-audience medium is critical to the effort. We learn from this the importance of narrative control, of power, over these accounts — we all have our own subjective strategic result areas, if you like. This is absolutely vital in the consideration of 'construction' — a term I have difficulty with — of narratives of national identity.

But first, the matter of control and power of narrative — the power over narratives. In the zone of foundational histories and of encounter stories, and of national identity as a subset of encounter, my favourite example of narrative control comes from the East Coast at Te Kaha.

Quite a few years ago, I was poking about the East Coast of the North Island, along the coast between Whakatāne and the Cape, collecting stories about whaling. Most of these were encounter stories — not encounters with whales, but encounters between peoples; between cultures, economies, languages, histories, technologies and so forth. They were incredibly rich stories which should not be under-characterised as being simply about the meetings of Māori and Pākehā. However, the stories continued to conceal the answer to a question that I really wanted answered: did Māori hunt whales at sea before the advent of European and American whalers? I went there trying to find this out and what I got was all these other stories.

I asked that question of old Pāora Delamere, then 90, who approached the meeting house where we talked by vaulting over a five-bar gate; his memory was every bit as good as that too. He was then the Ringatū Bishop at Te Kaha, and his answer — which was not an answer to the actual question but took the form of a story, or actually several stories — has nourished both my faith in and my scepticism about national narratives for the better part of 20 years. The story goes like this:

Rival tohunga of Te Whānau-ā-Apanui had their support teams competing on the beach, around the headlands and offshore in canoes, banging the water, rattling things and chanting karakia in efforts to distract and frighten the migrating whales, especially calves and pregnant females, and drive them into the bay and up onto the beach. Bishop Delamere reckoned that these rivalries between teams of tohunga were the precursors of the great hockey tournaments that subsequently took place up the Cape, but that is another story.

To cut the Bishop's long story short, all those people were out there competing with each other and trying to summon whales, and around the point sailed Captain Cook. To this day, according to the late Bishop, as far as Whānau-ā-Apanui are concerned, Cook didn't find them — *they summoned him*. It is a very important story, because you notice that similar narrative control is exerted by neighbouring Te Arawa, for example, especially Te Arawa whose post-contact history has involved tourism in the Rotorua area. Tourism is one zone where ownership and control of the nation's narratives are exceedingly complex, and where the social relations of exchange are seldom able to be drawn up in terms of alienation, exploitation, or victimisation, but are often a lot better understood in terms of story-telling.

Following on from Bishop Delamere's story, there seems to me to be a little swarm of narrative instances that are of crucial importance at this point in our nation's history. They are models of narratives, but they're most often thought of as topics or issues or problems. The Treaty of Waitangi is one.

The Treaty of Waitangi is a narrative, and not only is it a narrative but it produces narratives — it is one of the most productive narrative-producing devices that our nation has. It tends to be seen as either an historical event that is fixed in its meanings and capable of producing closures, or evolutionary, requiring revisionist thought and producing ongoing processes and stories. If you tend to the latter interpretation, as I do, then partnership models such as Charles Royal's for Te Wānanga o Raukawa make a lot of sense. This kind of model is another narrative-producing device and I'll briefly describe it for those of you who aren't familiar with his work.

In Charles' model there are three houses: the Māori house; the Pākehā house; and the Treaty house. Māori and Pākehā houses are constituted according to culture, not race. For example, we would expect Anne Salmond to have a place in the Māori house and we would expect Witi Ihimaera to have a place in the Pākehā house. While the Māori house and the Pākehā house will have different kawa and different protocols, different understandings of common law and the like, they proceed as partners. Where the discussion doesn't work, resolution is sought in the Treaty house.

This is not just a model of cultural organisation and social relations; it is a model for scholarship and mātauranga Māori, and therefore for narratives, especially narratives that involve national identity, because what people will be doing inside this model is telling each other stories — figuring it out. I think Charles' model is extremely sensible. The model of scholarship and mātauranga of Māori knowledge systems that Mere Edwards proposes also makes a lot of sense and seems to flow on from both the Treaty and from Charles' model.

In Mere's model, language and knowledge fall roughly into three groups: spiritual and religious beliefs, largely the domain of priests; knowledge of the natural world, based on experience and capable of generating predictability, and in the West largely the domain of research science; and moral and ethical values, in the West largely the domain of law and therefore of the legislature, both legal and political.

In many other knowledge systems, including in general the Western knowledge system, these three areas are separate. In the kinds of knowledge systems represented by mātauranga, they are seldom separate. In terms of knowledge and of our production and understanding of meaning, and of the narratives that convey meaning, this is clearly of immense importance when we speak of national narratives in New Zealand.

Following on from that, this is a critical consideration when you come to look at a case like the Wai 262 case, currently before the Waitangi Tribunal. Wai 262 is usually generalised as involving issues of intellectual property: Do you have the right to use the names of things? Do you have the right to use motifs like the koru? More particularly, do you have the right to genetically alter biological substances? And so on.

No one is going to make any sense whatsoever of a claim like this one if they insist on closure within a discrete knowledge system — one or the other. Only a way of narrativising the issue that takes account of models like Charles Royal's and Mere Edwards' is going to get anywhere. Wai 262 raises again this issue of official culture, the control of narratives and therefore such factors as definitions of common law. If you think that common law has nothing to do with national narratives, then try and understand — without a consideration of common law and who has the running of it — the difference in the definition of ownership, value and interpretation between taonga and European-derived cultural artefacts. You won't get far. From here we get very close to Michel Foucault's concept of 'regimes of truth' in respect of institutions such as the law. Foucault recognised that 'the truth' in narratives was directly a function of power in the institutions that were producing the narratives — which brings us back full circle to the issue of national unity agendas within those regimes of truth such as government, not excluding government projects for national identity.

This isn't a paranoid scenario — maybe a little bit paranoid — but it is a cautionary scenario. If you try and think about the nation's narratives outside of these issues, I think you will get into seriously confused and anachronistic endeavours.

Right now it is important for us to think of national narratives as being somehow part way between artefact and process. Once you tell a story it begins to take shape, it begins to have form, it has substance. At the same time, it is kind of fluid, and so I'm interested in thinking about why this term, 'the construction of national identities', bothers me a bit. I think that to go back to the issue of human agency and of the importance of the cycling-through of narratives through audiences and through storytelling is crucial. There are three stories about this that I would like to tell, very briefly:

Recently I went for a walk up Mt Matthews with one of my kids. It was in the middle of winter. Mt Matthews is pretty high; it's up the back of the Ōrongorongo Valley. It was freezing cold; the fog was freezing — probably where I caught this cold — and it was certainly primaeval. We knew as we went up there that theory tells us that nature is also cultural, it is constructed; that ideas about the wilderness, the wild, the primaeval bush are all narrative constructs. But I gotta tell you that when you get up towards the top of Mt Matthews and you're in that forest and the fog has come down and everything is covered in great festoons of dripping green moss, and you're walking through stuff that you could easily believe no soul had ever trod on before, then thinking about the wild, thinking about the primaeval, ain't hard, because you're there.

And yet, what's interesting about the situation that Jack and I were in as we plodded on, was that we were both whistling. At one point I stopped and said, 'What are you whistling?' and he said, 'Oh I don't know, I heard it.' I thought, 'Uh, it's actually an aria from *Carmen*,' because I was whistling the same thing; we were kind of going back and forth. We'd been to City Opera's production of *Carmen* not long before. So, there we were in the midst of the primaeval forest and, had there been ears to hear, they would have heard someone who whistled in the front of his lips and someone who tried to whistle with his mouth, doing *Carmen*. It kind of complicated my idea of what the primaeval is about.

Later that night we were playing Monopoly in the bush hut — of course, you always play Monopoly when you go up to the Haurangi Hut. Anyone outside in the dark would have heard a father exhorting his son to look after his capital reserves — not to look after his bush reserves; look after his capital reserves. That is what I like about the disputation of an idea-like construct — on one hand you know what the theory is telling you, and it's right, okay, but when you're up there, you're up there, and at the same time, there is this other stuff going on. I hope I've made myself clear.

The other story I like a lot, a similar one, involves a memorial night I spent years ago with a very dear friend of mine whose father had just died. We sat up all night looking at slides — his old man, who had been a taxi driver in Onehunga, had been a fanatical slide taker, and had trunks of slides — and it was one of the most moving and illuminating experiences of my entire life. We began about six in the evening and finished about ten the next morning. It was 'click, click, click, click', like this, on and on for hours and hours and hours; it was like a stop-frame showing of a movie. It slowed down an entire family history. Three things we saw in the course of it I remember most of all. The first was the table settings for Christmas dinner.

We saw the first slide of the Christmas-dinner table-setting when the kids were really little, with cups full of coloured lollies and coloured paper napkins and stuff, and the menu was the way it was — it was not a wealthy household, quite a struggling household — with fresh peas and potatoes from the garden, what have you. It was photographed with great affection and reverence.

From then on we saw the table setting and the menu change year by year as the kids grew up and as the family became more affluent and as the nation's times improved. Towards the end there was a moment of sadness, because the kids had developed their own sophisticated tastes, sophisticated by comparison with slide one — on the table were wine glasses and the coloured paper napkins had been replaced with Irish linen and there were bottles of wine. The middle phase of the Christmas dinner had involved enormous indigestible servings of turkey and red sauce and that sort of stuff; now there were rather new-agey salads and lighter food and a selection of vegetarian dishes and so on. Ah! it was a fabulous narrative.

Another one I remember was the bean trellis. The bean trellis went through generations of invention and optimism. The first was really down there, some galvanised pipe and chicken wire and it certainly held the beans up. Subsequently — obviously someone's bright idea; I suspect Bruce and his old man had got together and done a bit of backyard carpentry — there was a terribly over-constructed, over-designed weightily assembled bean trellis made of big chunks of four-by-two. They didn't do a very good job but it was there as a kind of monument to domestic inventiveness and had been recorded in a slide. And so on, until the last one, again a moment of sadness, because it was a plant-shop take-out pre-assembled trellis painted trendy green and the beans were happily growing on it. This was in fact the last bean trellis and Bruce's father was by then in hospital dying of cancer, and so the bean trellis was a kind of memorial to the last planting of beans that he made.

And then there was the backyard incinerator: The first was a falling-to-bits old 45-gallon drum, then we moved through subsequent generations of backyard incinerators and the last one was a nice concrete-block structure that masqueraded as a barbecue or something. Wonderful. Wonderful stories, and you learnt so much about national identity and particularities of that family and about social history just from sitting up all night watching those slides.

Another one: I once went for a kayak trip down the Whanganui River with a bunch of people terribly well-informed about what was going on there, which made it a wonderful trip. There was an ornithologist who would stop us every so often and we'd circle around his kayak while he told us about the particular ornithology of that location. There was a water man, a Dutch hydrologist who, incidentally, was one of the people who introduced me to the story of Dutch immigration. He would stop us every so often and talk us through issues of water in that particular stretch. There was a tree man, and there was Dave Young whose book about the upper Whanganui is about to be published. Dave knew everything, so it was a fabulous trip and we kept stopping and having nice little seminars on the surface of the river.

And at one point the bird man went very quiet for a long time. We thought maybe he's got a touch of the bug or something, what's going on? Maybe he's got sore arms from paddling. But no, he'd been thinking. He stopped, assembled us and said 'Listen'. We'd been passing through a stretch of river where he'd been listening carefully to the song of tui and bellbirds, bellbirds mimicking the tui. He was listening for the boundaries of their territories because, according to him, each territory is marked by a particular call, a particular song. He was listening for the moment when he moved into a new territory as he went down the river. And as he did so he claimed that what he heard was this: [whistles a phrase, followed by a throat click].

He couldn't work it out. It sounded so familiar, something about it, and so he went very quiet. And then he realised that about the time when early transistor radios began to be carted up and down the Whanganui River by people canoeing and kayaking, *West Side Story* hit the airwaves. His belief was that there'd been enough airplay for *Maria* — remember the song? [Sings] 'Maria. I've just met a girl named Maria' — for it to have been heard often enough in a territory of tui and bellbirds in a section of the Whanganui River for it to have been implanted as their territorial song. He didn't know whether to laugh or cry. That's another one; this is the nature/culture thing, okay?

Now we're getting close to the end of this. To close off, Nick Perry's marvellous new book *Hyperreality and Global Culture* was recently launched in Auckland. I came up to talk to Nick's class at the University of Auckland Sociology Department and I was thinking, 'What is it that I want to say here?', because I'm not qualified in this particular discipline at all. (The human sciences, as far as I'm concerned, are how you get on with your kids rather than anything else.) But there was really a wonderful paradigm, a thing to think with, that Nick's previous book had given me, and I wanted to think it through before coming up. I had fun doing this because I ended up in a place that I wouldn't have thought I'd get to, and I thought I might share this with you today.

I was watching television a couple of nights before Nick's book launch and having a laugh at the marvellous television commercial for the Audi Quattro, which, you probably know, is a cracker. There's an old, wise Eskimo man — he has to be wise — and a young Eskimo boy who of course has to be credulous. They're tracking across the frozen wastes and they see the tracks of a wolf and a bear, and finally the tyre tracks of an Audi Quattro, an automobile, right? This terrific ad made me laugh every time I saw it, not just because of itself, but because it reminded me of a little history that Nick Perry had told. This was his description of some commercials made for New Zealand television, in particular the famous commercial for Apple computers which, you'll probably remember, has a pub scene with a bunch of farmers standing around being a bit tongue-tied. There's a suggestion that the Missus has left and the dog had to be shot, and then they get into a bunch of jalopies and go tearing back to the barn, where there's an Apple computer glowing in a corner, a bit like a Christian creche.

The essay on the commercial, in which it is now immortalised, pointed out that while the storyline, location, cast and language of the commercial were all rural, its viewer constituency was overwhelmingly urban. The commercial — we're back to national identity now — played on an ironic and affectionate recognition on the part of its urban consumers that the rural wellsprings of New Zealand national identity were mostly mythological, or rather, perhaps, symbolic, and this trope has gone on working for us and for the advertisers.

Nick's insight has given us something to think with: for example, the late Barry Crump's commercials for Toyota, in which Scotty played our little urban lad's ingénu to Crump's Swanndried mad bastard; the current high-country mustering commercial for Speights beer; even the long-running series of Fernleaf butter ads. They have all worked brilliantly because we knew they were toying with an urban appreciation of the rural symbolism of national identity and with notions of naturalness, wholesomeness and grass-roots value.

For me it seemed to work very well, and this brings us back to our literary platform here. It worked very well as an insight into understanding one of the founding myths of our literary culture: that the laconic vernacular short story that Frank Sargeson produced as exemplary in the 1930s tapped into and showed us authentic New Zealand speech, and in so doing laid the foundation for a New Zealand literature.

True or false? Well, years later, when Sargeson wrote *Memoirs of a Peon*, in the arch literary style of his mature novels, we gained a clearer sense of the correlative between that urban/rural vernacular — a sophisticated business. It then became apparent that the vernacular plank Sargeson had laid to the literary construction of national identity was even more of an artifice than the camp style he later came out with. It is no longer possible to read a story like 'White Man's Burden' without finding ourselves in a cultural construct every bit as sophisticated as its short-fiction equivalent 50 years later, the Apple TV commercial. I'd go so far as to say that the most direct descendants in the 1990s of Sargeson's wicked vignettes of the 1930s are those television commercials which play on the correlatives of vernacular, rural truthfulness and literary metropolitan knowingness.

I also suspect that the homosexual subtext of Sargeson's mateship was reissued in Crumpy and Scotty, and more recently in the Speights musterers. The classic, of course, was the Steinlager homo-erotic rugby players, whose cover was extremely well-blown by Peter Wells. Another correlative process in the construction of national identity has been the intellectual play with anti-intellectualism. I'll leave you with the famous closing paragraph of Sargeson's 'White Man's Burden', absolutely exemplary in this respect, and it goes like this, in case you need to be reminded:

> I slept out in a shed that night, but it was hard to get to sleep because of the row in the bar that came across the yard. At any rate, I had Maoris on the brain. You see I was brought up in the South Island and never saw many Māoris. But I've seen the press photos of the Arawas turning out for Lord Whatshisname and the pictures in the art gallery. And once I read a couple of books by a man called Elsdon Best. Gosh, there's a great day coming for Abyssinia when civilisation gets properly going there.

Thanks all very much.

1999 VINCENT O'SULLIVAN

Fit to Print

May I say what a pleasure it is to be invited to this and also what a privilege it is to be here tonight with those two Rangatira of New Zealand poetry, Allen Curnow and Hone Tuwhare. What I'm going to talk about, and it will only be about half an hour, with a few readings interspersed, is random remarks on the civilisation of the West.

When I was a child, the civilisation of the West began at a very precise point — that was the modest but glittering silver-painted dome of the Post Office at the Three Lamps. And how that phrase, 'The Lamps', well before I went to school, carried such a ring to it. Just as looking up at those three iron lanterns, with their panes of frosted glass, threw one into a world whose shapes were both shadows and truly solid. Parts of those shapes were one's parents, one's relatives, one's family's friends, who were solid as the back porch steps, or the front verandah rail, and yet shadowy too in their seemingly endless talk of a time and a place, which was as real to them, the grown-ups, as this is to myself now.

I knew, for example, that places like Kerry and Cork were further than Freemans Bay and I knew that where I lived was on the 'other side of the world,' even as so many of those voices kept telling one, of somewhere else.

It was distant, that place, yet strangely real, but so was Ponsonby Road, before I was born, where the Three Lamps meant the flickering flares atop an iron post, while horse trams clattered to either side of it, and at night when the burglars killed the postmaster and took the keys, those lamps reflected on the gleaming haunches that drew the trams, and the shadows moved down St Mary's Bay Road, even earlier than the clink of milk cans, moving along our own street. And at the end of it all the wrong man was hanged, who hadn't done the murder, and his gravestone told you so.

Now, for a child I suppose reality is often something like that: what is so living and graspable and immediately in front of you, and what is quite as real, but one will never touch, the world of the seven swans of Glendalough, or whatever the stories happen to be that you hear. But also, that place that adults talked of, the enchanted distance of their own youth that you want so desperately to make a part of where you are, and that in a sense, it does become so.

For many writers I think there is a particular glamour in that blurred yet precise territory where you remember what is real yet want to push further than that into someone else's memories as well. Because that is what stories mean.

It was not my own memory for example, but a much earlier one, that I had heard of as a child, about horses escaping from the pottery, that open space down from Blake Street and the red-tinned factory of the Auckland Bedstead Company. The horses escaped and moved through the night and I took that in for the novel, *Let the River Stand*, and ran it together with a story of a boy who was brutally beaten by what my mother would have called, 'his mother's fancy man':

> The boy lay in bed one night and heard the horses outside, their hooves ringing out on the sealed surface of the road. There were the voices of men calling from further down near the paddocks, the high whooping sound of trying to round the horses up, to turn them back from their canter towards Jervois Road and their shying at the traffic. Then it was quiet for a moment, an absolute hush

like God had put his hand over everybody's mouth. The boy sat up in bed and pulled back the thick curtain. His mother stood there quiet on the verandah. Her thin back was only a little in front of him, then out beyond her was the great space of the sky above the houses on the other side of the road. There was this piece of silence as though it was in the middle of the night instead of only early, because he had hardly gone to bed. Quiet except the man was in the kitchen eating, making his fork scrape along his plate. When he stopped, it will be like everyone slept, that's how quiet it will be, the boy kept thinking. And why is Mumma still standing there, why is she still watching? Then he jumped with the suddenness of the noise outside, the unfolding, bursting clatter as the horses flung in different directions, the three sets of hooves breaking from where they had stood, arcing out with such awful noise. He heard someone shouting very loudly just outside their house, the percussion of hooves that must have been so close to the fence. A tall man stood there, just near their gate, the bridle shining in his hands. The horse flowed past him, so big and slippery under the streetlight from the corner. The boy climbed on to the small table at the foot of his bed. He held up handfuls of the heavy curtain, he saw the smear of streetlight melt along the horse's flanks as it turned at the corner then trotted with its legs very high, like it was pretending somehow, like he did himself when he played at moving like a horse.

… The man with the bridle ran down the little street towards the factory. The bridle hung and slapped against his back, and the boy could hear it leaping. As the horse went down the street in front of the man the light had slipped off its haunches like it was a blanket. For a moment he had seen the tail trailing out behind it, the flopping of its mane up and down. There was an echo from down in the shadows, the exploding nervous hooves that came through between the houses when he could no longer see the horse but thought of it running on and on, the big dark animal with the man trailing it, the jangle in the man's hand, that he would never tie it with. Down that little street now and past the factory and into the further streets where the boy had never been ... Then, the boy standing on the low table at the window, the curtain dragged up and bunched in both his hands, was knocked sideways and so hard by the man's opened hand his feet were lifted from the table before he began to fall. The man whom the boy never thought of by his name, but only as that, *the man*, who towered above his mother as he did above the boy himself. He had come into the bedroom and seen the child at the window. The sight of the boy with the bunched curtains in his hand like the stem of a large broadening fan angered him as all things did that declared he was not obeyed, even a six-year-old standing beside his bed in the excitement of running horses through the early night. So that he called out *Jesus, boy*!, stepping towards him from the door. His hand raised and struck out, then fell again after the clear impact against the child's head, fell back like a heavy knotted rope against his side. The boy saw the streetlight blur like a whirling sun, the burning haze behind the closed lids when he lay on the floor.

It was only when I was kindly invited to speak at this festival that it came home to me quite how much I had written — often when I thought I was doing something else — about the Ponsonby where I was born, the Westmere where I grew up, the Grey Lynn where I went to school. Even about Pt Chevalier, that tree-flecked promontory beyond the reef that spilled like an enormous ink stain as you stood on the shallow banks at Sunnybrae.

  Pt Chev. was that mysterious land across the shimmer of the summer tides, where sex, that even greater mystery, sometimes happened, so you overheard, beneath the blue pines and the yellow clay cliffs. And where, as I read so much later, that pullulating tribe of Sinclairs in turn looked over to the mangroved groins of Westmere.

  The reef that separated us, that long, low finger of volcanic rock, was where adventure occurred. It was where my brother's schoolmate stole dynamite from the quarry and hid it under our house until the police stood at the back door. It was where domestic tragedy could spread its own stain of grief.

And here's a poem I wrote about 30 years ago, about one of those occasions; a poem called 'Exit':

EXIT
Mrs Murphy in her plastic raincoat on summer evenings.
Her quick humble talk. Her quiet husband.
A daughter we called 'Spaghetti'.
         Mrs Murphy
crying, when the news says 'Fallen
from Mt Cook', although the photo beside the story
is of no one she has heard of.

Mrs Murphy one warm May morning
wearing her plastic coat
carrying a string kit for her shoes
walks down past Patersons
      past Smythes
and Kennedys and Quinn's corner
as a heroine in the stories passes
dragons between clashing rocks
across hot-plate expanses to the enchanted
well. The magic stone. To the pure sea
always so calm there off Sunnybrae
it works this little fret-work along
the sand.
    Down to those slight edges
Mrs Murphy walked then.
Puts her shoes in the string kit
and the kit beneath a big gum.
Sets her clothes in a neat pile
as a woman does who goes swimming

> in case a friend comes down to join her,
> who comes to wait for her swimming back, whichever.
> Her friend will see her clothes and know them.
> She folds her things on the beach neatly
> as that.
>
>   And the plastic raincoat
> again on her naked skin Mrs Murphy
> walks out towards the reef, 100
> yards before the water is at her shoulders,
> walks on until her feet lose what she stands on.
> The sea pours hot glass.
> Her quiet hands turn fists.
>
>   Mrs Murphy is leaving Westmere
> discreetly as a moth.

Now there's nothing so unusual about the West, or at least my small corner of it, that keeps cropping up in what I write. Most writers, as I say, have one place, which more than any rings for them with a particular resonance. And part of that nostalgia — to use that lovely word whose origin means, quite simply, the *ache* of not being home — part of it, as I suggested, is very much one's own. But part of it is what is just beyond one's reach. The Ponsonby of those who came before. That somehow one is jealous to own as well.

  It's obviously that West Auckland that the nun walks through on an early morning in *Believers to the Bright Coast*. This is in fact in 1929, when she walks to tell a friend about a death that's just taken place at the Home:

> An hour later, as I put on my long black coat and walk out into the sharp air, I think how such trivial events lie beside those of greatest moment. Statues — toys — are stolen; a woman dies in agony; an ageing nun walks into the remains of the night, a slit of mild silky

grey already there in the lower sky, across the school playground and through the lane into John Street, then up the slope of Vermont Street, past the Marist Brothers school whose asphalt spaces spread out, pale and bare, in the expanding light. As I turn into Ponsonby Road, it is as though bonfires have been lit beyond the rows of modest houses, their roofs black against the flare of the new day. The air rings with the clamour of birds in the big trees. A young man with a kind of hood pulled behind his head runs past me, his arms punching out as though at some opponent who feints in front of him. 'Sister,' he grunts to me as he runs past. ...

    Then the sky is again surprisingly dark. I am almost at the brick Police Station when the quick rattle stirs in the plane trees, and I feel the rain. The clock across on the building where the dentist does the sisters' teeth shows not quite six. In the smear of rain a baker's van moves shiny as a toy. The horse's head and back are steaming. I cross the empty, bald main road. A charwoman letting herself through a wooden gate at the back of the Star Hotel pauses with her hand on the upraised latch, watching me until I pass. I hear the latch fall behind me, and the gate scrape as she draws it back. I walk down the steep slope of Newton Road, into the warren of small wooden houses. It is another ten minutes until I begin the rise on the other side of the valley, St Benedict's riding high above it, making me think of a tall red ship.

In a similar way, it's an older Herne Bay than any that I could have experienced, yet one that I think of as mine, in those paddocks that once ran from behind the Home of Compassion in Kelmarna Avenue, towards the mangrove reek and the shallow sucking tides between Regina Street and Cox's Creek. Where even until the late 1940s a handful of tinkers, as my father called them, lived in their strange caravans, and timber from the old turn-of-the-century mill stuck up through the knee-deep mud.

    These are the paddocks where Spicer, the retarded young man in *Believers to the Bright Coast*, and the handyman at both a convent and a brothel, innocently masturbates on a summer's afternoon, as he tries to remember *his* own earlier years.

So long ago I don't remember that clear even when I try, when it's still and quiet down the paddock behind the Home and hot enough, it summer all right, not enough to lie in the cut grass smelling like it fresh and dying together, the best time when I always thinking what was it like at the beginning. Best of all I like it when the two cows hardly any way off, the munch in your ear good as, the stink of them sweet as well in the hot day, and you're just lying there with your eyes closed and it all pink inside your head and the swish-swash close to you, lovely like that, the quiet, and you kind of part of it, the paddock and all, so hard to say it, say what's happening but it's hardly you even any more, is it, the way you sinking, slipping into everything else? And sometimes Mumma in my mind those times, so close like she standing at the window in the old first kitchen. She turns from the curtain and where she sees down the long road to the bush right off far as you can, where Daddy works, she says, where Darkie. She got the sun behind her, round her head. She saying to me, Soon now, he coming soon. Her hands in close against me, touches me very quick, down my face, down my side, like that, like that. So light it nearly hurts, my own hand sometimes touching me that quick, that light, only there, the place you never talk of. I think better the nuns not see, and rub my hand clean inside my shirt. Then I sit up sudden in the paddock and the special colour gone from things like it's fallen somehow back to how is ordinary, one old cow pouring muck down on the grass and the other the colour of big tea leaves spread all over her tits, her juicy spit when her head come up and looks at me, spit like long soft shiny wires nearly hit the ground. But nothing else there, only the Home across the paddock and one sister on the long verandah holding some sick old bugger, walks him up and down so slow might as well be dead and call it quits. Bloody everybody nearly dying up there I reckon sometimes, or loony kids can't walk can't talk, nothing, only the orphan kids anywhere near half-way right, look nice all right those ones in their shiny clothes, the new ribbony hats.

In my own childhood mind there was romance enough around Ponsonby and Westmere, not in the romance of events, but the romance of people. Where Billy Murphy, for example, who's almost completely forgotten about in New Zealand sport, but was one-time featherweight champion of the world, lived in a small house at the end of Summer Street. Where Nat Gould, the Jewish bookie, who claimed he was related to the Marx brothers, raised his black Homburg hat each time his Irish dressmaker wife blasphemed.

Where bandmaster W.H. Smythe, whose band you actually heard on the wireless, flashed and wielded his tree-sized baton as he practiced in the backyard. There were the Ellises, a family so terrifyingly tough that you'd walk half a mile out of your way not to endure their silent contempt. The shame of knowing the Ellises didn't even think you worth bashing up.

There was a family near the little park in Turatai Crescent, where once you were old enough to be let in on it, a pair of handsome foreign sisters got undressed in a room that had no blinds. There was Mr Jones who talked like Dylan Thomas before his time, who collected money I think for some kind of insurance scheme and had fallen, he said, from the top of the Post Office in Queen Street, with no more than a flattened nose to show for it, but the assurance that every bone in his body had rattled like dice.

And there were of course the old diggers from the First World War. To me anyway, puzzling and enormously fascinating figures, who were too old ever to have been young. With their medals and their crushed rainbow ribbons kept in Queen Anne chocolate boxes. And this is a poem about those old diggers called 'Them':

Clarrie Smythe let's call him there was one of him
in Kotare Avenue I used to see him on my *Star*-
round sitting on a white veranda one hand slower than

the other, a daughter who called him 'Father' as though
old Clarrie gave a gippo's stuff for a bit of side; there was one
behind the shops he was Grace Wallace's grand-dad
that was enough for glory surely without the medals
he was supposed to have;
                        Arch Cook's uncle who sang on the trams
who took his teeth out so he could whistle a decent tune
was another of them;
                            there was one in Browning Street
down from the Weet-Bix factory he'd played in the Forces'
team after the Fighting; he liked more
than anything else to sit in the corner of a room
and hear someone do a turn on a tin-whistle or a mouth-
organ so long as the women bloody stayed in the kitchen
and no one asked him what he thought as he said
about bloody *anything*. Some good mates had died
for peace so let's have some shall we? (His fingers
mind you the ladies reckoned were ready
like a rake if you didn't watch where you sat.)

There were Clarrie Smythes but not many of them.
They were the old blokes who made sure the memorials
didn't hog the scene entirely. When they wore red poppies
they were letting on there's places bigger than Westmere,
places a danged-sight meaner.
                        There's quiet streets though and white
verandas you think of when the poppies are budding in mid-
air and all you want is to get back there in one piece.
They let us in on that one too.
                      If you watched them properly you knew
why they liked the reef's spread ink and the mangroves
changing colour a dozen times in a morning and to hold
a fish beating your hands down at Cox's Creek

was as good as an All Clear;
      Clarrie saying *By Christ boy*
it's a corker day knew what he was saying.

But among the men my father's age, the fascinating ones were not, I'm afraid, the steady earners and the hard workers, and the good natured and the decent family men. The ones who gripped one with a sudden fascination of a magnet, were the ones to which grown-ups dropped their voices when they were discussed.

 These were the shady two-timers, the ones who occasionally disappeared for three or six months at a time. And I'll simply finish with poems about two of them. One of them is the Casanova who never quite made it and the other is the molester who did:

Corner
For 10 years Mr King on the corner section
has been looking for a word like *Andiamo*
or a background with a dago *twang-twang*
to stir up the ladies —
      but has only, Mr King,
his dark half-moon-on-its-side eyebrows
to go with the word his tongue
      will never lay to.

All he has to fall back on
is the state-house porch where he stands at sunset,
where he tries the odd *risqué* phrase
to the hurrying-home mums
but Mrs Laracy's bonzer knockers
Mrs Gray's legs which don't quite tally
Mrs Davenport's eyes which sort of look up heavy
as the lid of a mussel surprised in steamy water —
none of them go much on him, somehow.

There are movies & movies
                        and some are sad right through.

Remembering Westmere
A man called Mr Carpenter at number 31.
Two pretty daughters. A wife with a crimped blue

hat, the same one for years. Mr Carpenter
did time. Little girls. Not his own,

at least, that was something. Mr McIntyre,
the British Israelite, Mr Jack House,

a milkman in a black singlet every
day of every season, Mr Snowy Lester,

who refused work as a teetotaller refuses
illicit beverages for twenty years,

called him variously a rampant
sinner, a poxing perve, a sponging bastard.

I remember seeing Mr Carpenter, five foot
and shag all as people described him,

wearing a suit, his moustache clipped,
his shoes shiny enough to escape on,

looking at the rest of the street as though
they'd been away. No one liked to say so,

panty-pirate that he was, but there was
glamour. Mr McIntyre knew it,

Mr Jack House knew it, Snowy Lester even,
who said what *he'd* give him was the knife.

On the way up Garnet Road, waiting
at the tram stop, the Carpenter girls

held his hands and he swung them high,
his teeth and his mo and his palaver

made you think of Errol Flynn. See
a photo now you'd say, 'Ah, the Forties!'

Thank you.

2000 DAME FIONA KIDMAN

Friends and Lovers

Thank you Murray and Naomi. Thank you for your welcome to this beautiful city. I'd like to add my thanks to Random House for their support of me too in coming here. 'Friends and lovers', what a wonderful theme to build a festival around. How easily the words tripped off my tongue when Murray rang and proposed this evening's address. Friends and lovers is a term all of us have used a thousand times. And so, of course, I did say I'd love to come, no problem. Concepts we all say we understand, and it gave me a warm glow as I put the phone down and started planning how I'd talk about these wonderful feelings we have for each other.

Then I began to think about it. 'Hey,' I said to my 17-year-old granddaughter, 'what do you reckon I should talk about?', and she asked was I going to talk about both at the same time? And did one mean the other and vice versa? 'Well,' I said a trifle uncomfortably, 'it's possible that people can be both.'

'Oh well,' she said, 'perhaps you should look at Plato.' Well I thought about that and I thought it wasn't a bad reference point, but when it comes down to it, platonic love is what has been described as love from the neck up, if you see what I mean.

In my day it used to be a bit of an excuse for long lunches, you know, the ones when the restaurant's empty and the waiters are hanging about waiting for their tea break. And you still haven't gone home and you can't order another bottle of wine and your two lone voices fall oddly in the big empty room and you say, 'We mustn't ... we won't ...' or 'Not this time anyway,' or so I seem to recall. Love, in distinction from friendship, is killed, or rather extinguished, the moment it's displayed in public, it's also been said.

So, how do we define friends and lovers, and should we take for granted that those who we perceive as friends and lovers really are? Orson Welles said that when you're down and out, something always turns up and it's usually the noses of your friends. As for Samuel Beckett, he spoke of that loneliness and recrimination that men call love; not to mention Mae West, who felt that love conquered all things, except poverty and toothache.

But still, let's not get cynical before we've even begun. For a start, we've got living proof that Going West is the friend's and lover's very own festival. So, a big welcome to Philip Temple and Diane Brown, who fell in love at Going West in 1998 and are still saying, 'I love you'. Philip and Diane, put your hands up and let's see you please. Welcome lovers! Yay! And hands up anyone else who's fallen in love at the Going West Festival. Come on, come on. Yes? No? You're not going to tell us. All right, welcome anyway and welcome to anyone who thinks they might fall in love at Going West 2000. Sounds a bit like the Destiny Waltz doesn't it? And save the last dance for me. Oh yes.

Seriously though, I have had some wonderful friends. One or two of mine go back more than 50 years. The long friendships that have been sustained are ones based on mutual interests and enthusiasm, not just because they are there. I think of my earliest friend, from my first year at school: she loves books and she's a visual artist, as well as a lawyer. My dearest friend from my teen years is a well-known children's writer. Those are marvellous constellations of coincidence and happenstance in little country towns.

So, on one hand I cherish friendships that endure, but on the other

I relish the new. As a teacher of creative writing I've had wonderful opportunities to make new friends, and not just new, but some of them young. And they've got the power to challenge and change me. Many, though not all, of my friends are writers. People do tend to think that writers only talk to other writers, but I don't think that's true. Not for *real* writers, the ones who are down there in the grandness and the splendour and the muck and the grub of it all, the passion of real life.

But you know, writing, as it's been said perhaps tediously often, can be a lonely business. You go to work in the morning and there's nobody there to tell you to go to write. Not even your long-suffering publisher, who's waiting for your next novel. No, the writer goes off of her own volition, to do the solitary act that might or might not please editors, publishers, critics and readers, and she sits alone and they work. Not everyone understands the way a writer's life really is. And let me say it's not too bad, it's just different. Little wonder that we enjoy talking and socialising with people who understand what our day is like, who know that the phrase, 'Did you get much done today?' is meaningless. People for whom you don't have to fill in the picture of your life to make it sound like a real job, even if it doesn't look like one from the outside. People who understand that when you say you want to be alone, that's what you really do mean, and no hard feelings.

People too, who understand that the condition of money is an erratic, fluctuating and constant anxiety, or it is for most of us. So I suppose it's like any union or association of workers, with simply a common understanding of the unspoken and a shared way of life.

I lost my dear writing friend of 28 years, the late Lauris Edmond at the beginning of this year, something I still find hard to talk about in public. I could say, perhaps, that I've discovered that friends are the people who infuriate you most when they're not there. Ours was a wonderful friendship, which we celebrated in conversations that took place two or three times a week and more, sometimes, for 28 years. We lived within walking distance of each other's houses and when we talked on the phone, we'd have to stop because of the planes flying overhead from Wellington Airport. I'd have to stop first and then the sound would reach her as the plane flew over to her side of the hill. Some days I'd simply think that the planes had got the better of us. But it's not like that, it's a long silence that I haven't got used to yet.

A lot of my story titles and books have the word 'friend' or 'friends' in them — 'Mrs Dixon and Friend', or 'Unsuitable Friends', to name a couple. Certainly, friendship is a concept that's been important enough to inspire me to go on writing about it in different ways, for some 30 years.

'Mrs Dixon' is a prime example of that, exploring not just the idea of friendship, but in fact, whether friends and lovers could be one and the same person. Bethany Dixon was the central character of a story called 'A Strange Delight', that I wrote for *Landfall* in 1972. The protagonist, as he was in that story, was her former husband Peter, who'd left her because he was a tidy hard man and she was erratic and reckless. The truth about their situation is that although they cannot live together, neither can they forget each other. And the ties that bind, of children and a shared past, include too, the fact that they'd once been friends as well as lovers.

I have to admit to a certain sympathy for Bethany as a person. She reminds me a lot of myself as I was when I was her age. She chose a different path in life to mine, with children by other lovers and more than one marriage. I look back and wonder why I wrote about her so intensely, and suppose now that there was an element of me that could have been Bethany if I had chosen a different fork in the road. But she's haunted my path over a quarter of a century of writing and every few years there'd be another spate of Bethany and Peter stories as I track their separate lives, their occasional enforced meetings, as family events unfolded, their eventual choice to meet again as friends and once as lovers.

There's a passage in the first book about the Dixons that I am particularly fond of. Peter comes back to the small town where he and Bethany lived and where Bethany still lives. Years have passed and she's a person for whom the town is still home, but he comes now as a stranger. It's her birthday and suddenly he wants to buy her something. It's decided that he will buy her a new dress. And this is a little extract from it:

In the shop, the proprietress hurried forward, a woman of ageing chic, whom he dimly recalled had once had a much smaller and less well-presented shop in the main street. Since then she had clearly prospered and the clothing on display was stylish, as if she had learned to buy well. A couple of younger women with heavily jewelled hands, broadcasting rural affluence in tweed capes and slouchy suede hats, were choosing outfits for winter race meets. Bethany looked at ease among them, even though he guessed her clothes, neat as they had become, were seldom, if ever, purchased here.

'Hullo, Mrs Dixon, how nice to see you,' the proprietress greeted her. It was a shock to hear her called Mrs Dixon, as if he expected her to have some other name that did not associate them, did not bind them in a multiplicity of acts from which they would never recover, however much they might believe they had. Surprising, too, to see Bethany recognised and greeted as a respected woman of the town.

He had intended ordering events as he would have done if buying a dress for another woman — announce his mission, discretely suggest a price range, stand back and let the women believe they were taking over. As it was he said nothing. Already Bethany had said that she would look around for a few minutes, and that her friend would wait while she chose a dress.

Again the words struck him as curious. Her friend. On reflection, as he watched her flicking through a rack, he decided that he liked it better than husband.

Finally, two or three years ago, I wrote what I think is a definitive version of their relationship in a book, *The House Within*, where all the stories have been collected, some new ones added and the Dixons, having become grandparents, can reflect on their separate but entwined lives. Bethany, I should say here, has now become a renowned writer of cookery books. Peter's third wife is called Val, and this is them saying a sort of goodbye:

He doesn't want Bethany to come out in her dressing gown, but she does anyway, walking barefoot across the lawn to where the car is parked. The grass is frosted and very cold; her footsteps leave a silvery trail. There are stars fading above them, and the pad of the first joggers starting their morning run.

'I nearly forgot. Val asked me to get your autograph.' He takes her first book from the car - *Bethany Dixon's Traditional Cooking*, fossicking in the glove-box for a pen. 'Embarrassing, eh?'

Bethany hesitates. He can see her asking herself what to say to this woman to whom she is finally bequeathing the past.

'Good wishes?' she says, reading his thoughts. 'Of course, I do wish her well, but that's what you write for strangers. I feel I know her better than that.'

'Kind regards?'

'God, no. Too formal.'

She turns the pen thoughtfully over in her fingers, and for a moment he thinks she won't write anything at all. In the end, she writes her name, Bethany Dixon, her usual flowing, slightly rounded script, and flourishes a line beneath her signature.

Then she kisses him on the cheek. 'See you round, sweet Pete.'

Perhaps for many couples who part, this is a bit of a fairytale, but it's one I enjoyed writing and I miss the Dixons as they settle into older age without me. They were my friends too. I look back and admire Bethany's youthful recklessness and I fancied her sweet Pete.

Of course, our friends change from time to time, in the same way that fashions do. Try being friends in politics. When British Prime Minister Harold Macmillan massacred his cabinet in 1962, someone quipped, 'Greater love hath no man than this, that he lay down his friends for his life.' Well, in politics it might be said that things only seem to change. I must say from where I'm standing, going into politics looks like one of the loneliest jobs in the world. I thought about it once or twice, seriously, and saw the light.

As for writers, well, we're friends a lot of the time, but you'll probably have fewer friends when your book is remaindered. Some of you may be familiar with a poem full of gleeful malice that begins, 'The book of my enemy has been remaindered and I am happy.' You can bet your last alphabet cookie that those writers are friends at the launch parties.

We can have friends who, as in one of my stories, were unsuitable. We grow up and get over them. Even if we're 50 when we meet them. We discover that people are not true friends after all, or they don't interest us in a lasting way and so on. But there are some friends, who, if we are serious about them, and they about us, we owe something to, and they to us, if we are to be true and constant in our friendship. Not always literal truth — Bertrand Russell wryly observed that if we're all given the magic power to read each other's thoughts, the first effect would probably be to dissolve all friendships. The thing is, most of our friends are flawed, imperfect human beings just like ourselves but if they don't need reminding by us, I think a kind of trueness should prevail that is in the end, truthfulness, as each one of us understands it.

Which brings me to another matter. As Murray has already mentioned, he heard me speaking on Kim Hill's programme about the death and its aftermath of my friend, Leigh Minnitt, who died at her husband's hand in 1980. It's difficult to talk about this too, but it's difficult in these circumstances not to either. I am aware of the dreadful pain that discussing this topic still causes many people.

For those of you who don't know what this is about, briefly, Dr David Minnitt shot his wife in their bedroom after an argument. It was a May and December marriage, as they say; he was some 30 years her senior. For a long time it worked well. They were childless, but they had affluence and status. And they were enthusiastic supporters of various liberal causes. He was our local family doctor and she was my good friend, as she was to many others. Things fell apart after Dr Minnitt had major heart surgery and in the three years that followed, he suffered an extreme change of personality and became, by turns, withdrawn and violent. As she wrestled with these problems, Leigh developed some demons of her own, like drinking too much.

Finally, — who of us didn't in those days, or even now — she fell in love with someone else and tried to leave. Only she didn't — she couldn't because, he killed her. I was one of the last people to speak to her on that fatal day and I do know that the use of a gun had been threatened. Not something I revealed at the time, for a variety of what I now think of as complex reasons, among them, fear. Fear of cross examination in court and the invasion of my own privacy — after all, the defendant knew the most intimate details of my life. I'm not proud of this. Times were different in 1980, but that's not quite good enough. Dr Minnitt was found guilty of manslaughter in a notorious trial, notable for the defence of provocation and the blackening of his wife's character. He was found guilty of manslaughter, spent about three years in jail and, after his release, returned to the practice of medicine.

I've been reported recently as saying that I thought that evidence I held back would have brought in a verdict of murder against Dr Minnitt. I have to say that if I gave that impression it was not entirely the one I had hoped to convey. In a sense, I believe the verdict of manslaughter was probably correct, not so much because Dr Minnitt was provoked, although he may have felt that he was, but because he was crazy. Guilty of manslaughter on the grounds of insanity. Good doctors don't go around shooting people, particularly their wives, because of arguments. It's the sort of thing you'd have to be crazy to do, wouldn't you?

I read a recent *New Yorker* piece called, 'When Good Doctors go Bad', in which the writer said, 'The real problem isn't just finding aberrations, it's what you might call every day bad doctors. In medicine, we all come to know such doctors: the illustrious cardiologist who is slowly going senile and won't retire; the long-respected obstetrician with a drinking problem; the surgeon who has somehow lost his touch. Good doctors can go bad and when they do, the medical profession is almost entirely unequipped to do anything about it.' So finally, there it was, something which sort of said it for me after all these years, and yes, medical and lay people did know about Doctor Minnitt's health problems.

So why now? What made me speak about it so long after the fact?

Well, because of friendship really, and the belief that friendship doesn't die with someone, although something can die with a friend. In my case, it was what was left of my innocence when I was about 40 about what people can do to each other. I learned that friendship demands a degree of courage, which I didn't have enough of at the time, but I don't think it's too late to seek it. For the word to be made true, if it's possible.

And Leigh wasn't one of those flawless human beings, those mythical, impossible characters. But whatever her failings, she was also beautiful, vivacious, generous and intelligent and all of this got left out of the record, the story of her life. The bad things became legend and the good forgotten and every now and then the media serves a story up like cold fritters, when people are looking for easy excuses for the inexcusable. And I asked myself one morning when I saw the story rehashed in the newspaper yet again, 'What would I want of my friends, if I was left marooned in history like this?' And I still come back, troubled but unequivocal, with a view that this was something I had to do. It *hasn't* been easy speaking out about it after all this time and perhaps this where it ends. Perhaps this *is* in fact enough.

Except perhaps to add this: it occurred to me more than once that it might have been something, a very small something, if Dr Minnitt had acknowledged a crime of passion. He might have said, 'I loved her so much, that I couldn't bear the thought of losing her. It drove me crazy that she would have gone.' We might just have begun to understand. Passion is so much easier to understand than righteousness.

So where do we as a nation stand on the subject of passion? Are we really a nation of 'passionless people'? Well, I don't think so. A couple of years ago I was commissioned to select a collection of New Zealand love stories for Oxford University Press. Over the space of about 18 months I read some five or six hundred New Zealand short stories, looking for expressions of love in our short fiction. And the conclusion I came to was this: we are a very passionate people indeed, but for a variety of reasons we have become inarticulate about expressing love to each other. True, we know the words of pop songs and crooners. How many of my generation first heard the words 'I love you' on car radios in the dimly lit back seats of cars? Words nobody had the courage to actually say to each other. 'True love', 'Oh baby mine', 'Look what you've done to me', 'I get so lonely when I dream about you', borrowed words, not our own. I did begin to wonder whether it's this suppressed voice that drives us to dark acts instead of tenderness.

For it seemed to me as I read, that many of our love stories on the surface are about everything but love itself. You could say it's a shyness, I suppose. And I guess we have to go back to our colonial past to understand how that came about. How, for instance, did one declare themselves a lover on a ship seemingly going nowhere, on a voyage that took months, amidst the crowd of people who inhabited your cabin? How did you stop to declare yourself a lover as you whacked down the bush and built a rough shelter for yourself? How did you say 'I love you' when you were scared and wet and cold?

Although, in fairness, people did write letters to their sweethearts and there was a marvellous exhibition at the National Library, a year or so back, called 'Posted Love' curated by Sophie Jerram, that exhibited New Zealanders' love letters to each other, and then there followed a book based on the exhibition that came out afterwards. I do recommend it to you. I'd like to read you one little extract by Truby King's father, Thomas King, writing to his wife during a period of separation in 1860:

> I am not ashamed, my darling, to tell you how I love you. How in the lonely nights I feel the blood coursing through my veins when your image rises before me. If I were to cease to love you I would cease to be happy. For no other woman is as fair and the remembrance of your embrace tells me of the bliss I am deprived of in my darling wife's absence.

Going back to the Oxford collection for a moment, I was very happy with the one that eventually emerged, although there are gaps and omissions, which I would love to fill. The need to collect stories from earlier times meant that some of the more recent language of love didn't get an airing and there is definitely more of it around. It seems to me that we as a people have never stopped loving each other but it's in recent times that we've learned to more eloquently articulate our love for each other. And on the whole, I think we are happier and freer for that. And as for me and who I love, well I think I've reached the age of discretion.

Lot of biographers around here. One of them, who shall remain nameless — oh, Michael I am sorry, I will never call you nameless — threatened to write my biography. Well, he does say that it was a playful comment and he doesn't really mean it, and he'd better be right.

I'd like at this stage of my life to be thought of as the lover, rather than the beloved. Who can really know who is doing the loving, except what one knows of themselves? I know I love children and grandchildren and yes, I do love my friends too. And each and every love is different.

I thought the place to end might be with a reading from a sequence of poems, which I could describe as a short history of love for my own friend and lover for 40 years. His name's Ian Kidman. These are the last four verses from the poem 'Wakeful Nights':

> 3
> *Leigh, North Auckland* the Jolly
> Fisherman's Lodge, approached
> from the wharves over slatted
> wooden bridges, suitcases
> in hand.   Your letter arrived
> for my birthday 1960:
> 'surprise surprise two letters
> from me and none from you, send
> me a telegram when you
> decide.' All I did was read
>
> all week watching the spinifex
> turn over in the sand. Only
> when the distant lights of boats shone
> through the shadow of the navy
> sea burning beyond the granite

cliffs, the haunted clay,
was it cool enough to consider
your proposal;
               in the end
I said yes, a strange
place to choose a life.

          4
In the dark the children's faces
like magnolia flowers on the pillows.
Whose turn to chase the milkman's
night delivery down the frosty road
the forgotten bottles clanking
against our dressing gowns? Those
children drank 8 pints a day.

          5
These wakeful nights went hand
in hand with grit, mad laughter
and tears; they were bodies turning
left to right right to left
against the gaunt, the red-eyed
dream. We listened to the winds
that sweep across
        Te Whanganui a Tara,
their muttered *kiss gasp kiss*
at the window pane, as we sought
each other's bones.   Instead
of resting, we tore the blankets
from side to side, avenging
late parties, nightmares, ordinary deceits.
Oh, in the end, we said
                        enough.

6
As the last light star
dissolves above the sea, you
place the white cup beside
the bed, love so various
has become kind: 'how did
            you sleep? the ritual
enquiry;
                'not badly'
I tell you,
     remembering
   one thought leading
to the next as the Judas
sheep leads its brothers up
the slaughterhouse ramp and
slips away, words ever
treacherous; the notebooks
go on filling night
        by lighted night,
those hours at last are friends.

   Do not think me changed, my
fabled fault and virtue to
love persistently, nothing
changes that.   I have simply
learned to guard the word
beyond the powerful dark;
        the sun fans along the hill
tops, I watch the bay, the sky
the heavy heavy languor
of the green curtain lifting.

2001 MICHAEL KING

Never Lost for Words

Thank you, Murray. It's wonderful to be here again and I feel very lucky to be invited back to the Going West Festival. It's also a great privilege to follow Fleur Adcock. I seem to have been associated with Fleur's extended family one way or another over a very long time. I've always greatly admired her, and we think she still belongs to us, even if she's still not sure. It's funny, when you talk to people in London about Fleur, as we were doing about two months ago, they speak of her as that English poet who sometimes goes to New Zealand. We of course think of her as that New Zealand poet who somehow got stranded in London and feel that she'll come back, if someone gives her the opportunity. But wonderful poetry Fleur, thank you — wonderful to hear you live for a change.

I won't reiterate things that have been already said, except to say that what I had proposed to say and what I'd been thinking about saying was rendered utterly inappropriate by the 9/11 events of this last week and it meant that the words seemed inadequate, the jokes seemed inappropriate, and the whole way I was approaching the topic, in the light of what we've recently experienced, seemed full of hubris. So I'm going to do something else. Something, as they say, entirely different, if you'll forgive me. It strikes, I hope, the right note, and does in a kind of Byzantine convoluted way, come back around to the topic of this festival.

I'm going to tell you a story about my great-uncle, whose footsteps I was tracing three months ago in Eldridge Street in Lower Manhattan, under the shadow of the World Trade Centre towers. I also want to tell you this story because it has Auckland and West Auckland connections, and because of the knowledge that we're going to hear this weekend from a wider range of voices than simply the Anglo-Celtic ones of mainstream New Zealand.

For me however, the story begins not with the great-uncle, but with his son, Roy Belgrave, who married my mother's sister. Roy was my godfather and my favourite uncle. He was one of those adults with the rare capacity to be relaxed and genial in the company of young people, and this at a time in my life when most adults believed in the maxim about children being 'seen and not heard'. Roy, for example, bought me chewing gum, which my parents forbade us to eat as vulgar. He made homebrew in the garage in his home in Takapuna and he let me slurp spoonfuls from the jars of malt that went into the beer. He also let me drink small glasses of the brew itself when I was ready, and at home I wasn't allowed to touch any form of alcohol until I was eighteen. And, I had this unspoken understanding with Roy that I didn't tell my parents when I got home exactly what I'd been doing in his garage.

Best of all, however, and what I remember with most pleasure, Roy would take us off with my cousins for swims off the coast of both sides of the Auckland isthmus, including Muriwai, Piha and Karekare, chugging there and back through the dust — all those roads were unsealed in those days — chugging there and back in his ancient but reliable Ford Anglia. On colder days we went as far as the hot pools at Parakai and these weekend expeditions were for me, a Wellingtonian, my first taste of West Auckland. They were also punctuated by the sounds of horse races on the radio, another pastime my parents strongly disapproved of.

Most of all I have to say, I enjoyed Roy's sardonic view of the world.

He was scathing for example, about the number of Power Board workers, each feather-bedded by union demarcation, who arrived one day to rectify a simple electrical fault. On another occasion, he told me how preposterous it was that his next-door neighbour had made a fortune manufacturing women's underwear. Women's underwear! While he, a civil servant, responsible at this time for Naval Stores, involved in activities that actually allowed the country to function, earned a fraction of his neighbour's income from underwear.

All this was communicated to me in what I thought of as Roy's old-fashioned accent, one that was actually closer to Australian speech than modern New Zealand. The long vowel on *school*, for example. It was no accident that he and Frank Sargeson, who had an identical accent, recognised themselves as fellow Hamilton High School old boys, when they met on the long North Shore walks they both took in old age.

There was one topic that I learned however I could not discuss with this very affable uncle and that was anything that verged on criticism of the one Holy Catholic and Apostolic Church. Roy was a stalwart member of the Takapuna parish and belonged to the Knights of the Southern Cross, a kind of Catholic/Masonic organisation, modelled on the American Knights of Columbus, and formed initially to work unquestioningly and sometimes underground on behalf of the Church's bishops. When I had run-ins with the late Archbishop Liston in the late 1960s, Roy would take no criticism of the octogenarian prelate. 'Jimmy Liston's a saint,' he told me on more than one occasion. 'If you're offside with him you'd best look to your own conscience for an explanation.'

There was another quality of Roy's that made me uncomfortable though it was not uncommon among Catholics of his generation. He was mildly anti-Semitic. More than once I heard him speak disparagingly of Jewish lawyers or Jewish businessmen as if such people formed a fraternity based on religion or ethnicity, that sought to shut others out, and as if they were only interested in money and in protecting their own. What made this quality of particular interest in Roy's case, was the fact that, good Catholic though he was, and Irish as he was via his mother's ancestry, there was a question mark over his own ethnic background, or to be more precise, over the cultural and geographical origin of his father, Maurice John Belgrave, a prominent businessman in that part of Hamilton that used to be known as Frankton Junction. We didn't know much about 'Mr Bel', as my mother always called Roy's father, my great-uncle by marriage. A large swarthy man in later years, Maurice Belgrave had turned up in New Zealand from London in 1908. Initially he sold fabrics, needles, buttons and thread from a handcart in the small communities that bordered the main trunk line in the central North Island. He had a gift for salesmanship, and he loved the patter and the banter that accompanied it. He worked hard, he lived frugally and by 1911 he'd been able to open a drapery store in Frankton Junction. In 1911, Maurice became a Roman Catholic in order to marry 22-year-old Margaret Josephine Hartnett, later known to her family as Nim, who worked in the Frankton shop. Maurice was at this time 29, solidly built, strikingly handsome, moustached, and charming.

He told Margaret's Irish Catholic parents that he was a Gaelic-speaking Scottish Presbyterian, which explained the slight accent and the ignorance of Catholic liturgy and culture. On his marriage certificate however, he gave his birthplace as London and his parent's names as Alfred and Sarah Belgrave. Whatever cultural and religious antecedents Maurice Belgrave had abandoned in the Old World, he indicated to his wife's family that he was happy to convert to Catholicism and no further questions were raised about his background. The marriage was solemnised with a nuptial mass. A lengthy report in the *Waikato Times* gave generous space to details of the bride's family — her father worked for the railways in Hinuera — and none whatsoever about the groom's relations.

In due course, the Belgraves became established in Frankton as a prominent Catholic clan with three boys, of whom my uncle, Oscar Roy, although he never used the Oscar, was the oldest. They attended Mass together on Sundays and worked when called upon to do so on behalf of the parish.

The Frankton business prospered, particularly after the railways built extensive new housing in town for their employees. By the 1930s, the family was well provided for. They owned sections in other parts of Hamilton, and they began to build a bach at Eastern Beach on the coastal outskirts of Auckland.

Even when the drapery store was well established however, Maurice still liked nothing better than packing suitcases with samples and supplies and setting off for days and sometimes weeks, to sell on the road. This habit became a matter of comment within the family. Was he an inveterate wanderer? Was he addicted to the patter of salesmanship, or was he simply trying to get out from under his wife's regime of solid respectability? Nim Belgrave had become by the 1930s, a matriarchal figure of substantial character and authority.

It was about this time that my mother's family came into contact with the Belgraves. Roy, an intelligent and ambitious young man, began work in the Government Printing Office in Wellington, in the early 1930s, with my mother's brother Bernie. Bernie brought Roy home for meals and for musical evenings on Sunday nights. And Roy began to court my mother's sister, Mona, whose beguiling soprano voice was on display on these weekend evenings around the piano in Ngaio. In the course of their courtship, Mona went to stay with Roy's family in Frankton. My mother, two years younger, went along as chaperone. In no way did she resent this role. She enjoyed the ebullient Belgraves, all of whom had a well-developed sense of fun, loved picnics and card playing and singing around the piano and followed the horse racing meetings around the Waikato countryside.

When Roy and Mona eventually married in 1939 after a long engagement, my mother was a bridesmaid and Roy's brother Claude best man. Relations between the two families became strained however. First Nim Belgrave demanded that the wedding be held in Frankton, even though the bride lived in Wellington, then she insisted on a mysterious gap of several hours, between the mass and the post-wedding function. After the nuptial mass and the photographs outside the church, Nim and Maurice shocked my grandparents by heading off to the races at Te Rapa. The suspicion grew and indeed it seems justified that the Belgraves had wanted the wedding conducted on their own patch solely so as not to miss one of the more exciting events in the year's racing calendar.

Years later my mother told me she'd been sweet on Claude Belgrave, although she hastened to say it was in the years before she met my father. But her strongest words of affection were reserved for her 'Mr Bel', Roy's and Claude's father. He had been, she said, like an uncle to her and this in a country where she had no flesh and blood uncles of her own. He teased her, he encouraged her, he showered her with affection. Told her she was beautiful and in general made her feel good about herself. Like my mother, 'Mr Bel' sang and played the piano, and this was a further source of the rapport between them.

By New Zealand standards however, one has to say, 'Mr Bel' was eccentric. While he took care to avoid any disclosure about his possible family background, he was nonetheless careless of convention and didn't give a damn about what other people thought of his behaviour. One of his routines was to strip to the waist in front of an outside mirror and basin in front of his shop and shave there each morning, greeting and conversing with passers-by. His customary way of attracting the attention of his family in a crowded public place was a high-volume whistle. 'Ignore him,' Nim would always say to her children. After having to stand all day in the shop, he liked to soak his swollen feet in a basin of water in the evenings. If people called to visit, he would stand up to shake hands, but his feet remained in the basin, just as they did when he played cards.

I have no first-hand recollections of 'Mr Bel'. He died in 1944, one year before I was born but I knew Nim and their three sons and the offspring of those three sons, with whom I grew up and played as cousins. And they were, and are, an unusually talented lot. John Belgrave, now chairman of the Commerce Commission, is like his father Roy, a public servant with a penchant for administration. Michael Belgrave, is like me, an historian and a former research director of the Waitangi Tribunal. Kate Belgrave is a feisty journalist and so on.

What we didn't know in childhood and didn't begin to discuss until a much later time, was where the Belgrave name and patrimony might have originated. Were they all descended from Scottish Presbyterians? Were they connected to the respectable English Belgraves, whose name in Old English meant groves where Martins live? Maurice Belgrave's marriage certificate alleged that he'd been born in London in 1882. His passage to New Zealand on the steam ship *Paparoa*, also originated in London. On the strength of this evidence, my cousin Peter Belgrave searched for a record of his grandfather's birth in Somerset House in London in the 1960s. He found nothing. This raised the possibility that Maurice John might have had origins that were, to our Anglo-Celtic minds, more exotic than British roots. Might he in fact have come from Europe and changed his name to Belgrave?

I put this question to my mother, when I was compiling tapes on family history in the late 1980s. 'Well,' she said, 'I'd never really believed the Presbyterian story', and there was evidence that it was a fabrication. Maurice and Nim had in their household a woman named Annie Jones, known to the family as Ciss, who acted as housekeeper and child-minder. In August 1944, Ciss had come upon Maurice in his living room. He was listening to a BBC radio programme, with tears glistening on his cheeks. On air, a journalist was speaking about Nazi extermination camps in Eastern Europe and the fact that the majority of inmates and victims were Jewish. 'Those are my people,' a grief-stricken Maurice told Ciss. He was already seriously ill, suffering from the effects of diabetes. Days after hearing this broadcast, he was dead from a heart attack. After hearing about this episode from Claude Belgrave, my mother was sure that Maurice was Jewish and had fled Eastern Europe, possibly to escape pogroms in the years before the First World War. 'The name Belgrave,' she said, 'mightn't even be his. He could have been in London preparing to board a ship to New Zealand and seen a sign saying Belgravia and invented a name like that to disguise his identity.'

My mother had first-hand experience of the kinds of unpleasantness which might have led to such a ploy. Her first job after leaving school had been with a firm of Jewish furriers in Wellington. The owners of the company were excessively frugal; they spent little money on staff amenities and tried to discourage workers taking morning and afternoon tea breaks. This was not viewed as a tendency on the part of employers in general to screw down labour and production costs; instead it was attributed entirely by the Gentile staff to the fact that the owners were Jewish, and therefore expected to be mean with money. Nothing was said within earshot of the employers. Out of earshot however, comments were of a sharply derogatory and decidedly ethnic character.

I have no precise recollection of when I first became aware of Jews as people supposedly different from other New Zealanders. In the enclosed world of pre-Vatican II Catholicism in which I grew up, the cultural frontier in New Zealand, reinforced by separate education systems, appeared to be between Catholics and Protestants or to a lesser extent, between Pākehā and Māori.

I do remember the nuns at convent school telling us that the Jews had been God's chosen people, that he had promised to send them a Messiah and that when that Messiah arrived in the form of Jesus Christ, the Jews had not recognised him. Worse than that, they'd put Christ to death and thus became guilty of the monstrous crime of deicide: killing God.

This view of history was reinforced annually by prayers in the Easter liturgy for the conversion of Jews, which was sandwiched between those for heretics and schismatics and the conversion of Pagans, and this particular prayer went thus:

> Let us pray for the perfidious Jews, that the Lord our God may take the veil from their hearts and that they may also acknowledge our Lord Jesus Christ … Almighty and everlasting God, you do not refuse Your mercy even to the faithless Jews; hear the prayers which we offer for the blindness of that people so that they may acknowledge the light of Your truth … and be delivered from their darkness.

The gospel of St Luke, read on Easter Wednesday, painted a picture of the Jews apparently intensifying their guilt. 'Crucify Him, crucify him!' the crowd cried when Pilate offered to release Christ and most tellingly, and most often quoted in the gospel of St Matthew, 'His blood be upon us and upon our children.'

The consequence of this iniquitous behaviour, Sister Isidore told us, was apparent in the fact that the curtain that hid the Holy of Holies in the temple at Jerusalem was rent in two at the moment Christ died; and that the Jews, from being God's Chosen People, became an accursed people doomed to wander the earth forever, rootless, despised and persecuted and still waiting, ever more hopelessly for the Messiah who would unite and save them. The role of Judaism in the eyes of Catholics, shrank to that of a precursor, or an anticipation of the real business of God, which was a relationship with humankind transacted through Christianity.

Another story of Sister Isidore's chilled us and thrilled us with its implications. She said that when Christ was carrying His cross through the streets of Jerusalem to Calvary, He rested for a moment against the doorway of a Jewish shoemaker. In Jerusalem, not surprising. But that was always said, 'a Jewish shoemaker'. This man opened the door and told Him to move on. 'I shall move on,' Christ was reported to have said, 'but you will be condemned to wait for me until I return.' That shoemaker, Sister Isidore revealed, as a consequence of his lack of recognition and lack of compassion, was thereafter condemned to wander the earth until Christ's Second Coming. He had been seen in Europe on authenticated occasions throughout the Middle Ages. He was known as the 'Wandering Jew' and in all probability, he walked the earth still to expiate for his sinful rejection of the Messiah.

There were contradictions in the nuns' view of history and theology that had already become apparent to me by the time I was debating religious issues at secondary school. If it was the will of God the Father that His Son had to die to redeem humanity, then how could that be the fault of anyone other than God? And surely, had it not been the Romans who introduced crucifixion as a punishment for troublemakers throughout the

Empire, and Roman soldiers who had driven the nails through Christs's body? Even more puzzling in this context of Jewish culpability, why was it never put to us that Jesus Himself, his Holy Mother, His stepfather St Joseph, and every one of the Twelve Apostles were also Jewish? And why was it that in the religious literature of the day, the *villains* of the gospel story, Judas Iscariot, the Sadducees, the Pharisees, often looked evilly Semitic, with bushy eyebrows, hook-noses and snarling features, while Jesus and His Mother and the Apostles all looked distinctly Aryan and pious?

I tell you as a sidebar to that: an American student solved this for me when I was teaching there earlier this year by saying, he'd been told at school what happened and 'Oh it's quite simple. Jesus was Jewish until they crucified him and then he became Christian.'

Two other stories from that time remain with me. One of the priests who taught me at secondary school told us how his father would gird himself each year in fancy dress costume for the parade associated with the Wairoa A&MP show. He put on a mask with an enormous false nose, a top hat and a long black coat to appear as 'Ikey'. There was no racial malice involved, simply an assumption that that was what Jews looked like and they were amusing in Anglo-Celtic eyes.

The same priest spoke of coming across in the seminary library the *Protocols of the Elders of Zion* which he said, explained that 'the Jews' were responsible for revolutions, the threat of revolutions and the control of the international financial system. The contents of this book were not made the subject of formal priestly training, but neither was there any information attached to the volume which made it clear that the work was a notorious forgery, designed by the Tsarist secret police to discredit Jews and add momentum to anti-Semitism in Russia.

That set of school-time memories is utterly clear. What is less clear is when I became aware of real Jewish people and of anti-Semitism outside the context of explanations of the gospel story. In my secondary school years, we took annual winter holidays on Mt Ruapehu and belonged to the Ruapehu Ski Club. Here there seemed to be a plethora of what I eventually recognised as Jewish families or families that had at least one Jewish parent. I remember the Bohmers, the Bolots, the Shenkins, the van Dingles, the Mitchells, the Turnovskys, the Munzes, the Geiringers and the Priors.

And I remember one particular girl, spectacularly attractive and athletic, who was to be seen out skiing each day with one particular boy. I had given no thought at all to the young woman's ethnicity, until I overheard the father of the boy say to his wife, as they put on their skis outside the lodge, 'I don't want him hanging round with that greasy little Jewess.' To say I was astonished and appalled would be an understatement. I was 14 years old and I was literally for the first time, and for about half a day afterwards, struck dumb. I had to physically remove myself from the company of others, so that I would not have to participate in conversation. All I had been exposed to in the past was a sectarian religious view that Jewish people were unfortunates, who had missed an opportunity for redemption by failing to recognise, and then killing off, their own Messiah, and that they'd been made to suffer for this error of judgement. I had never before encountered first-hand evidence of unmistakable dislike for someone because of their ethnicity, nor could I see the relevance of the accusation. The young woman concerned was beautiful and well-groomed. There was no sign anywhere on her person of anything that might have earned the epithet 'greasy'. Nor had I previously heard the term 'Jewess', and the manner in which it was hissed clearly redolent of venom.

It was soon after this that I had an experience that almost everybody my age can recall, seeing for the first time in a cinema, documentary footage of the opening of the death camps in Eastern Europe at the end of the Second World War. The condition of the wretched survivors, the spectacle of emaciated corpses, the sheer number of those exterminated, all this implied an evil so vast, that it was all but incomprehensible to an adolescent mind. I felt physically sick if I brought these pictures back into my mind. How could people treat any sentient creatures that way, let alone fellow human beings? And yet even as this thought occurred to me, I still had the fresh memory of a respectable church-going Wellington businessman, a good family-man, and a generous contributor to community projects, who had served in the Second World War, saying with such passion, about a child from a family socially very much like his own, 'greasy little Jewess'. Was there some connection? Wasn't anti-Semitism something he had chosen to combat by fighting Hitler's forces? I didn't care to discuss this juxtaposition with any adult. I now, not for the first time, mistrusted any sense with which the adult world might reconcile these two events, one cosmic, the other local. They pointed to a horror of such proportion that I shrank from exploring it. That fear was that there might be people in my own community or my own country, otherwise decent people, who might condone, or worse, approve of what had been done to Jews in Hitler's Europe.

At this time, I lost the ability to laugh at any joke, however harmlessly intended, that poked fun at or caricatured Jewish humour. When my Christian Doctrine teacher at secondary school referred to a cash register as a 'Jewish piano', I shuddered with reverberations of what else he might believe. Had I been more courageous, I might have got to my feet and left the class. He, I imagine, would have put that comment in the same category as the jokes he also told which cast doubt on the intelligence or common sense of the Irish. But he was Irish, and there is a difference between self-deprecation and deprecation of others, and while there had been persecution of the Irish, disastrous famines and an Irish diaspora, there had been no Irish equivalent, recent or otherwise, of what was increasingly being referred to as the Holocaust, or the Shoah. Nobody had set out systematically to annihilate the Irish in Ireland or elsewhere.

It may have been a vestige of this feeling, even an intuition that Christians owed Jewish people some kind of atonement, that drew me in the direction of Jewish students at university. Or it may simply have been the coincidence that Jewish students were involved in university cultural and political affairs in numbers far out of their proportion in the student population. Whichever it was, after I turned eighteen, my world seemed to be as full of people who were ethnically, if not religiously Jewish, as it had been previously of Irish Catholics. I flatted with Tony Haas and Paul Peretz. I was involved with them and with Michael Hirschfeld in student politics. I socialised with Carol Bohmer, Monique Block, Helen Schwartz and the Lenart brothers. I courted Linda Sacklin. Peter Munz was far and away my most stimulating teacher in history and Eric Geiringer became my doctor.

In all our various interactions there was scarcely any discussion of our respective ethnic or religious backgrounds, except when marriages were in prospect and parental difficulties anticipated over the business of marrying 'out'. They knew I was Catholic. I knew they were Jewish, without knowing precisely what that meant to them. And I was aware that, while there were no Jewish schools in Wellington, some of them had had previous contact and developed friendships through membership of the Jewish youth group, Habonim. Some, including Michael Hirschfeld were Zionists and went to Israel to work on Kibbutzim and actively promoted within the Labour Party, policies sympathetic to Israel's position.

Tony Haas my flatmate and later my best-man, when under stress, would occasionally cry out, 'Oy vey! Oy vey!' in a kind of caricature of himself. But because I never visited a synagogue, nor ate with the families of Jewish friends on occasions of religious significance, I never saw them behave in ways that were appreciably different from those of my own family. I was aware however, that some of the parents of these friends had what were, by Anglo-Celtic New Zealand standards, exotic backgrounds. There were for a start, the Central or East European accents, which to my ears were redolent of culture and charm. There were occasional references to life in Russia or Czechoslovakia, or Poland, or Lithuania or Austria. There was a degree of sophistication in the business of eating and drinking and the serving of wine with meals, which we run-of-the-mill New Zealanders regarded as 'Continental'. And there were hints, just hints of unspeakable circumstances, that had propelled these families as far from Europe as it was possible to travel. There was also an unspoken but ever-present acknowledgement, sometimes in the location of framed photographs, of the loss of other family members in those same unspeakable circumstances. It was the subject of too much gravitas to be raised in conversation by, or with, a non-family member.

Over all these years however, and the years that followed, and in the course of those and other relationships, the one group of people I never thought of as Jewish were my Belgrave cousins because they were *not* Jewish in any sense that mattered or was visible or documentable. Like me, they were Catholic. They'd had the same kinds of upbringing as I'd had and, for the most part, gone to the same kinds of schools. Despite the question mark over their grandfather's origins, if they had any kind of ethnic identity over and above being New Zealanders, it was Irish Catholic, like my own. And that was the sole context in which I placed them, until I took a telephone call in Dunedin early last year.

The voice was American and unknown to me. The caller said that he was a psychoanalyst from New York, named David Belgray, and that he'd just been given my number by cousin Kate Belgrave, with whom he'd just had dinner. He had come to New Zealand to try to make contact with members of his extended family and that family he said was, or had been, Jewish. Their name in Europe had been Bilgoraj.

The Bilgorajs had originated in that enormous corridor of Jewish settlement, that had grown up in an arc from the Baltic states through the western provinces of Russia and down to the Black Sea. That so-called 'Pale of Settlement' embraced what is now parts of Poland, Latvia, Lithuania, Byelorussia, the Ukraine, Romania and Bulgaria. Until the Second World War it had contained the largest Jewish population in the world, and the greatest reservoir of Jewish culture. As David Belgray's family members had sought to escape poverty or persecution there, and made their way to various sanctuaries in the New World, they had anglicized their name: to Bilgrei, Bilgrey, Belgray and Bilgoray in the United States; to Bilgora and Bilgorri in England; to Belgrave in New Zealand; and to other versions of the name in the countries that were not English speaking. My great-uncle, he told me, had been his father's first cousin and his name in Europe had been not Maurice Belgrave, but Moshe Bilgoraj. He had made his way to New Zealand via Vienna, the East End of London and the Lower East side of New York.

While this news was confirmation of something I had believed since my discussion with my mother a decade earlier, it was confirmation with a degree of particularity that I, a professional historian, had thought would be impossible to achieve. It was more than 80 years since my great-uncle had turned up in New Zealand with no evidence of any past. The idea that the family might be able to trace his origins down that corridor of time, without even knowledge of his real name, or the country in which he had been born, had seemed preposterous. A search for a needle in the proverbial haystack. And now, without any warning, an arm had reached out of the haystack and handed me the needle. I had gone in a matter of minutes from knowing *nothing* about my great-uncle's family, to having an instant context of considerable breadth, depth and complexity. That revelation was, and is, a great gift and I propose to make use of it the way I suspect any writer would.

I'm haunted by curiosity to know what life was like for a man who came out of the Shtetls of Eastern Europe, who knew the fields and hills of Galicia and the forests of the Carpathians, to push a handcart full of fabric and buttons through the steep limestone valleys of the King of country. Who, in order to conduct business there, had to add English and Māori to the Yiddish, German and Polish he already spoke. I wonder too what might have been the psychical price for severing all connections with his family of origin, his culture, his birth religion and reinventing Moshe Bilgoraj of Southeast Poland as Maurice John Belgrave, Roman Catholic businessman of Frankton Junction.

Most of all, I'm haunted by the image of my mother's 'Mr Bel', normally the most cheerful of all men, slumped in front of a radio, head bowed, weeping at the monstrous fate of East European Jewry, and I can't help but wonder if his death only days later, was a consequence of that revelation.

In investigating this topic, I will be writing about a New Zealand that was not in those pre-World War Two years, welcoming of people who were neither British nor Irish. I will be writing about a mainstream culture that heard and wanted to hear its Anglo-Celtic voices and not those of New Zealand Māori, Jews, Dalmatians, Italians or Chinese. It is an era that has ended mercifully, as a richly variegated programme of this festival reminds us, but it is an era that contains the cultural soil in which our Pākehā culture was nourished, and that offers a basis for understanding what is past or passing or to come. Most urgently of course, I shall investigate the topic the way a writer does, via language. Because language is the only vehicle we have to pursue thought, feeling, memory and action and to attempt to make sense of our individual and collective experience. And because, thank God, until we are felled by death or incapacity, the one commodity of which we are never short, is words.

And thus, I do in the end, finish this presentation with what has been chosen as the title of this festival, as it is the title of Amelia Batistich's most recent, marvellous book, *Never Lost for Words*. Long may it be so for all of us.

Shalom. Kia ora koutou. Zdravo. Thank you for your attention and patience.

2002 DAME MARILYN WARING

Tracking the Vernacular

Taupiri te maunga. Waikato te awa. Te iwi Pākehā. Tēnā koutou katoa. 'Tracking the vernacular' — I worried this subject for weeks. Of any title I might comfortably have arrived at to speak on, this one would not have entered the picture. For the first time I've been asked in New Zealand to speak about writing. So, I'd be driving along uttering the mantra — tracking the *vernacular*, tracking *the* vernacular, tracking the *vernacular*? Etcetera. After some weeks of this, my mind led me home, quite literally, to a line in a piece I had written for the *Waikato Times* on 'nostalgia'. It was to be the first in a series from old local identities and mine was on Taupiri, where I grew up. Near the middle of the essay I'd written:

> For most travellers Taupiri is a blur on the map, with nothing to distinguish it from a myriad of similar towns around the country. But for me as a child, the whole place was a playground. We could rove and roam pathways, riverbanks, school fields, sports grounds, backyards and paddocks freely, as if they were our own. I remember the shock of the UK immigrant newcomers, who were building their house, telling us we were trespassing and couldn't take the shortcut

through their property from the dairy factory on our way home from school. Trespass wasn't the sort of word you used in Taupiri.

'Trespass' wasn't the kind of word you used in Taupiri — in remembering that I arrived at my beginning. Perhaps I could track my vernacular, with all its twists and turns, and see where that led me. I recognise that my vernacular is very culturally and environmentally determined, but the impacts of these influences were felt in quite distinct ways. I'm able to trace some of that through my writing and a couple of selections from the writing of others that influenced me at different times.

So, let me begin again. I wrote a piece called 'On Claiming a Pakeha Identity' in January 1996:

We'd been horse trekking for three days between Pakiri and Te Arai, around the Tomarata Lakes and along glorious beaches — clean air, clean water, rarely seeing other people.

On the way home the 17-year-old, a prefect that year in a private girls' school, began a conversation about what it meant for her to be a Pakeha New Zealander. This had been provoked in part by her indignation, on registering at the school for 1996, to find that she was expected to identify herself as 'European'.

I had also been indignant about the issue in days past, when I'd read an opinion piece by the then Minister for the Arts Simon Upton labelled, 'I am European and proud of it'. It purported to be about cultural identity. 'I'm European', he wrote. 'Their culture is my culture … If, as a European New Zealander, you want to understand why you think or speak as you do, your search will lead you back to European roots.' It claimed, 'we shouldn't be trying to deny who any of us are or where we come from'. Well, Simon and I both come from Ngaruawahia, on the Waikato River, bordered by the Hakarimatas. Coming from this place certainly informs why I think and speak as I do, and it's a considerable distance from any land mass regarded as European.

Where I grew up, in Taupiri, all of us went home for kai, wore potae, took a mimi behind the trees, observed the tangi at the end of the road, talked about different tane and wahine, and kuia and mokopuna in the village. It would have been a foreign language for any European child, even a British one.

Of course, this time of our childhood coincided with Macmillan and de Gaulle bantering over whether Britain could be part of Europe, and the cultural cringe of that time was the notion that to be British could possibly mean being European. Britain's joining the European Economic Community has always been the moment in my lifetime when I think a large sector of the population of New Zealand grasped the opportunity to cast off a toadying deference to roots then four to five generations old.

To the young woman asking, I expressed my notion of being Pakeha, beginning with my inability to describe my identity and where I come from, without speaking te reo ... I spoke of topographies and colours, of long and wide uncluttered spaces, of the textures of feathers and fauna not found anywhere else, of the remnants of dinosaurs called tuatara, of kakapo and kiwi, of kauri and puriri. I again resorted to that non-European language ...

And when I moved to speak of the music and fashions of my generation's culture, I resorted to the lyrics of two other local Waikato lads, Neil and Tim Finn, who began a song on an album released at the height of Split Enz fame in 'Europe', 'I was born in Te Awamutu'. I was delighted to find in another publication some days later that Tim Finn was fond of quoting Gertrude Stein's line: 'People are the way their land and air is.' Upton probably doesn't agree: after all, he was a transplanted US citizen. But to be European in the way their land and air is? Spare me. The rainbows are layers of the varieties of suspended pollutants. The mosses of Denmark will radiate Chernobyl's poison for 10,000 years.

'There's something a little immature, Upton wrote, 'in the habit of some New Zealanders trying to define themselves without reference to their European cultural roots.' In which case this privileged well-travelled Pakeha, who could afford to leave Aotearoa and sample the opera of London and Milan, the architecture of Rheims and Wurzburg, the galleries of Amsterdam and Florence, and feel inconsolably homesick all the way, will wear the immaturity with pride.

Aroha Mead says citizenship is about identity. There's something privileged and arrogant about refusing to embrace being Pakeha, and a cowardice I smell there too. I cannot avoid the conclusion that if generations of your family have been born in Aotearoa New Zealand, to choose to call yourself European is to deliberately and consciously choose to continue the process of colonisation, not only of the tangata whenua, but of all others here too.

Cultural identity is a cutting edge debate, inviting a personal decision which varies with experience and information, for those who are willing to embrace cutting edge debates. I was amused to see the deft kick for touch made by the Department of Statistics in their 1996 census: *Are you a New Zealand European or Pakeha*? it asked, and neatly trapped Upton and me in the same identity.

I'm sure that many people who have passed through Taupiri might think that the vernacular of Taupiri would be limited in terms of its politics and international engagement with the critical issues of the late 1950s and early 1960s, when I was growing up. In my *Waikato Times* piece on nostalgia, I recalled, 'Everyone knew everyone. Several times a year I knocked on every door in town selling Girl Guide biscuits or the gestetnered school magazine or tennis club raffle tickets. And every year the local Seventh Day Adventists … and the local IHC collectors would knock at our door.'

Harry Clarke also knocked at our door. Harry was a member of the Beijing-aligned New Zealand Communist Party. He was known to everybody and nobody worried about the CPNZ. In Taupiri when people knocked at your door you gave what you could. When I was nine, my father bought me Bertrand Russell's *Common Sense and Nuclear Warfare* from Harry. I read:

> In reading of the plans of militarists, I try very hard to divest myself for the time being of the emotions of horror and disgust. But when I read of plans to defile the heavens by the petty squabbles of the animated lumps that disgrace a certain planet, I cannot but feel that the men who make these plans are guilty of a kind of impiety ... I hope, though with much doubt, that some gleams of sanity may yet shine in the minds of statesmen. But the spread of power without wisdom is utterly terrifying, and I cannot much blame those whom it reduces to despair.
>
> But despair is not wise. Men are capable not only of fear and hate, but of hope and benevolence.

Hope and benevolence. Perhaps I might have expected something of that in the vernacular of my next twist of fate. At the end of two years at the Ngāruawāhia High School, I was sent to the Waikato Diocesan School for Girls. On my first day there I added to my vernacular: Mercedes-Benz, Porsche, Citroën and Jaguar. They were not the sort of words we learned to spell in Taupiri and Ngāruawāhia. Within my first week came a letter from my dad and a small book inscribed 'For no particular reason'. You can ruminate for years on why he sent the *Rubaiyat of Omar Khayyam* to the Waikato Diocesan School for Girls.

But along with this also came litanies, liturgies and epiphanies — the last of which I certainly didn't experience very much. And at a time when my C-drive (C for cerebral) was just hitting the fast lane, it was filled with the lyrics of 636 *Hymns, Ancient and Modern*. Thirty-five years later, I know most of the words on Sunday radio broadcasts.

From Diocesan I went to Victoria University to study law and politics. At first I was confronted with complexity and — to give a taste of that arcane world that I entered — I brought along *The Poverty of Historicism*, by Karl Popper, who once refused a professorship at Canterbury University.

But I opened it just a little while ago and I really don't think that I can subject any of you to the turgid complexity of this, except I'll just share a little bit because he's comparing sociology and the social sciences with the natural sciences. I can say in his defence that this was probably written before quantum physics got close to chaos theory, but it was certainly post the Copenhagen school of relativity and complementarity. So, when he says things like 'In physics we are dealing with a subject matter which is much less complicated. In spite of that, we further simplify matters artificially by the method of experimental isolation', I wonder how he would have dealt with quarks.

It was possible to read this, and Schumpeter, and all the other turgid texts we were subjected to in politics, and to have only clinically detached thoughts, which was encouraged in those of us who were students in the social sciences in the early seventies. But other lectures and the stirring of the new phase of the women's movement made clinical detachment more and more difficult. I managed to stay in law school until I had to study Criminal Law and I joined the feminist movement.

Something I wrote before major law changes, gives an interesting reflection on the law school vernacular I had to leave:

> Some women believe that there is a law that protects their physical integrity, the protection of the right to choose whether, when and with whom to have a sexual connection. They're wrong — the essence of the crime is theft of another man's property.
>
> It is called 'rape'.
>
> There is a belief that marriage is a partnership of equals, a relationship of mutual rights and obligations. But you cannot, it appears, violate your own property, so that, 'no man shall be convicted of rape in respect of his intercourse with his wife'.
>
> This is called 'spousal immunity'.
>
> There is a belief that increased awareness of the horror of rape has changed the system to lessen the trauma for victims. Throughout the country, when the victim reports to a police station she is led

through locked doors, along cell-lined corridors full of those under arrest, to a converted cell, cramped, badly equipped, often poorly cleaned, for a medical examination.

She may have a policewoman with her. It is unlikely she will be examined by a woman doctor. She is unlikely to have any close friends with her as support.

This is called being 'treated sympathetically'.

Women believe that in saying 'no' they have demonstrated lack of consent. Men believe 'no' means 'yes'. So if you're raped after a fight with your husband or lover because he wants to 'make up', or by someone in authority over you ... or because you are blackmailed into it ... or because you know from years of experience that the peace is easier than the resistance, then the law is subject to the House of Lords decision in Morgan's case on consent.

With all the massive legal adherence to the standard of the reasonable man (and notwithstanding the compounding problem of this sex bias), Morgan's case sets a different standard. A defendant should not be convicted of rape if he genuinely believed that the woman was consenting, whether or not his view was based on reasonable grounds.

This is called a 'successful defence'.

It is generally believed that rape is a crime of violence. But the law says it is possible to be raped without violence, so that the media will report and judges will repeat: 'Fortunately the complainant was not injured.'

This is called 'rape simpliciter'.

People who have never attended court hearings before and who are called as witnesses to a rape case cannot believe that defendants, especially those who raise consent as a defence, can remain silent. The victim spends her time on trial in the witness box, often for more than a day. The defendant is innocent until proven guilty; the victim is guilty until proving herself innocent.

This is called 'centuries of legal tradition'.

I dropped out of law school. This was assisted by the voices of women in New Zealand, and some born in New Zealand, who were publishing texts that were recommended reading by the time I hit my Honours year — Juliet Mitchell's *Woman's Estate*:

> The assimilation of Women's Liberation by the media into colourful reportage may be symptomatic of something more than its hungry lust for sexual objects in any shape they come. As individuals, many men react to women's claims with fear or, alternatively, with bemused, compensatory tolerance. But there is no indication that as yet, despite its enormous growth, the organized movement can claim more than nuisance value. All previous revolutionary movements have had, at their centre, at the crucial times, to be clandestine. It is not just that the media gives Women's Liberation publicity, it is that in concept and organization, it is the most public revolutionary movement ever to have existed. Able, too, to make the most revolutionary statements in public without anyone seeming bothered. This raises many questions, not only about a society which sees women as always unserious, but perhaps, more critically for the immediate future, about the nature of the movement itself.

I graduated, and there was a magic year of studying music in London, attending productions at Covent Garden, the South Bank. The Old Vic was still there. I learned the differences between Romanesque and Gothic and Perpendicular arches. I understood Baroque music because of the architecture of Wurzburg and Regensburg and Rottenburg. I tried unsuccessfully to understand all of the characteristics of Pointillist and Cubist and Impressionist paintings — never got there. I saw theatre which I remember today with great clarity: Vanessa Redgrave in Peter Handke's *The Ride Across Lake Constance*; Laurence Olivier and Joan Plowright in *Pirandello*; Peter Hall's productions of Shakespeare — learning a vernacular that was almost impossible for me to speak of on my return home to Taupiri and Ngāruawāhia.

But it was not long before I was turned in another direction entirely. A place of estimates and appropriations, of men giving Maiden Speeches according to Standing Orders organised by Whips.

In the weeks before I was to leave Parliament, the *Listener* asked for a reflection on being a Member of Parliament, and the very first of the *Letters to My Sisters* was written. There are times when I still find it hard to read. But we'll try a little bit, which is a reflection on the first term:

> I watched the games and lines of caucus for the first time not recognising them, taken in, not realising I would become used to these moves. The most testing agenda items left until 12:45 p.m., with a conclusion of 1:00 p.m.; issues like a national price for milk or national two-channel coverage for television, popping up and being a safe bet for an inconclusive and wasted hour when there was major electoral discontent that should have been aired.
>
> The good old pre-Budget kite-flyers, to make the backbenchers feel they've been consulted: prescription charges, indirect taxes … When just enough new members enter every three years, and just enough older members think they might jeopardise promotion chances by getting involved, and just enough don't want to get involved, and just enough think it's a pointless waste of energy anyway, old dogs don't need new tricks.
>
> I become involved in my first abortion debate and it highlights what I've slowly learned of the diversion of being beset by sisters … and the abject humility of being understood.
>
> There is the re-writing of the Security Intelligence Service legislation, and Michael Minogue wins a commitment to an Official Information Act. I take down every word of caucus for this year and keep it with a copy of the official caucus minutes (it's in the Turnbull) — still the student, I think the comparison may be of interest some day.
>
> There's too much to do, so much to learn, don't see clearly, so much I don't say — but Huntly needs $1 million of energy resources

levy (because of the power situation), and a National Roads Board priority for a bypass, and a poll for a Trust tavern, and I'm meeting Eva Rickard about the return of the Raglan Golf Course …

I do as much as I can … I arm myself with Katherine Mansfield for bold encouragement, and on my wall I write her words: 'Risk. Risk anything. Care no more for the opinions of others, for those voices. Do the thing hardest on earth for you to do. Act for yourself. Face the truth.' It joins T.S. Eliot's lines from 'The Dry Salvages':

> And right action is freedom
> From past and future also.
> For most of us, this is the aim
> Never here to be realised;
> Who are only undefeated
> Because we have gone on trying

In the years that have passed I've been a farmer, a development worker, an academic, a consultant. I've always been an avid reader and prized those New Zealanders who have written in a voice that I have recognised as distinctly ours. I was thinking as I drove here of Frank Sargeson's writings, with the uncle on the farm in the King Country; coming through the North Shore thinking of Janet Frame's *Living in the Maniototo*, which loads of people found a grim book and I laughed out loud on aircraft whenever I was reading it; Owen Marshall's stunning short stories and Patricia Grace's gems — I believe that 'Butterflies' is one of the most important, staggering short stories in our vernacular ever written.

It's a skill that I treasure, but not one that I would claim, but there have been moments when I've felt my voice to be distinctly ours. And I'd like to finish with a reading where all these tracks to my vernacular find a home. One which I think a number of you might be able to share.

In June 1995, the G7 summit, as it was then, was to be held in Halifax in Canada and the National Film Board of Canada had decided to premiere the documentary *Who's Counting?*, which was based on my book *Counting for Nothing*, at the People's Summit, held in conjunction with the leader's meeting. This award-winning film was made by director Terre Nash and because the premiere was to be held at the People's Summit, I was asked to write the open letter from the 'people' to the 'leaders'. And this is it:

Gentlemen,

Last Sunday I was dressed in a winter-weight wetsuit and handed an old inflated tyre tube. With me were two adults and four children, one of whom was an eight-year-old boy, Sam. We descended a small path through native bush to a tomo, wound our way down to a tunnel entrance and launched ourselves afloat on a small river.

Lit by a myriad of glow-worms, the fossilised remains of shells were clearly visible in the limestone above us, rock carved by the ocean millions of years ago. And all around us shone stalactites and stalagmites, their extraordinary shapes and textures alive with the quiet drip of water — each one of these staggering forms 'growing' before our eyes at a rate of one cubic inch every 300 years.

The farmland above had preserved bushstands. This land had not been poisoned with fertilisers and chemicals, but had sustained indigenous people in traditional and modern farming practices for 800 years. It produced food. The caves lived on below.

We followed the path of the river for a kilometre underground to emerge through more bushland, teeming with nesting birdlife, and returned with our hosts to a traditional family marae, where we showered and were fed soup and toast. All tribal protocol was observed, without pretension.

On this Sunday, May 14th, New Zealand had won the America's Cup in yachting. In this country, it was churlish not to follow the news. I turned on the radio.

More cases of Ebola were counted in Zaire. The disease had spread because of the lack of absolutely basic medical supplies in hospital. I remembered that two-thirds of Zaire's GDP is controlled by Unilever and other multinationals. Into my mind flashed a scene from my UN field work in Bangladesh. Coming upon the WHO vaccination team in a village, I watched the same needle and syringe being used repeatedly. I grimaced. 'It's OK,' the team leader assured me, 'on children this age, you can use the needle up to ten times before it gets blunt.'

The news continued. China had conducted another nuclear test, and France was rumoured to be commencing underground testing at Mururoa in the Pacific. Japan had increased its storage of nuclear 'waste' material. The International War Crimes Tribunal had announced a list of Serbian leaders it wished to prosecute for their part in a war for which, by 'international agreement', weapons had long ago been 'banned'. In Iraq there continued to be a shortage of basic medicines, as a result of the Gulf War.

I remembered how our countries rallied to defend 'democracy' in the Gulf War, in Saudi Arabia, where there's no universal suffrage, and in Kuwait, where half of us are not entitled to vote. I compared this with G7 resolutions in respect of South Africa. I remembered words from an interview in the documentary *Who's Counting*? Ben was speaking in a nuclear silo, of the way he and his colleagues have been drilled — to fire nuclear weapons. He said: 'We're trained so highly ... that if we had to do it, it would be an almost automatic thing. There wouldn't be time for any reflection until after we had turned the key.'

Finally on the radio, there's an interview with the New Zealander who designed the mast of the yacht that won the world's oldest sporting event. What was his proudest moment? he was asked. 'People said nice things about the mast,' he said. 'It didn't give any trouble. It never fell down.' When asked how he had competed from his basement garage with the likes of designers from Nasa, he quipped: 'If you don't have money, you've got to have ideas.'

Gathered together at your 1995 G7 summit, you will count your growth statistics, your GDP figures, your currency values, your unemployed, your interest rates, your investments, your surpluses or deficits, your export receipts. You will count your money.

Outside, we wait for the ideas — those that spring from the real world, where too many of us are refugees, too many of us are pre-literate, too many of us are anaemic or malnourished. Where too many trees are felled, too many of us are poisoned by the by-products of what qualifies as production, too many of us are dependent, too many of us are the subjects of corrupt political regimes whom you welcome for their business and capacity for exploitation. Too many of us have no fresh air anymore.

Most of us are women and children. Most of our lives and work don't count in your statistics. We notice that you are all men. Do you remember from your childhood the sense of wonder in Sam's experience in the cave — the awe, the amazement, the capacity for utter humility in the face of millions of years of unalloyed drama in the kind of world from which your office now excludes you? Do you remember this boy in you, and what he valued?

Outside your room where the G7 summit meets, a different sense of values operates for most people on the planet. Six weeks ago Sam was with me in the ancient kauri forests of northern New Zealand. In early autumn here, the cones exploded, showering seeds on the ground. Sam picked them up, more than 400 of them, and is planting the offspring of 800-year-old magnificence (that we viewed for free) to sustain life and to defy the political and economic pathology that governs your agenda and your lives.

Gentlemen, I do not address you cynically, or lightly. I retired after three terms in the New Zealand Parliament: I have some small experience in that profession. Close friends say I'm a consummate apologist for politicians. So I ask you: do you have the political will and the personal commitment to plant trees that may live 800 years, or to preserve living, growing fossilised caves for millenniums?

Or is all imagination spent?

My vernacular.

2003 GEOFF PARK

Wild New Zealand – Voices from the Landscape

Tēnā kotou katoa. My greetings to you all and my greetings to Waitākere, one of the few parts of New Zealand where houses sit amongst trees. As Michael King and I walked down here this evening we spent a few moments discussing that there are not many parts of New Zealand like this. It always appeals to me, coming up to this part of the world. I do so from another corner of the country, where it is also just possible to live in proximity to trees — that precise corner where Katherine Mansfield wrote in 1907, 'On the one hand is the sea stretching right up to the yard, on the other the bush growing close, down almost to my front door.' As I said to Michael, most of my week I live a stone's throw from where she sat and thought of those words.

That same bush with the same ancient beech trees that Mansfield knew — they're still there, thanks to her contemporaries who preserved it as scenery from the suburban subdivision that otherwise would have taken it.

I'm up here because Murray Gray and I were at the same Karekare party, back in March. Murray's invitation to speak tonight was as casual as it was warm, so it went to the back of my mind, where it still was when he rang me some months later. By then my schedule was onerous and I was in a lesser mood to oblige — but it is after all to the Waitākeres that I was asked to come.

Just moments before Murray rang, I'd been in a library following a lead on one Herbert Guthrie-Smith, author of *Tutira: the story of a New Zealand sheep station*, for many years called New Zealand's most famous book. It was the sort of lead that had me pulling all of Guthrie-Smith's books off the shelf. Fallen down behind was a delicate little book called *Where Bell-Birds Chime*, by an author I'd never heard of: Edith Howes. It was one of a series published in the 1910s called 'The Dainty Booklet Series', with a few other authors I did know about: James Cowan, Beatrice Baughan, J.C. Anderson and Jessie McKay.

Under the heading, 'The Romance of a Forest', Edith Howes wrote:

> The islands of New Zealand lie like green gems flung upon a sapphire sea. From end to end forest greenness gleams down the land, filling its valleys, climbing its mountain slopes, descending its shores, there to mirror forms of fairy beauty in its deep fiords.
>
> Towns of shiny newness break its ancient course, wide planes of waving corn or tussock waste intervene, but still the forest crowns the land, sheltering and befriending and enriching it, standing for ever majestic, noble, beautiful as the forest of a dream.

My talk tonight is actually called 'Writing into the Bush', not 'Writing into the Wild' as announced. But it is about the bush, that forest part, able to be entered and experienced, and in a few corners lived in, like the Waitākeres and where I live in Days Bay. But apart too — something of our imagination and our dreams. That's the bush of which I'm going to speak.

I'm going to speak about writing into the bush in a particular vein. In my book *Nga Uruora* I wrote that when poets, painters and novelists compress a sense of place into its essence, it is inevitably that elemental connection between people and the land's non-human life. Its sparse presence in Pākehā art and literature is symptom enough perhaps of the land's native spirit vanishing before the immigrant culture could evolve any bonds of affection for it. That recently got picked up in the poetry anthology *Spirit in a Strange Land*, with the following passage:

> New Zealanders, predominantly urban since the 1880s, have also long worshipped the bush of a mythic rural New Zealand. They developed a kind of nature spirituality, a transcending of this land. This was sometimes a simple romanticism, or mysticism of place but more often a generic and abiding love of the bush as a living link with the primordial and settler culture. Tramping in the bush along pilgrimage trails was to return to a purer form of pioneer life; a life lived in close proximity to the spirit of nature itself under the southern skies. In art and poetry this was always slightly out of focus and unconvincing. This spirituality was explicitly linked to national identity in Monte Holcroft's 1940 prize-winning essay and since then this theme has seldom been far from the definitions of New Zealand and New Zealanders. Finding a language for this bush spirit has been more difficult than Holcroft envisaged. And tramping can no longer be quite so innocent as we all come to realise how the land has been transformed and how we have constructed the very bush itself, and how little that is original remains.

It was in exactly that regard that I wrote in *Ngā Uruora* that where most of us live, the evolution of modern New Zealand culture from its colonial beginnings has been paralleled by nature's relentless vanishing from sight and mind. And as we have become a culture poor in people who have been able to read country and feel it, we have been losing our capacity to know the life forces that sustain nature and to intuit with them. Yet no piece of New Zealand has been colonised so long that its native spirit is a reality no more. Even in the most Europeanised plains, like the Manawatū's or Canterbury's, traces of forest, or history's archived paintings and settler diaries, reveal nature's intent: what ancient Europeans also knew as the places of genius. I also wrote of the genius of place, an idea with a long literary tradition in a slightly different sense.

A century after the advent of British settlement, the genius loci — the tenderness of place, the sense of intimacy mingled with a habitual and inseparable surrounding — was the great historian John Beaglehole's chief concern for New Zealand. While it pastures its soul in fields classically English, New Zealand's identity, he ventured, was where the bush perpetually and in silence renews its green inviolate life.

I said to Murray Gray when I agreed to speak that it definitely wasn't going to be a lecture. What I'm going to do instead is give you a series of eight things — I'm calling them 'eclogues'. It's an appropriate term for a literary festival perhaps. You won't find the word in the *Shorter Oxford Dictionary* but it's there in the supplement: 'eclogues'. Florio in 1591 uses the term: 'How revellers blanche their passions with eclogues, songs and dances and sonnets.' The term comes from the Greek — it's about the discourse of goatherds. An eclogue is a short poem of any kind, especially a pastoral dialogue.

But perhaps in New Zealand, given what Beaglehole said about the pastoral and the forest, eclogues should be ecologues. Certainly, delivering something like this in Waitākere 'Eco-City' we should keep them as ecologues. Ecologues are brief, not just their sentences but their whole. I'm not going to stick with that rule, I'm going to give you some fragments. I'm not going to link them together — you can do that.

Passion
Each one has a name; the first one I've called 'Passion'. The reason I was chasing Guthrie-Smith of Tutira Station was that I'd just read an obituary of him in the *Journal of the British Society for the Preservation of the Fauna of the Empire*. Yes, there was such a society. Enlarging on the New Zealand writer Alan Mulgan's obituary of Guthrie-Smith in Wellington's *Evening Post*, the Society's journal said how Guthrie-Smith's writing of his tale *Tutira*, about how foreign plants and animals proliferated across the New Zealand countryside in the wake of European colonisation of Māori

territory, was with something approaching passion.

It was hard to discern whether it was a bit of a put-down of a colonial or whether it was praise. Mulgan wrote of Guthrie-Smith's close and accurate observing of nature and his love of wildlife. We've had naturalists more renowned but none who wrote so well. Usually limpid, his writing could become a spate when he was aroused. His warnings should make us pause and reflect, before it is too late. And Mulgan quoted, as an example, from Guthrie-Smith's writings:

> In the 1870s a species of insanity would seem to have permeated New Zealand. The country was apparently no longer to be New Zealand at all. God's work in the South Pacific [dog's work in the South Pacific perhaps we should say] was not good enough—the Dominion was to be transformed into a sixth-rate Britain. Our own native plants and native birds were unworthy of us. It was given out and widely accepted that the former were of no great beauty, that the latter must inevitably perish. The Maori race was presented as doomed.

I recognised immediately, when I read that, a type of writing with which I was familiar. And in outlining what my 1995 book *Nga Uruora* was about, I wrote:

> When the smoke of the colonists' fires cleared at the end of the nineteenth century, New Zealand had become a different country. Māori had lost their most precious life-support system. Only in the hilliest places did the forest still come down to the sea. Nature was no longer neighbourhood. Huge slices of its ancient ecosystem were missing, evicted and extinguished. Our histories, though, don't explain it. They've had neither the sense of place, nor ecological consciousness to do so. There is, as Janet Frame says, much to expose in New Zealand that for some reason wasn't there before.

Guthrie-Smith's own experiences, his fears, his learning, his regret and delights, are vital components, vital organs really, of his narratives. There's that remarkable thing in *Tutira* — the shift of realisation from the confidence of 1921, when the book was first published, to the preface to the 1940 edition in which he asks, 'What have I done, to wash my part of New Zealand into the Pacific?'

And in a society that's been called 'the passionless people', it seems to me that all you've got to do to have your writing called 'passionate' — it's been levelled at me — is to put yourself in the story.

My choice of reading from Guthrie-Smith is a very biased one, as you're going to find tonight: I talk a lot about kererū, the wood pigeon. I spent the afternoon sitting under a tree working through this talk and there was a pair above me; as there was at home when I was working on the text. So, I'm going to read you some extracts from a chapter called 'The Pigeon' from his 1910 book *Birds of the Water, Wood and Waste*. 1910 was the same year that human involvement with kererū — hunting it, keeping it in captivity — was made illegal by the Animal Protection Act. 'The Pigeon': a few quotes:

> The boundary rivers of the run are gorges from watershed to within two or three hundred feet of sea level, and many of the paddocks are almost completely bounded by cliffs and gorges. In the crannies of their sheer sides all sorts of interesting plants find foothold, and where one stratum overlaps another, limestone over papa for instance, the superposition is marked by a long line of greenery, sometimes flax and toi, but often rangiora, fuchsia, mahoe, etc., and it is on their lateral branches, jutting out into the air, that pigeons love to nest ...
>
> Often I hear the Pigeon termed a stupid bird, and just as an honest man among rogues is called a fool, so, perhaps the Pigeon's trust and guilelessness does deserve that name amongst those who shoot him sitting at close quarters. (It is 1910 after all.) Otherwise, he is by no means a fool. ...

Probably under natural conditions the young birds retire during the worst period of the moult to the very depths of the bush, and there in shelter and comfort, build up their strength.

But at other times, Tutira's kererū preferred a very different habitat.

In the event of a prolonged absence we would find the birds waiting for us in the drawing-room, or one of the bedrooms off the verandah, and we'd get a friendly whistle and a shake of the wings as welcome.

The Pigeon has several notes, one a single low "ku," which may be taken to express watchfulness and caution, perhaps recognition too; then there is a louder, more interrogative signal "ku," by which alarm is indicated. (This from a bird that came in from the wild, attracted by the lifestyle of the few domesticated *kererū* that were around the Guthrie-Smith homestead at Tutira.) ... There is also the almost inaudible, sharp, sibilant whistle of welcome, hardly, perhaps a whistle, or, if to be so designated, then a whistle ethereal, spiritual and sublimated to attenuity. I often hear "Uncle Harry," perched in the pear tree, shaking his wings and whistling thus when he spies me on the lawn and welcomes my approach. Then there is the curious double sound of grunt and whistle, noticeable when food is not at once forthcoming, and which may perhaps express impatience.

Passage
The second eclogue is called 'Passage'. In Brian Elliot's 1967 book, *The Landscape of Australian Poetry*, he wrote how 'The first need in a new country or colony must obviously be in one way or another to comprehend the physical environment. In poetry we find this need reflected, in colonial times, in an obsessive preoccupation with landscape and description.'

Passage, it's called. At first the urge is merely topographical, to answer the question, what does the place look like? The next is detailed and ecological: how does life arrange itself here? What plants, what animals, what activity? How does man fit in? The next may be moral, how does such a place influence people? And how have they developed it? Next come subtler inquiries. What spiritual and emotional qualities do such a people develop in such an environment? I am going to deal with 'Passage' by simply giving you a couple of quotes from two guidebooks, I could call them. The first touches that moral urge — it's Elsdon Best's words, with which he entered the bush in Te Urewera in 1895, and wrote up in a travelogue called *Waikare-moana: The Sea of the Rippling Waters*, a copy of which I've just been lucky to acquire from our host Murray this evening: This is what you read in the early years of the last century, when the book was a popular one, when you entered Urewera with this guidebook in hand:

> ... as there comes to all who truly love to view the face of mother Nature, the desire to look upon the unwrought wilderness and note the war which has waged for untold centuries between it and primitive man—neolithic man, who has opened up the trails through the great forest he could not conquer—trails by which the incoming pioneers of the Age of Steel shall pass along (Best is also meaning the road, constructed from Murupara to Waikaremoana, so, it is both a road of history and an actual road), to leave behind them peace in place of war, thriving hamlets for stockaded pas, fields of waving grain for jungle and for forest. And with this there also comes that strange sensation of vivid interest and pleasing anticipation which is felt by the ethnologist, botanist and lover of primitive folk-lore when entering a new field for research. For the glamour of the wilderness is upon him ...

If I'm a botanist, I'm a precocious one, one who learnt the names of plants of my bush as part of my childhood. And I know a little of Brian Elliot's subtler enquiries; the learning about the pleasure in the pathless woods, that Allen Curnow learned just along the road from here; to look hard at nature. It is the nature of things to look and look back harder. Botany is panic of another description.

I remember the moment, a century, almost exactly, after Elsdon Best wrote that entry passage to the Urewera forest, in which I wrote the following passage. An epiphany, it was a kind of *Going West* moment. This is the only reading from *Ngā Uruora* tonight. I thought it would be appropriate, as it's just been republished, so that's something to celebrate. This is one of my favourite bits of my own writing. It is about a landscape of wet mud, of a western estuary, the Whanganui Inlet. It's another piece about entering the forest, in this case from an estuary, walking inland:

> First thing in the morning, autumn's light just touching the tips of the forest, the serenity of the bay—to a city dweller—is unforgettable. Only the canoe wake betrays the stillness, and the illusion that the big trees are keeping their distance. Ashore, a heron breakfast along a band of raupō in front of them wishes I would keep mine. Stepping into a run and flexing its wings in a great downward arc, it sweeps noisily out over the calm water. ...
>
> There is enough anxiety in the reaction of a kererū to decide on its leaving. The flash of its white underbelly in the sun, like a signal that there's an intruder about. The low-lying country that fraternises with estuaries and tidal inlets has long been on the receiving end of humanity's fondness for wiping out nature. As it has shaped a nation of coast dwellers, it has become one of New Zealand's most altered environments. Its indigenous life is dying faster than most and has become the most easily forgotten. And if ecology tells us anything, what's more, the signs are that worse is yet to come.
>
> The brute facts of our contaminating and annihilating every place like it, our reluctance to let the other species be, are what makes this little bay such a novel experience. Once, before we brought our farms and towns to bear on this kind of ground, there must have been countless like it, all round the New Zealand coast. Had Europeans settled New Zealand in less of a rush, and with less anticipation of a low-lying country spread awaiting them, a few more forests of big trees might still stand on its tidal flats.

For all they evoke of the presence of the past, the tall trees are unassuming. Kahikatea, rātā, pukatea—loaded with shiny, flaxen clumps of epiphytes, they appear to stand at the water's edge. But like the same pattern of plants at Petone that—momentarily—had the New Zealand Company believing their desperate search for a great alluvial plain was over, it's an illusion. At Petone, the low line of forest that seemed to come down to the harbour's edge, turned out to be behind an invisible belt of swamps and hollows. Just as unapparent from out on the water, the bands of manuka scrub and sun-bleached raupō and rushes in front of those big trees are actually broader than the trees are tall. Spread between the tide and the trees is a diversity of life we've made a rarity—sea rushes lap by the sea at one end, shaded palms and delicate ferns beneath them at the other, and in between, a succession of plants, each progressively less salt tolerant. Yet unless the quirks of ecology or the search for level land attracted your gaze, you might notice none of it. The meeting grounds of forest and sea are always fascinating places. Yet few have this diversity of life.

Ecologists talk of such places as communities, but any sense of a co-evolved alliance between its plants is more illusory than real; just another fantasy acted out about nature; forced upon us by our urge to divide and classify. As easily as our eyes pick out concentrations of colour and texture, we are tempted to see zones and boundaries, as if—to be able to inhabit them—the plants of places like this must organise themselves into something like societies.

But the lives this place attracts are no more than cohabitors, sharing affinity for the edges of tidal inlets. What seems co-ordination, a design, a special natural system to keep the sea from the trees, is revealed on close investigation to be just a collection of plants thrown together by fate and their ancient histories. Each Darwinian species preoccupied by itself, elbowing its neighbours, sending its seeds to strive at the limits of their abilities.

Regret
Regret's pervasiveness in the landscape of the New Zealand nature writer is something you can't ignore — its classic expression perhaps William Pember Reeves' late Victorian valedictory, 'The Passing of the Forest: A Lament for the Children of Tane':

> The blackened forest ruined in a night,
> A sylvan Parthenon that God will plan
> But build not twice. Ah, bitter price to pay
> For Man's dominion—beauty swept away!

Reeves wrote in another book, *New Zealand*, his 1907 guidebook for English tourists:

> A hewing down and a sweeping away of beauty compared to which the conquests of the Goths and the vandals were conservative processes, for those noted invaders did not level Rome or Carthage to the ground; they left classic architecture standing. To the lover of beautiful nature, the work of our race in New Zealand seems more akin to that of the Seljuk Turks in Asia Minor when they swept populations, buildings and agriculture and Byzantine city and rural life together in order to turn whole provinces into pasture for their sheep. Not that my countrymen were more blind to beauty than other colonists from Europe. It is mere accident which has laid upon them the burden of having ruined more natural beauty in the last half century than have other pioneers.

And then we may be going to that place called Waimahia with Frank Sargeson in his regret. In his *Once is Enough: a memoir*, it is his uncle's mistake, 'cramming into seven years a sort of small-scale repetition of this country's history, repeating in his ignorance, as he would later on admit, some of the worst mistakes the pioneers had made.' Sargeson's uncle discovered under the fern and manuka that began in the new grass even before the forest's burnt stumps had rotted away, as he says, 'the distinct beginning of a new forest; tiny tendrils and seedlings that promised to become kahikatea, tōtara, rimu, matai, great trees that could live and flourish hundreds of years after you were dead'.

Sargeson's own looking around and expressing so well what my own domain — and history landscape — is all about: '... one only had to look around to see a remarkable variety of country:there was the untouched bush, and on the maori land, a very great deal (although it was my uncle's belief that much bush throughout the country had been burnt by the maori, perhaps sometimes by accident, long before it was ever seen by the white man) some was still being cut, and where it had been burned you saw land in every stage of reversion ...'.

'So although I couldn't know exactly what my uncle's land had originally looked like, I only had to visit his neighbours to see much going on that most certainly represented all that I regretted having missed.'

In talking about regret. I need to talk about that particular regret for a kind of bush that we can hardly imagine; the bush that *Ngā Uruora* is set in really; the bush of swamp and swale, eddy and eel, flax and flow, flood and fecundity, teal and tall trees, waterway and waka, mahinga kai and maemae, that vanished in the blink of a nineteenth-century eye.

Once Sir Joseph Banks said he had seen a far southern land of swamps which might doubtless easily be drained and which sufficiently evinced the richness of their soils by the great size of the plants that grew upon them: 'Indeed, in every respect the properest place we've seen yet for establishing a colony.'

The confidence with which Britain took Aotearoa's wet plains from swampy bush to grids of dairy farms, effecting in the process one of the most dramatic losses of wetlands on earth, had its roots in Joseph Banks's own swamp drainage operations. As Banks wandered the Pacific with Cook's *Endeavour*, his hard engineers at home were transforming his childhood landscape of England's Lincolnshire fens.

How interesting then to find how, to Banks, this childhood landscape became one suffused with regret. It was gout in 1808 that first gave Joseph

Banks a taste of his fallibility — Banks, who we have known and blamed and honoured for many things, but not literature. However, as Harold Carter has written it was in the gouty gloom of January 1807 at Soho Square, with William Cartlich at his elbow to transcribe his evanescent thoughts, he called up 'The Mire Nymph', which Carter describes as 'a sort of satirical self-flagellation'. It was a poem addressed to the Proprietors of the East, West and Wilmore Fens. It is a long poem, and this is just a piece from it:

> ... From easy couch of soft alluvial Mud
> Unmoved since Noah landed from the flood.
> Uprose the Murky Naiid of the Fen
> Seldom before beheld by honest Men
> Her head was crowned with Sedge, her bosom bare
> Eels crawld like Lice among her clotted hair.
> Deep were her Eye balls sunk, her aguish cheek
> Shone deadly pale, above her Peat staind neck,
> Why will ye, shriekd she, torture my repose
> Am I a prisoner to my deadly foes
> Has barbarous Banks prevaild ...
> Are come my muddy Dykes & Sykes to scour
> To starve my Geese, banish my Water fowls
> And seize my Fishes in their native holes
> Rip up the bosom of my favorite Slough
> With the fell Harrow & detested Plough

And regret, we should remind ourselves, is not just distant history about attitudes to the bush long gone. In the summer of 1979–1980, Peter Hooper, West Coast friend and provider of verse to be painted to the Westie Colin McCahon, wrote about the New Zealand Forest Service, seven years before its demise, burning a native forest to establish pine plantations on the West Coast. As Hooper says, 'A forest belonging to the people of New Zealand being destroyed at the taxpayer's expense.' I was working in these same forests as an ecologist when this happened and when he wrote in *Our Forests Ourselves*:

> On one of those calm, pellucid days which make autumn the loveliest season of the year on the West Coast, Forest Service workers will be strategically stationed around the perimeter of the forest. For months, the dead and dying trees will have dried out, but the Forest Service takes no chance of a damp gully being saved from destruction. Helicopters using Comet and Aphid attachments will shoot flaming diesel around the perimeter of the area to be burned. The day must be calm so that the ring of fire will burn inwards to the centre and not be wind-driven beyond the perimeter. Although the trees had been felled months before, there is already new growth on stumps, from roots and fallen branches. Under the pale lime-green umbrella of fern fronds, seeds are thrusting to the light already.
>
> And there is life in the wrecked forest. The larger flying birds have gone, but fantails pirouette in the shadows. ... At the appointed hour, the fire-ships with their flame-throwers roar into the attack. Within minutes flame and smoke are boiling upwards in a terrifying mushroom cloud. No living creature within that narrowing perimeter of flame has any chance of survival. Small birds are whirled upwards in a scorching, suffocating wind. ...
>
> This suffering remains in the earth and air of such places, and can be experienced decades later as an ashen greyness of spirit which appals the wanderer in these haunted solitudes. The Coast is studded with the ruins of former forests, places of monumental despair.

The primeval shadow

There is one key word in the European reading of the New Zealand bush and in the writing of the New Zealand bush; it is there from the very beginning of the European encounter with the New Zealand bush. Jerningham Wakefield in Queen Charlotte Sound in 1839: 'Nothing can be imagined more magnificent than this scenery or however less suitable for cultivation. It was impossible not to be struck by the majesty of this primeval forest.' And for an agent of a land settlement company who viewed native land and native people with such an eye, shaped deep in England's landscapes of enclosure, Jerningham goes on, 'They knew not of any further right to a district covered with primeval forest, far too vast to be of any use to descendants of their tribe. The first clearer became the acknowledged owner of a tract of hitherto intact land. The first axeman in a primeval forest laid claim to the surrounding trees.'

But it was really Monte Holcroft who gave us the term in our literature. In the early 1930s, in his book of essays, *Timeless World*, he wrote how he sensed in New Zealand, 'a primeval quality of earth which will yet find its expression in literature; become its secret strength not in novels or tales of our small, isolated life here, but in the manner of writing and in the substance of thought.'

And in a more famous 1940 essay on the subject, Holcroft called that quality of New Zealand 'the primeval shadow'. He considered it an unsettling quality. To stand on the edge of the primeval forest is to encounter something that is not ours, 'something that has never belonged even to the Maori, but has known centuries of an undisturbed stillness or has contained some dream of life too strange for our minds to grasp ... something to be feared.'

Nothing new in that; another European sensibility, the Frenchman Dumont d'Urville in 1826 remarked how a solemn — almost sinister — atmosphere pervaded the New Zealand forest. However, like the spiritual grandeur of Janet Frame's dark foliage bush in which the forest and the land are clearly the parents — the ancestors making their presence known, and what else may people do but rebel against a life of such dependence — Holcroft believed it would have immense cultural consequences. Until New Zealanders found a reconciliation with the forest, Holcroft forecast, they would remain cut off from any real depth of spiritual life. When nature's primordial forests were recognised, the forest would become an unexpected source of power in an adventure of the spirit.

Inscape

I was privileged a couple of months ago to attend the thirtieth birthday of the Waitākere Ranges Protection Society at the Henderson Valley hall. It was one of those events where there were many people to honour, and in presenting Don Binney with one of the Society's awards, the President, my good friend John Edgar, thanked him for giving us 'an aesthetic'. This struck me with its accuracy, and I remembered a few weeks later when I read the review of Damien Skinner's book *Don Binney: Ngā Manu/Ngā Motu* in the *Forest & Bird* magazine. I don't know who the writer was — I looked for it, but the editors left the name off the review — but it's pretty good. It goes: 'Looking at Don Binney's painting calls to mind the poetry of Gerald Manley Hopkins, in his endeavours to capture what he called the 'inscape' of the natural world. Don Binney produces a similar but visual poetry.'

One interpretation of Hopkins' 'inscape', a *Shorter Oxford* definition, is 'the unique unified complex of those sensible qualities of the object of perception, that strikes us as inseparably belonging to and most typical of it, so that through the knowledge of this unified complex of sense data, we may gain an insight into the individual essence of the object'. More simply perhaps, inscape and nature is what Les Murray, the Australian, calls wild sound that low aggregate susurrus which emanates from the landscape. And I'm leaving inscape there, because it's a quality that is so sparse in our writing compared to the painters like Binney and certainly McCahon too, whose deep familiarity with Hopkins' poetry must have meant that he had an understanding of inscape.

Bushed

It is true of course, as Elizabeth March in her recent wonderful book *Local Voices*, on Waitākere's Te Henga Valley and its people, recorded Tyl von Randow saying, 'The bush-clad ranges are not human habitat. They are not for the hunter nor the gatherer, not for the ploughman nor the herdsman. Not for the artisan, money lender nor scribe. … The bush-clad ranges can do without us.' It's not quite what Augustus Earle observed in the Hokianga in the 1820s:

We travelled through a wood so thick, that the light of heaven could not penetrate the trees that composed it. They were so large and so close together, that in many places we had difficulty to squeeze through them. To add to our perplexities, innumerable streams intersected this forest, which always brought us Europeans to a complete standstill. While we were toiling with the greatest difficulty, our natives were simply jogging on. So completely accustomed to it, that they sprang over the roots and dived under the supplejacks and branches with perfect ease, while we were panting after them in vain, our bare-legged attendants loaded as they were, scrambled with all the agility of cats or monkeys.

We'll come back to those folk in a minute. Meanwhile, wherever there's bush there's hunters. And hunters, more than anyone, more than most New Zealanders, have a very strong sense of that great scary line, derived from our history and its ensuing landscape, and expressed in that extremely un-New Zealand phenomenon *Harry Potter and the Philosopher's Stone*: 'You're going into the forest, after all. You've got to have your wits about you.' As a 1961 James K Baxter poem warns, if you don't have your wits about you it can be awful indeed. So this is 'Bushed':

Bush country. The tree spiders build
Their houses to the east, when the sun can enter

Gossamer tunnels. Also
Grass flows to the north, bent over

By southerly winds. A man from Te Kuiti
Told me this, lest I should be caught

Without a compass in bush country.
And walk in circles through the blinding hills

> Filthy, foodless, frantic, lame,
> Mocked by the bellbird's requiem
>
> Till some roofed creek or tangle of green lawyer
> Had gripped me ...
>
> We shared a cabin on the southbound ferry.
> Perhaps he came too late. I do not know.

Bringing home the bacon
A hunter's writing into the bush caught my eye a week or so ago in the Saturday edition of the *Dominion Post*. It was the antithesis of walking in circles through the blinding hills, and of frantic foodlessness. Andy Lyver is the editor of *New Zealand Hunting and Wildlife* and a self-declared passionate hunter, not least because of her discovery, in her words, that the depth of flavour of food is directly related to the intensity of the experience in harvesting it.

> Setting out from a valley tent camp, just as dawn was breaking, soft light in the eastern sky, pushing back an indigo blanket, I followed the stream up the narrow valley. The frosted grass sparkled in the shafts of early sunlight. Across the stream, I headed for an overgrown track that led up a ridge.

After a steep climb, the track levelled out and Lyver was free to focus, she says, on stealing forward and looking for game:

> It was exhilarating to explore the tranquil environment, shrugging between the tree trunks and stooping under branches without making a sound. Birdsong was magnified in the stillness and at times I paused just to allow the bush sounds to fold around me. No breeze stirred the trees; not a leaf turned. And then I saw the pig.

Of course we cannot put bush writing and hunting in the same room without reference to that great tradition in New Zealand writing that, were we to call it 'Crumpian', would be as meaningful to the New Zealand chapter of Eng-Lit as the term 'Dickensian' is to the whole book — at its root, that sense of being inside something and comfortable inside it. As Jack Lasenby recently recounted to Kim Hill on Radio New Zealand, when he and Crump entered the Urewera bush, 'we stepped into it and pulled it round us like a blanket'. So here's a piece of Crump himself, on the run from the law in the Urewera in *Wild Pork and Watercress*:

> Sneaking through the bush always looking for something to kill and eat. Having to do it. Needing the meal. There was something savage about it, something kind of primitive. And there was always the nice things like the birds ... I always liked birds and I got to know most of them in the Urewera. ...
>
> We did have one memorable meal about that time. We were skimming through some of the best huts, but there weren't many people in the bush at that time of year. The last thing we'd eaten was half a weka each and a packet of instant noodles we'd found in the Onepu Hut—and that had been hours before. We'd crossed the Kahikatea Range and dropped down the steep shingly tawa creek-head of the Otopukawa Stream. And suddenly we saw dozens of wood pigeons eating the miro berries. We were finally going to eat.
>
> We chose a good spot in a grove of miro trees and waited for the pigeons to come flapping in, whistling with weight, to land on the branches. Then we plonked them with a .22. They were so fat that some of them burst, an inch of bright yellow fat all over them, when they hit the ground. We set up our camp by a trickle of water and smothered the birds in clay (feathers and guts and all) until they looked in the firelight like a row of loaves of bread. [And those not eaten on the spot] we wrapped in leaves and took with us when we moved on to Manuoha the next day.

Kūkū/kererū
What's interesting is that as I transcribed that just the other morning, sitting with my laptop, a couple of kererū flew by whistling with weight into the old cabbage tree above me, which leads nicely to the next eclogue: the incredible survival of kūkū or kererū. In this eclogue I acknowledge Gary Snyder's *The Incredible Survival of Coyote*. Against the grain of the modern American West and also paying homage to Snyder and via him to the discipline of nature writing, I'm about to go to an international muster of nature writers in Australia. An interesting word: not a term you'd hear here in New Zealand: 'a muster of nature writers' — there wouldn't be many of us.

Remember those Ngāpuhi forest men that Augustus Earle described scrambling with all the agility of cats and monkeys? 'Where the finest examples of the human race are to be found, the largest and finest timber grows,' Earle wrote of the Hokianga. One village, literally buried in a forest, was near one of the most beautiful wooded valleys that Thomas McDonnell could remember. Some of Earle's party may have even been with McDonnell when, as the valley's kūkū or kererū finished fattening themselves on fruiting miro trees, he went into the forest with the ropu kaiwhakangau, laying about five kilometres of the valley floor with snares, and the old men placed it under strict tapu. This is McDonnell writing; I tracked this through Elsdon Best who got it from McDonnell and his relation Gudgeon:

> In fact, it was never thought that anyone could have dreamt it possible to go into places of this kind, not being one of the tribe, and death would have followed to a certainty anyone who so transgressed tribal rites. The usual take, or harvest, of birds in one month, during the full fruiting of the miro in its season, was from four-and-a-half to five thousand birds, mainly pigeon, but also parrots and tui. But even in my time, when I was a youngster, I used to accompany old Toenga Pou, when he went out bird snaring into this valley, and have helped to lift between three and four hundred birds from

the few hundred yards of the stream he had prepared in the way I have described.

Like knowing a little bit about coyote before guns and the American West, before cattle and private property, knowing about the once-was-a-birdsville quality of our forest past is vital knowledge for imagining the future — in this case, a passage in a recent essay about a bush track in my neighbourhood, being upgraded to cope with the growing numbers of walkers. Whether the label on their lips has the wilderness unwrought, or unoccupied, many more people are coming along this track in quest of it. When flights of treated timber steps began appearing a number of years ago, part of me accepted them as the necessary consequence of more feet. But other senses missed the close-to-the-groundness of the old path, its intricate stepping from tree root to tree root. Flights of quite another kind — the soundful sweeping of the forest's disturbed kererū — inform us that whatever we imagine the forest to be, whoever we believe it belongs to, it's without question theirs; their home.

Towards the end of Patricia Grace's *Potiki*, Hemi and Roimata express ecology's power, the same process that Sargeson saw on his uncle's hill country, if with a different take on it — the connections of whenua:

> The hills are quiet now. They went from our hands long ago but we do not need them in our hands. We only need them to be there, to be left to heal, to be left for trees to grow on. With trees on the hills again our own corner is safe and we are who we are. For now it is safe. With trees on the hills, we can keep our ground productive, our sacred places safe, our water clear.

And in the same forest of mind that Edith Howes — with whom we began — saw, 'the hills will be scarred for some time and the beachfront spoiled but the scars will heal as growth returns because the forest is there always, coiled in the body of the land, helping the fact that even if we with our eyes can't see it, the forest is always there'. And a vital player in this process of the hill's healing is kūkū or kererū.

And kererū, for those who haven't noticed, have been an evident player in tonight's narratives from me, as they are in last eclogue of the writing into the bush story. An old friend of mine has until recently been the Department of Conservation manager on Matiu Island, in Wellington Harbour, which is being restored to its indigenous cover as a sanctuary for native birds. Both of us are Hutt Valley kids, and both of our work since our university days in the 1960s has involved us in conservation, and does more recently in 'ecological restoration' as it's now called.

Richard Anderson has worked mainly with birds and the introduced predators that threaten to eliminate them. I've worked mainly with plants and vegetation. But we have long known that central to what both of us have done, or worked in, is what Pérrine Moncrief called 'the timeless, intimate co-existence of New Zealand's native birds and plants, the one interacting upon the other so delicately that without each other neither could flourish'.

Whenever I visited Richard on Matiu our talk would inevitably make some reference to the new native forest growing apace around him and the birds it would increasingly attract, if not brought to it by their human benefactors. When, we asked ourselves, would the first kererū arrive? An injured kererū sent to the island's sanatorium from Eastbourne soon flew back to its beech-forest home, but there was no doubt in either of us that it wouldn't be very long at all before the first kererū came to stay. I mentioned this when I spoke last year to the Writing the Landscape course at Victoria University's Institute of Modern Letters, a course coordinated by Dinah Hawken. The following day they were going out to Matiu on a field writing trip. 'Don't just look at the landscape you're going to write about,' I told them, 'If Richard's on the island, talk to him'.

I end with hope that nature writing, as Australians and Americans call it, is really going somewhere, and I was thrilled to have some connection with this. And so the last little pieces I will read are from the booklet that the course prepared, called *Matiu/Somes Island: birds, stones and bones*. The first one is from 'Fishing' by Celestina Sumby:

Fishing
(For Richard Anderson, after seven years on Matiu)
1
He travels through his house.
A housed island
he always dreamt of
while hanging on to one end
line dipped
in sun-drenched

water caught by the sun,
and curved against
the edge of an island
all green and rock.

He dreamt of
covering its bare secrets
of setting animals free from the ark.
…

2
To think that he could land this place.
And then the bare bones of it.
The birds acknowledging his presence
fought his landing from above.
An island is a lonely place but
not so lonely as to be left alone.

3
After one day and seven years he still
couldn't see behind his ears.
Such stories were always told in two halves.
He waits for the natural outcome.

In which trees form their roots
in childhood fantasy
a boy goes fishing for islands.
Phone calls are received through
invisible wires.
Reward is delivered on the wings
of a bird.

This is from Morgan Lawrence-Bach:

Matiu/Somes, 17th August

...

This island is at the centre of what we call our home, a point from which the harbour and the hills are a ring. The island like the centre of a spiral, the last bit to unfurl. Layers of history are peeling out, opening, lying in a line from then till now, like leaves running off the stem of the fern.

The kererū has come back to the island. It has reappeared on its internal map. A soft fat bird, feasting on the tree, starting, slowly to pick this spiral open.

From the introduction to the booklet:

Students who stayed over were able to listen to Richard Anderson ... talk about the island's history and character. At the end of his talk, while out by the plant nursery, a wood pigeon flew into a nearby tree. Richard's face lit up brighter than the stadium lights; he told the group that this kererū was probably the first to return under its own power to the island for at least a century, maybe longer. The 20 years of stalwart planting efforts by Lower Hutt Forest & Bird had borne fruit, literally, and the birds were returning to the re-forested island.

And the last is two verses from Airini Beautrais:

Looking back from Matiu

I see Matiu from my everyday roads, the grass slopes in the day, the winking beacon in the dark. this place where everything was dug too deep is spilling light into the water wounds. deforested, replanted, self-seeded in its own forms of sea-cast knowledge. the humming night, the ocean smile and the mended cloak of green. the resting place of seals. the guardian place of stone.

from here, whoever watched could have seen the harbour change, the city thunder grow. this eye has watched while its green was burnt, while people came and lived and died. right whales are coming back, pods of orca have been noted. today, the first kererū to return of its own accord was spotted, fat and lolling through the tree lucerne.

Thank you.

2004 DAME CHRISTINE COLE CATLEY

Between the Lines: A Tribute to Michael King

Well, our interesting Mayor Bob Harvey, and his Council, Tangata Whenua, Murray and the Going West helpers — this is a marvellous yearly occasion, and the rest of Auckland is so jealous of those of you who live here. We can at least come and join in your festival.

It was a great honour to be asked to talk about Michael King, that generous presence who has been at every Going West festival since 1998. I can hear him say, 'For God's sake Christine, make them laugh!' and I'm going to try to do that.

That wonderful phrase Murray must have dreamt up: 'Between the Lines'. All of us here would have read so much of what Michael has written over the years — almost 30 books — so I'm going to try, in various stories that come to mind, to tell you something of the man 'between the lines', this quite extraordinary man. I do have to remind myself, for goodness' sake, celebrate his life, it is the only possible thing to do. It's particularly good — and I do thank Murray for having brought Tainui Stevens here tonight — that we can see some of that marvellous 1974 classic television series *Tangata Whenua*. I looked at some of the notes which Michael sent me at that time — even before email became prevalent, we sent each other a great many notes. And the problems — which no doubt Tainui will tell us something of — they had making this film: assembling people, getting to know and understand them, and the fun that they had. Also, the knowledge that everyone working on *Tangata Whenua* knew they were doing something really important, because this was the first time that Māori faces and voices were really given a prominent part on our television. So, it's so fitting that we're going to be seeing something of that tonight.

I could not stand the idea of Michael King when I first heard about him—absolutely dreadful. I had reason, I thought: he was going to be arrogant, petty, a fusspot, narrowly toeing the line. Almost all the things, in fact, which Michael was not and could never be. You see, this was the situation. In fortuitous circumstances I had been given the marvellous job of heading the first journalism school in New Zealand. This was at Wellington Polytechnic in the 1960s and we'd advertised for another tutor, our fourth, I think it was. Now as an old journalist I knew perfectly well — or I thought I did — how important it was that we got just the right sort of person for this job: someone intelligent and knowledgeable of course about his craft or trade; somebody to teach the basics. But much more than that: somebody with standards, ideals, I would say, with dreams of improving our media; somebody who would be able to lead students and improve our teaching team. It was a very important appointment for me. Now at the stage (I must be careful of libel here — that was always one of my better lectures at journalism school) but at that stage and understandably, journalism had never been taught before, and the course administrators were people from high schools or in some cases universities of New Zealand and tended to be somewhat bureaucratic. They had little or no idea what journalism was, what news was, and they expected us tutors to provide a detailed year's timetable of what we would be teaching every day, every week, for the whole year. I provided a broad list of topics of course, but that shocked them, and one of them said to me, 'There, I've put you down to teach grammar in August.' I said grimly, 'We teach grammar every day.'

But this bureaucratic administration was good hearted. They promised to let me know as soon as interviews had been set up with applicants so I could return to Wellington and take part, as this was in summer and we were off cruising in the Marlborough Sounds. We set up twice-daily watches for our personal news; nothing came for me. I was really perturbed as to what had happened. We detoured to Nelson, tied up and found a telephone so I could ring Wellington. That's when I learnt that they had decided, they'd taken it upon themselves, not to spoil my holiday. They had interviewed all the applicants and they had appointed somebody called Michael King. I was absolutely horrified. I can remember to this very day tearing my hair out. I had the darkest forebodings of what he would be like. Well of course, a minute or two with Michael and I had yet another lesson in the folly of rapidly jumping to conclusions, because by the greatest good luck, Michael was of course, everything that I, and hundreds of students then and since, could possibly have hoped for.

Michael and I began laughing and, in memory anyway, continued laughing until March 30th this year. Which is five months and eleven days ago. Time enough indeed for us to be celebrating his life, because when I think of Michael, I think of all these things: laughter; warmth; generosity; a passionate concern for the many things which matter; for social justice; for helping everyone to try to live life to the full; and for employing the best words he could find at the time, with his very considerable intellect, to express these hopes and ideals.

In his 1999 book, *Being Pākehā*, Michael put it this way, 'The most profound satisfactions are to be found in living a life in accord with the natural world, exercising the human capacity for friendship and altruism, engaging in creative and personal activity and experiencing an allegiance to one's origins.' Rousing words! Live the best life you can and do what you can for your fellow humans, is what he meant.

So, it is Michael the man — in love with life, in love with this country, courageous, generous, laughing — whom I would like us to celebrate this evening. Yes of course he was our great biographer, and I think the greatest historian for the ordinary, intelligent New Zealander. He wasn't an historian's historian, in the sense that he didn't really advance new theories, but he explained us to ourselves; taught us to be proud of what he called our Pākehātanga as well as Māoritanga; taught us that Māori weren't always the victims and Pākehā weren't always the plunderers and stealers. He didn't go along with fashions or ways of thinking or excessive talk. He looked for the facts and he looked at them straight. Then he wrote and he stood up to be counted. And sometimes it took courage.

I think, from my knowledge of him, that what hurt him most in his professional life was when some Māori activists, understandably, attacked him for daring to write about their history. For daring to invade and capture their territory through his writing. The impacts really distressed him — well, I have to say they infuriated me, because I had seen a bit of what was going on backstage — and so Michael asked me if I'd write a letter to one of the papers, I think it was the *Waikato Times*. And I did, about what I'd seen — there were various instances, such as the time I had driven him to some remote part of the Uruweras. For much of his life, Michael was hard up. He didn't have a car at that time, and he wanted to go there so he could interview a very, very old woman, a kuia, in the Māori language, which he was learning with the help of an interpreter.

I can see this dear old woman now, how she clasped his wrists. I can see her thin hands holding onto him. She did not want him to go because here was somebody who was really listening to her story and she was obviously trusting him to remember it, to record it and to tell others. Somebody — Michael — was listening.

Now if Michael had not recorded this story it would have been lost forever, and I would like every Māori, every Pākehā, to remember that fact. Nobody else was doing this just then. This was what, in the seventies? Nobody else was talking with Māori before it was too late. He talked to leaders such as Te Puea and Whina Cooper, but there were so many men and women, nameless except to their own tribes, whose stories would have been lost if Michael King had not gone forth, in spite of all the criticism, and won their trust, and recorded what they had to say.

But you see, Michael, being Michael thought he could do something else for Māori —Māori history — in another way. He moved on to Pākehā biography and history of course with the lives of Frank Sargeson, Janet Frame and his many other books and of course his *Penguin History of New Zealand*. But while he was doing this, he did his very best to help interested Māori to learn more of what really was necessary if you wanted to advance in the world of researching, recording and writing.

We tried to persuade more Māori into our journalism course at Wellington Polytechnic. Michael joined that very good educator Gary Wilson, who's done so much for this cause, in running special courses for young or youngish Māori to help them to compete on more equal terms for acceptance into journalism training, because more and more journalism courses were being set up. He brought me in to help in Wellington and in Rotorua, and I saw once again his instinctive rapport with students, his great-hearted giving of himself in any way he could. It was the same with writers' workshops we ran at Victoria University in the 1970s. They were the progenitors of the great Bill Manhire classes—Fiona Kidman's classes were in-between.

Now if Michael could help anyone he did, no matter how ill or how stressed he was himself. I'm beginning to make him sound like a saint, which indeed he wasn't — I'll come to some of his mischiefs in a minute. But I would like to tell you something of what he was up against so you'll have more of an insight perhaps into what I really call his enormous courage.

As a child, he had polio. It could have been worse. But post-polio syndrome continued to dog him. In 1984 he fell victim to what was at that time called Tapanui flu, or chronic fatigue syndrome. I know, I got it myself, we got it from the same source. This exhaustion with Michael was always there waiting to return, so that he'd have to go to bed reasonably often just to recover from the fatigue. Then he developed diabetes and it was probably only Maria's loving and careful care with his diet and her wagging her finger at him that enabled him to work on as he did.

And then last year, just as he was working so hard to finish his monumental *Penguin History of New Zealand*, and to comfort Janet Frame in what they both knew was her terminal cancer, Michael learned that he too had cancer. Not just any cancer — if you can say that casually about cancer — but one which struck at the very root of his ability to communicate. I use the word root: it was a tumour at the base — the root — of his tongue. Now at the same time, he was receiving requests from overseas papers, 'Please would you write an obituary about Janet Frame. We understand she may not have long to live.' And of course, Michael took that very seriously and as he wrote, he must have been thinking, *who will write mine and when?*

He asked questions of his doctors and he got answers. He knew that his radiotherapy and chemotherapy regimens would be horrendous. Seven weeks of treatment and then after that would be the wait to see if they were successful. Of course, we know, thank goodness, that he had that lovely time when the doctors said they had been successful and he said to me, 'I feel like Lazarus risen from the dead.' But Michael knew that it might just be remission. He had been given just a very few days before this gruelling treatment was about to begin, and this time he had to break the news to those near and dear to him, particularly to Maria, herself stricken with multiple sclerosis, and Maria was perhaps Michael's greatest source of anxiety. How would it be for Maria? He had to help with all these people with their shock and grief. He had to finish promised pieces of writing and plan promotional reviews for his *Penguin History of New Zealand*. Michael was the consummate professional, you see, the author. Oh, that all publishers had authors like Michael. He couldn't let down Penguin and Geoff Walker, his oldest friend from student days.

And he had to front up to the big occasion in Wellington, where Helen Clark was to give to him and to Janet, in absentia, and to Hone Tuwhare, her very first awards for literary excellence. And then the next day he decided he really should go public with the facts of his illness while still carrying out his promise to do interviews with people like Kim Hill, John Campbell, I think there was Paul Holmes, the dailies, strings of people. All this he did in that short time after first undergoing some really distressing procedures when his cancer treatment began. The most painful was to have all his bottom teeth out because the radiation would have poisoned their roots. What sort of person is this, I wonder? I think for a lot of us probably, good old New Zealanders, (I was brought up, father back from the War), good soldiers never cry. Felix Donnelly might have had something different to say about that, but I think the New Zealand thing is, 'Right, we'll soldier on, we'll do the best we can.' But how many of us, I wonder, could really have behaved, have lived, as Michael did at this time? Always bearing in mind that so many people, he knew, were looking to him for advice, for help.

He did all this with grace and courage, for the most part keeping his troubles to himself and always mindful of the needs of others. During his treatment he lost 16 kilos. He could take no food or drink by mouth for a long period of time. His great Christmas treat, he told me, just last Christmas, was to be given one cup of tepid tea, a great Christmas treat. And he laughed about it, of course he did. His enormous courage, his generosity, his discipline — I think sheer niceness and goodness is another way of putting it — saw him continuing to fire off notes and emails to all manner of people. Michael was the great encourager. We should know, this audience, how important it is; we should all do it more. When we read something, particularly by somebody young, beginning, about which we think, 'Oh, yes!', we should all just sit down and write a note of thanks, encouragement, appreciation. I write so many of these notes in my head; Michael wrote them in actuality.

He'd always been a mentor, you see, helping people. I didn't know, because he didn't ever mention this to me, but throughout this cancer treatment he remained an official mentor of one writer. What that must have taken, what discipline and what thought for that person. He received some 900 messages of love and support from New Zealand, from overseas, from many places, and he even tried to answer a number of these. Maria and his friends and family said, 'No, no they will understand.' and he would say, 'I'd like to reply if I can.'

I'm sure a lot of you here would have sent him messages and if you didn't, he would have known that so many people were thinking of him.

He was to say that he was absolutely certain that these messages had a direct effect on his immune system. I would believe this too—I really would. We Sargeson House trustees — Michael was a founding deputy chair right at the very beginning — put together a small book called *A Small Book for Michael*, in a limited edition of 50 copies. He loved to laugh of course, so we collected in this book some of our best ever Michael stories, in the hope that while he was having this treatment for cancer, he'd be able to read them and look at them and remember and laugh.

I thought I would read you just the last piece in this book because it introduces Michael's mischievous side. Now many of you will remember how Michael and C.K. Stead duelled for weeks in the correspondence columns of the *Listener*. Readers used to wait for each weekly cannonade. Well, sometime after this, I was publishing a collection of Michael's and I was very gratified that he offered it to me to publish, because Penguin really was his publisher. It was a collection of essays and occasional talks he'd given, called *Tread Softly for you Tread on my Life*. He'd dedicated it, he told me, to someone who needed a dedication. I love that; he knew what pleasure dedicating it to this person would give. Well, suddenly he phoned me from Opoutere, 'Is it too late to change the dedication?' I said, 'Well, I can get the proofs back from the printer,' and so on, and he said, 'I'll dedicate to that person in another book'. But for this one, he said that he wanted to change it. This then became his famous dedication:

> For C.K. Stead
> who, like execution,
> concentrates the mind.

Of all the messages received during his illness, he especially cherished one — and so he should, when he showed it to me — he said, 'what can one say, when Karl displays such sensitivity, humour and charm.' Because this is what Karl wrote to him. Karl had been one of the original Sargeson trustees too of course. Karl wrote to Michael:

Your interview this morning with Kim Hill (that must have been the day after Helen had given him his big award) was so good. You always do these things well, but this one was exceptional. Such good things said in such perfect tone and pitch. I'm not praying for you, you'll be pleased to know, because everyone knows who that Stead person would pray to, if he prayed at all. But I'm hoping for you and wishing you all the best.

Well of course, Karl spoke for so many people and that meant a very great deal to Michael. He loved the incongruous, the quirkiness — no wonder he and Janet Frame got on so well together. He had so many stories. He particularly loved his story about Janet playing scrabble. With her linguistic facility she was a devilish opponent. Now Janet had on the board, 'silltits'. 'Silltits?' said Michael, 'what on earth does that mean?' 'Oh,' said Janet,' (I can just hear her voice), 'It's what all those women in New York get when they spend all day leaning out of tenement windows and watching the action in the street.' So of course, they allowed her the word and of course she won the game.

One of Michael's great friends was Irihapeti Ramsden, whose father Eric Ramsden was on the Christchurch *Press* for a time when Allen Curnow was there. Irihapeti Ramsden was a considerable woman, an old, old friend. She was dying of cancer, and she asked if Michael would conduct her funeral. Irihapeti being the sort of woman she was, it had to be an occasion where people laughed and rejoiced. Michael told this story at the funeral.

He had been at a significant function with Māori and Pākehā where a number of people had been asked to sing a song or recite a poem to show something of their respective cultures, their cultural inheritance. On came Irihapeti (Irihapeti was very beautiful) and everyone was confident she was going to launch into a waiata of great resonance and antiquity. She didn't. Irihapeti was half Māori, half English: Eric's father came from Yorkshire. Irihapeti didn't sing the waiata, she told Michael later, as she was fed up with all the portentousness and banality and so on. And she sang instead a song which she said her father had taught her:

> Gentlemen will please refrain
> From passing water while the train
> Is standing at the station in full view.
> Workmen working underneath
> Will get it in their eyes and teeth
> And they don't like it any more than you.

Now you can see how somebody like Irihapeti and somebody like Michael were — of course, it's a funny expression — 'soulmates', but they were; they could perceive each other. There are far too many stories but that's probably enough because I want to read a few lines that Michael read at Irihapeti's funeral, lines which I love, and which a lot of you probably know.

Before I do, I would just like to say that the Michael King Writers Centre Trust are, we hope, on the track of a magnificent property. (Not the one behind Frank Sargeson's — we couldn't raise enough money for that. Who knows, someday we may be able to do that too, to win back Frank's land.) This [the Signalman's House, Tarapunga Mt Victoria, Devonport] is a place, we all feel sure, that writers, that Michael himself, would be delighted with. And if any of you do feel like making a contribution, up at the back at Murray's bookshop I've left a receipt book and you'll get a receipt and much gratitude from us.

These last few lines are from Rex Fairburn's, 'To a Friend in the Wilderness'. Michael read them at the end of Irihapeti's funeral, and I thought you would like to hear them tonight:

> Old friend, dear friend, some day
> when I have had my say, and the world its way,
> when all that is left is the gathering in of ends,
> the forgathering of friends,
> on some autumn evening when the mullet leap
> in a sea of silver-grey,

then, O then I will come again
and stay for as long as I may,
stay till the time for sleep ;
gaze at the rock that died before me,
the sea that lives for ever ;
of air and sunlight, frost and wave and cloud,
and all the remembered agony and joy
fashion my shroud.

And the word I'll leave you with is — joy.

Thank you Michael.

2005 NIGEL COX

Word of Mouth

Thank you, Murray, it's great to be here. As Murray Gray said, I've been overseas. I've been living in Berlin for five years where I worked on the Jewish Museum Berlin. Murray asked me to say a few things about what it's like coming back, and when he asked me, three or four months ago, I was all set for it. It just didn't occur to me it would be one week before the election, and it's a kind of different mood in the country, a special time.

I called this talk —because I kind of like these pompous titles — 'Before I Went Blind' and the idea is — he says, changing glasses — is that you get an impression of your country *[finger snap]* as soon as you get back here, and then after you've been here a while, it kind of fades, and you just are here. And so, I wanted to try and capture what it was like a little bit in those first few days. So here we go: Before I Went Blind.

So where do you start? Winston Peters? I don't think so — but coming back, your eyes fall on such things and you think 'You! Still alive!' I want him gone by lunchtime. The inner groan when you see that Judy Bailey is *still* reading the news, and such news! That's the news? Surely, New Zealand is at its worst in the run-up to an election.

But you're pleased to be back, that's what you keep telling yourself — you've thrown the dice, there's no turning back —so of course you're pleased to be back. But in fact, you are. For the first couple of weeks, I walk around with a big dopey grin on my face, loving everything: fish 'n' chips in the rain under a Norfolk pine at Mission Bay, magic. The wine. The food. For five years we had the pick of European food and wine and what we have here, I'll take it any time. And so cheap! And so good!

Of course, for the first few weeks back after five years, wine with fancy food in the company of old friends is what takes up most of your day *[pats stomach]* — not too much wrong with that. And all the no-brainer stuff: the All Blacks with a decent scrum; everyone speaking English. It's like a return to real life. And that's the problem. You can feel real life setting in, and although, you don't want to, you can't help noticing a few things.

Where to start? In Germany, maybe. As I said, I was there for five years with my wife and two kids — in fact we came home with three — working on the Jewish Museum Berlin. Now that museum is a whole other topic and I don't propose to go there tonight, but what it meant was that unlike other countries that I've spent time in — drinking their wine, eating their food, it's amazing how those things loom so large in my life — that job really meant I did go into German society, or at least some way in. I look at myself now with a Kiwi eye and I think, 'So, are you more serious?' 'Are you less flexible or is that just age?' 'Are you taking yourself more seriously? Or is that just hubris?' The casualness of New Zealand, this is not a big feature of everyday life in Germany.

It's one of the big things that strike you here, this casualness. I want to start now on a long slow circle into the middle of what I have to say tonight, and out at the edge as I start, what I get is the greeting from the heavyweight Māori guy who inspects my passport at Immigration: 'Great to have you back fella. Welcome home.' After cops with machine guns, you've gotta love that. The bloke getting you into lines for Customs clearance: 'Look everybody, we're a bit overloaded here, just go over into those two outbound lanes would you — just ignore the markings on the floor.' Ignoring markings! — never in Germany.

And then you step outside, and everything is so open — the skies for one. In Berlin, there's always a building rising right in front of your face. There's no horizon, no distance. I can't tell you how lucky we are to be able to escape so quickly from the 'enclosing-ness' of cities. And the freshness of the air! After a year in Berlin, my nose was like a chimney that needed a sweep, and it stayed like that for the next four years. I'd been back a week when I noticed it was getting better. It's all the exhaust emissions etcetera in the air, and there's no wind in Berlin to blow it away, well nothing that we'd call a wind. It did blow a bit one day, and all the dead branches came down off all the trees, killing seven people and closing the roads for weeks.

Okay, now quickly on the weather: it's too soon for me to be missing the way the seasons are articulated in Europe, but I know I will. It's not so much the snow — though I did love the way that white blanket smoothed everything back to elemental shapes — it's the changes, the way you can so strongly sense the world turning, and your life going through its seasons. It makes you more reflective — somehow, instead of seasons, what we have here is weather.

And what's that weather like? Well, we don't really notice. In New Zealand we are increasingly of the idea that the weather should be constantly warm and permissive of outdoor activities, and any weather that's not, is somehow an aberration, an insult to our idea of our lives. Accordingly, we wear warm weather gear no matter what. To see people in Courtenay Place, Wellington, during a southerly in a tee-shirt and shorts, is to remember what Jock Phillips said, in this case about New Zealand men: that the culture of not giving expression to pain has become a culture of not giving expression full stop.

Just to do a little truck-stop here on clothes: the unbelievable casualness of the clothes New Zealanders wear is one of the things that poke your eye right out, right up there with the popcorn quality of the TV news — TV in general, actually — and the obsession with violence (more on that later). Peter Jackson on set reminds me of Les Murray's great poem, 'The Dream of Wearing Shorts Forever'. Guys wearing to work the jersey they use to wipe the dipstick, jandals at the dinner party, the lawn-mowing trousers. At the same time, New Zealanders have become a lot more conscious of style. Travel back with me if you will, to my boyhood in the Masterton of the 1950s — please, we don't want to stay there too long — what I can see walking down Queen Street is the daggy, the saggy, the raggy and the self-rolled tobaccy. Now not too much of that about these days, outside of Speights commercials. Lots of people seem to have one eye out for that TV camera that might suddenly put a frame around them and make their day. So the style is, be casual, but with streets of cool.

When you pause and look around at the skies here, one of the things you see everywhere is wires. Black lines cutting the open into pieces — telephone wires, power lines looping, sagging, making cobwebs. Doesn't anyone care what things look like? The Germans have been getting rid of power lines for years. And signs. Our cities are thickets of signs. The whole country has gone berserk on marketing itself. Every little Lotto outlet and heel bar has a brand and a tagline and they just have to get it poked right into your eye. Doesn't anyone want the cities to breathe a little? Oh, that's right, our cities are for commerce not for people.

And all that marketing competes with another category of signs — you know the ones — which read, 'In case your eye catches this sign instead of the thing right in front of you, those are 'stairs', which means you have to lift up your feet or you'll have a nasty accident.' Doh! If we didn't have so many of these signs maybe we'd see the stairs better.

The wires-in-the-sky thing extends to pylons. So, we're really going to have pylons marching across all of our landscape? Is there no money in this country for beauty? Or do we think we have so much of it down south, that up here where most of us live, we don't have to care? And wind turbines. In fact, I think wind turbines are relatively interesting looking and I'm all for eco-friendly sources of power, but has anyone looked at what's happening in Germany? There, they've had serious investment in wind power for over 20 years. Thanks to significant government subsidies, many farmers erected big propellers on their land and sold the power to the national grid. You see stately forests of them, seeming to cartwheel across the horizon when you take a train journey. They're intrusive yes, but not ugly. Nevertheless, just recently the Germans have concluded that the propellers are not an economic source of power, and they're going to abandon them — just as we are about to invest heavily in this area. And Germany is a country with an infinitely greater commitment to ecological sustainability than us — is anybody paying attention?

Of course, the eco-commitment of the Germans can get tedious. To get rid of your rubbish you need to sort it into at least five types, each of which must go into precisely the right bin down in the courtyard. These bins are used communally and when you move into a new apartment block, you're given comprehensive instructions on how to sort your rubbish and how to deposit your stuff — it's detailed in your lease for God's sake — and woe betide if you get it wrong — phalanxes will arrive to set you straight. Colour code your empties into the correct white, brown, or green bin in the bottled area, or face a good dressing down. If you buy a takeout bottle of beer, you pay a 50c surcharge for each bottle, for which you're given a receipt — hang on to that. So long as you've kept the receipt, and the bottle, you can get a refund when you take them back, to that exact shop. If you buy it here, and drink it there, tough! you lose.

When you move out of your apartment, take it back to the bare white walls you started out with — the exact shade of white naturally, which is also spelled out in your lease. No question that any improvements you might have made would be worth keeping, everything must go. Is that smart? When we left Berlin, I spent four blasted days unbolting a massive mezzanine floor, that was so big and solid, you could have landed the space shuttle on it, and the next tenants were planning to put it back up again. Remove the light fittings. Fill the screw holes and leave only bare wires. So, you know you can't check the place, there's no lights. Remove the sink bench, leave only the outflow pipe. Now what do you do with the sink bench, which was custom-built and won't fit anywhere? Well, there's no market for it, actually there's no market for any second-hand stuff. I guess it's because for the last few decades Germany has been so incredibly wealthy. Maybe that's about to change, unemployment is way up and rising steadily; economic growth is non-existent. But, for now, what you do is get your friend with a van to come round and take it to an urban recycling centre. It's what Berlin has instead of a dump. My first visit to one of these amazed me. For a start, it's so clean you could hold a picnic in the middle of it. No smell, none whatsoever. It's simply another urban facility standing cheek-by-jowl with crowded apartment blocks and shops. Men in bright, clean overalls direct you where to put everything — they *are* all men.

It's men in charge in Germany. When Helen Clark visited the Jewish Museum, all my colleagues said, 'Your Prime Minister is a woman?' Angela Merkel, who's very likely to be Germany's next PM, faces hatred from the men in her party, who resent being told what to do by a woman. Would never happen here, would it?

Back to the recycling centre: everything is divided into shipping containers which, when full, are shipped off for use as raw materials. Neat, clean, self-serviced. But it does feel counterintuitive. You want to get rid of your perfectly good old desk, so you break it down at the recycling centre, using the crow bars they provide, into splinters for wood pulp. Is that necessarily a good idea? Your old chair, which isn't good for recycling, is dragged away somewhere and crushed. Unless it's an antique, hardly anything is ever used again. All the old fridges, washing machines, dryers — in a container for scrap metal. It does make you wonder.

But there's no question. German ecological practice makes this country look like a cowboy outfit where anything goes. We met a German eco-freak who, during Ronald Reagan's 'Star Wars' era, terrified that Europe would get caught up in a nuclear war, emigrated to New Zealand because it was, he figured, the cleanest, greenest, furthest away place he could think of. And he was shocked by what he found here. He stayed as long as he could bear it, but it was the state of the rivers, the way we think about land use, the dumping of fertilisers, the way we build things: it was just too hideous, and he faced his fears and went back. In fact, many Germans spoke to me about this: New Zealand does not care enough for itself. For a country that says it's clean and green, that sells those qualities, we're not trying hard enough. After living in Germany, it's difficult not to think: the only reason New Zealand is as clean and green as it is, is because we have a small population. Look, this is where we live. We're so lucky we don't have acid rain dropping in from the primitive economies across the border. We don't have a thousand years of manufacturing as an inheritance. So, what are we thinking about?

I suppose that's where, circling, circling, I start to bear down on what is at the centre of what, after five years, I find in this country. I mean I love it here. I can't tell you how I maundered on about New Zealand to my poor colleagues at the Jewish Museum. I explained our recent history. They all know what the Treaty is. They're sick of hearing about our extraordinary founding document. I was like a one-man promotional campaign I couldn't stop myself. I ignored their glazed looks, I just kept on singing. It was a kind of homesickness I think, and maybe an anxiety that the place wasn't really as good as I made out. Pride. National pride is such a spooky business. The Germans by and large don't have it. They're hugely conscious of where national pride once got them. They all exit Germany constantly. Not like us, because we have to see the world, but because they want to escape their own country. They're huge travellers as you know. Though when you hint that they might come down here for a visit, they all say, 'Such a long way.' New Zealand for most Germans is a paradise they would love to visit but won't. Nevertheless, I kept plugging away with the boosterism, despite which, because they're very tolerant, the Jewish Museum offered me a permanent contract. So, you see, we could have stayed in Germany. We chose to come home.

And it's as though, having done that, somehow you end up holding your country to account. 'I committed myself', you say, 'So you better deliver.' It's unfair really. What part, tell me, of the modern world really measures up? The problem is when it doesn't, then you feel: okay, so I don't have to either. After a few weeks various things started to come to the surface. The visual clutter, the casualness — which in the main I see as a huge positive — the obsession with superficial style, the indifference to beauty; all done too with great confidence.

Confidence, now there's a thing. The magazines, *Metro*, *Next*, *Pavement*, various magazines I found on people's coffee tables, had pictures of us, New Zealanders, shot from below, gazing confidently into the middle distance. A gas station attendant with a good tan — what a hero. A king of business — look at the guy. Look at those haircuts powering their way along Lambton Quay. Yep, there's real confidence here these days. It's as though we've come through. Come through what? Well, I guess that would be Rogernomics — we took the pain and suddenly here we are out on the other side, and thriving. And why not? It's good to be confident. It's good to love your country.

But magazines, I mean, whatever happened to *New Outlook*? *New Republic*? *Quote Unquote*. They're gone. Okay magazines do come and go, that's their nature, but what's replaced them? Style bibles, full of heroic portraits, full of flattery. Where's the *Listener* as it used to be? *Metro* as it used to be? Does no-one want that kind of serious consideration of the country anymore?

My most recent novel, published earlier this year, received in total about half as many reviews as the first one published 20 years earlier, because the review spaces don't exist anymore. The reviews for the new book were very positive, but actually, trivial, essentially fluff. I mean, positive — I'll take it — but what's going on here?

Within a few weeks of being back I heard three times in various media broadcasts people saying, 'Oh, you're not trying to get into that old 'national identity' crap are you?' 'All that navel gazing about national identity. The national identity discussion is such old hat.' I found this hard to believe. Okay, the literal phrase, 'national identity', has probably done its dash, but all over the world people are debating the idea of their nation — in France, in Germany, in the States. The whole world has, since September 11th, had some hugely fundamental questions thrown at it: Can we live with one another? Can we keep living like this? Surely the discussion about who we are, about what the essential it-must-not-be-lost quality of this country is — that's a discussion, which one way or another, has to go on forever. But coming back I pick up a great reluctance to talk seriously about these things, to consider who we are, where we're going. The only question everyone seems happy to address is, 'Is it good for business?' What are we, Switzerland? Because that's what I'm getting. That this is a nation obsessed all over again with material satisfaction, that anyone who wants to discuss things in any context except, 'what will it do to the share-market?' is just causing trouble, 'Come on, wanker, get your boat shoes on, get down to the Loaded Hog.' You know, it's like a return to the 1950s. We're all right. We're satisfied. We got what we wanted. Everything's okay. Don't frighten the horses.

Of course, there are things that people mention. The violence: it's hard to get good figures for comparison, but it seems that Germany has about as many murders, per capita, as New Zealand. But you'd never know that from the news. The same is true of violent crime. There's an obsession about these subjects in this country, but no commitment to discussing *why* it might be. A friend remarked recently that this was a 'country full of rage'. Is it true? Why? Sure, the media kick things around — but always in the context of who's the winner and who's the loser, the big concern is, who lost face. Politics in particular: never focusing on, 'Where is this taking us? What are we becoming?'

The public transport systems: the clear message they give you here is, 'If you can't travel by car, you're just shit, and that's how you'll be treated.' On the bus to work each day, I can't sit down properly because I'm too long from hip to thigh for the moulded plastic seats. Come on, I'm not *that* tall. Who says our buses should be so squashy, so noisy, so jerky, so ill-lit? Is it because public transport isn't the stylish way to go, so, it's okay to default to like-it-or-lump-it? German buses, compared, are like limousine luxury. Everybody hates our public transport, but does anyone have anything to say, except 'That's what the market dictates?' I don't mean just moan, I don't mean find out who is to blame, I mean ask ourselves, is this who we are?

The media: everyone bellyaches about it, but then we just tune in just the same. The news. There's Judy saying, 'Today the fig leaf of political respectability was torn from the bleeding body of Rodney Hyde, who was exposed as having sold his principles down the drain when he dot, dot, dot.' Isn't she trying to say, 'Today the Act Party changed one of its policies.' After five years of listening to the BBC World Service, the *language* of the news here is just astonishing to me. It's as though it's been 'tabloid-ised' for a tabloid nation.

The cultural scene: there's a powerful sense that there's a rich cultural life, that terrific work is being produced, amazing stuff and lots of it. The *Small World, Big Town* exhibition, for instance, at the City Gallery in Wellington is full of art that is at least as exciting as anything I saw in Berlin galleries, but does anybody care? Somehow, it's work in which there's nothing essential at stake. The nation has found a way to consume culture, without being affected by it. And the practitioners feel that, and they turn their faces towards each other, looking in towards the 'higher ground' of aestheticism, towards 'those who know'. The cultural arts are segmented, the literary arts cut off from the visual, architecture cut off from theatre, and all of it cut off from 'real life'.

Isn't this what people used to say about New Zealand way back? Aren't these the clichés I grew up with in the 1950s? Maybe they're coming back to bite us. Or was it that they never went away, and we just forgot about them?

It's only a few weeks since his death, but the passing of David Lange really gave me pause. I can't help but remember that time, that first year when he came to power and, even though our economy was on its knees, we found ourselves. Remember the excitement of us going nuclear-free, of having a Prime Minister who could make us laugh. New Zealanders laughing — that was a real breakthrough. New Zealanders who could really talk: Kim Hill; Derek Fox; Bill Manhire. Suddenly that's what New Zealanders were, interesting talkers. That same year, Keri Hulme won the the Booker Prize for her book *The Bone People* and after Lauris Edmond and Dinah Hawken won the Commonwealth Writers Prize for poetry — we all read those books, and everyone was talking about them. Janet Frame's *An Angel at my Table* — first the book and then the wonderful movie by Jane Campion. The Treaty settlement process was launched; the rugby tour to South Africa had been stopped. There was a sense that we were going somewhere. The Greenpeace ship *Rainbow Warrior* went down, sunk by the French at Marsden Wharf. Suddenly we were a country worth attacking, and we had a heightened sense of who we were.

In 1991, I had lunch in Paris with Judith Trotter, who at that point had been our ambassador for four years. She said, 'This nuclear free nonsense, New Zealanders have no idea what it is costing us.' And I got on my high horse, which is a very rare occurrence, 'I think you've been away too long,' I said. I think New Zealanders *know* the price and they've decided to pay it. That's the thing I ask myself now. Is there any price we're prepared to pay, for anything? What are we prepared to forego, in the interests of, 'something better'? Tax cuts?

It's interesting when you turn to Germany. This is a nation defined, even today, by the terrible things done in its name 60 years ago. It's true that 15 years back, the fall of the Wall did provide a new focus. But then the problems of reunification gradually swelled, most visibly in the unemployment numbers — which are terrible — at the same time as economic growth subsided. So that today, the country is at a loss, unable to afford the strong social provisions it has regarded as eternal, but not yet ready to give them up in favour of a market-driven society. Good on them, I say. Hang in there Germany. Of course, in many ways there is no real comparison possible between the two countries. Totally different histories, languages, geographies, climate and social makeup. Levels of discussion: in Germany they really know how to give an issue the complete 360 — by Judgement Day you've heard all the angles. Is that true of us? My impression is New Zealand is made up of what I call 'agreement groups'. People only associate with people they agree with. Are we afraid everything will fall over if we say boo?

Our books: after 20 years in the book trade here, what I think people want from a new novel is one, to be flattered; two, to be comforted; and three; that the book be decorative. Doesn't exactly sound like Günter Grass does it?

And yet Germans are ready to feel a great affection toward New

Zealand, an affinity. They see us as who they'd like to be, if only. There's a shared sense that it's the human that matters. And they're right. The human side of New Zealand *is* amazing. I mean I'm sorry, I know I've been having a good old moan, and everybody hates a moaner, me especially — so throw your bananas now but it's the people here. Ken Gorbey and I didn't get the Jewish Museum open when no-one else could because we were such good museum makers, because of our brilliant skills at synthesising cultural history: it's because we're Kiwis. Sorry if that sounds a bit trite, but you can't overstate, I don't think, the way that New Zealanders know how to solve a problem, how to cut through the crap, how to focus on what really matters. This is the upside of the casualness: we have a terrific sense of how far to go, of the unnecessary. Jandals at the dinner party: it isn't going to break any bones. When you say of Germans, 'They didn't know when to stop', a real shiver goes down the spine. 'They didn't know when to pull back.' But do we?

As most people know, I'm pretty keen on pop music, so I've been catching up: Trinity Roots; Fat Freddy's Drop — these are CDs you might pick, over music from anywhere in the world. While I'm sitting there listening, I like to look at photographs, at the moment, two books in particular: Marty Friedlander's Godwit collection; and Ans Westra's *Handboek*. Mostly, what you've got there is pictures of the 1960s and 70s. Wonderful pictures, so expressive, but not timeless. On the contrary, they're very much of their time. It's the faces, our 60s and 70s faces, that amaze me. I stare at them. Those people are astonished to be here, and at the same time, they're not sure of where they are. You couldn't say that these days.

Those heroic photographs I saw in *Metro* and the other magazines. New Zealanders are so self-possessed now, so expert, so competent. So aware of their competence. We know where we are. We know who we are. We're in the middle of our lives, in the middle of our world, here in the middle of the Pacific.

But what are we *doing* with this knowledge that has been so hard won? Have we arrived at the end of our history? Is this it? Is *this* what we had in mind? Or are we bored with the idea of issues, or are there no issues left? Or is it that the media reduces everything to porridge? Or we're just too busy with our own struggles to care what kind of society we're making? Have we arrived, New Zealand, at the place we were going to?

Thank you.

2006 PATRICIA GRACE

The Truth About Stories

In an ancient Māori tale, there is a woman called Rona who went out one moonlit night to fill the calabashes with water so that her children would not be thirsty. As she made her way along, a cloud passed over the moon causing the night to darken. In the darkness she tripped and fell, and on getting up she cursed the moon for its failure to light her way. The moon was greatly insulted by this and, by way of punishment, began to pull Rona skyward. In desperation Rona grasped hold of a manuka tree, hoping it would anchor her to the Earth. But the Moon's pull was too strong. Up Rona went, tree and all, until she reached the Moon. Ever since then, when the Moon is full, Rona can be seen there inside the Moon, holding on to her calabashes and clutching the little tree. Which all goes to show that the first man on the Moon was a woman. Not only that, but the first man in the moon was Māori.

It was through such stories that people of ancient times explained their world, defined themselves, reinforced what their values were and enlivened and enriched their lives. The truth about those old stories is that because they are of exceptional quality they have withstood the test of time; they have withstood translation into modern concepts and idioms and translation into other languages.

In a few weeks' time my fifth collection of short stories, titled *Small Holes in the Silence*, is to be published. One of the new stories is a retelling, expanding on the ancient story of Rona, which I always thought was too short anyway, or the version I knew was. For example, it doesn't tell why the children were alone when Rona went out. Where was their grandmother? Where were their aunties? Where was their father? My version is called 'Moon Story'. It begins like this:

> On the night that Rona had bad-mouthed Moon, she did it because she wasn't in her right mind. Even before she tripped and fell, she was feeling stressed. So much had happened that day and at the end of it she'd been left with far too many responsibilities.
>
> Early that morning, in an enemy attack, one of their men had been killed. They'd been taken by surprise, and though at first they tried to defend themselves they found themselves greatly outnumbered. Some of their houses had been broken down and most of their stored food had been stolen from the pataka. All they could do was take their children into the forest and hide until it was over.

So, it sounds like a usual scenario.

The truth about stories is that they can be renewed; they can be edited, expanded, updated, adjusted to suit the time and place of telling. And there will be something new to be found in them every time they are retold, re-read, or heard again. There will be new thoughts and ideas, new messages. And in this way they will continue to be meaningful because we have made them our own:

> Once the raiding party had gone on its way the men followed at a distance to make sure it was leaving the territory. They knew that one day there would have to be a reprisal but that would have to wait until they had built strength by making suitable liaisons ...
>
> After the men had gone the women and children set about

fixing the houses, consoling the widow and finding enough food for everyone to eat. They also had to tend to one of the grandmothers now lying in the death shelter which had been erected for her.

The truth about stories, whether ancient or modern, is that they explain and define our worlds, or the worlds of those who tell or write or listen to them. They tell us in a contemporary way about what is important to us and the people about us. They tell us our histories, mirror our contemporary lives, help us understand our futures. They give definition to the self, or to someone's self, defining all aspects of living, including our lives of speculation, deep thought, feelings and dreams:

> While others had the task of seeing to the needs of the widowed and the dying, much of the responsibility for providing food and replenishing stocks was left to Rona and any children who were old enough to help.
>
> It was late at night before she realised that the water containers were empty. There was no water for children who might wake in the night and no water for the dying grandmother who had not taken solid food for some days. Most people had fallen asleep by then or were keeping watch around the shelter.
>
> So although her baby, sleeping on the mat by his grandmother, was now stirring and would soon wake and begin crying to be fed she thought she'd better go to the spring to fill the calabashes.
>
> There was a cold wind blowing, Rona put a cloak over her shoulders and took up the containers, tying two at her waist and stringing the rest together to carry, then began running as quickly as she could along the track through the trees. The way was bleached by moonlight. The pumice path, the undergrowth, the fringes and fronds, the trees, the swathes of hanging kiekie were all decoloured except for a tinge of blue like mother's milk.

The truth about stories is that they retell our physical world — of the particular land and forests and seas and cities, people, systems, houses, workplaces, that are part of their everyday existence. Or they tell us other people's stories. They will tell of other circumstances and experiences, other countries of the world or of the universe real or imagined; and in this way, enlighten and enliven our world and our lives:

> Rona was not halfway to the water hole, flying along, leaping the rocks and tangles along the way, when a big hairy cloud, dog-shaped, ran right across the moon's face, causing the pathway and the whole night to blacken. Running in darkness she did not see the looping tree root across her track. Rona tripped and fell, letting go of the calabashes which shattered against the stones and trees.
>
> It was a heavy fall in which Rona banged her head hard enough to be knocked out for some minutes. There was a broken bone in her foot, she had bitten off the tip of her tongue and there was blood coming from a gash in her shoulder.
>
> Rona put full blame for her fall on the moon.
>
> Perhaps in her stupor it didn't occur to her that it could have been more the fault of the passing cloud that the light was blocked out, or the wind that had whistled the hairy-dog across the moon's visage. Once she had gained consciousness it was all she could do to grasp the trunk of a small tree and pull herself up to sit with her back against it as the scraggy dog ran off and there was light once more. But because of her concussed state, and after all the stresses of the day and the anxiety about her baby, maybe she could be excused for sounding off at the moon the way she did. Maybe there were extenuating circumstances.
>
> Although really, no matter how you see it, it was an enormity to look the moon in the eye the way she did then, and call it a big bowl of boil-up in which the moon's own head simmered and steamed along with the mess of fern root, kumara, vegetables, fruits and a variety of berry-filled birds.
>
> No excuse for it.

The truth about stories is that they verify customs and values and behaviours and tell us what is important or not important to us, or they may, and often do, challenge the well understood order of things:

> There was no greater insult in the universe than to be compared to cooked food — for it to be insinuated that your mana was to be taken over by one who would eat you, and to imply that you were to be chewed, swallowed, digested and excreted. There was no more low-down state of being than that of cooked food, and therefore no greater profanity than what emanated from Rona that night.
>
> 'Pokokohua. Stupid Moon,' she yelled. 'Look what you've done. The calabashes are broken and I can't fetch water. My ankle is broken too, so I won't be able to make it to the spring anyway. I'll have to crawl home now but my head is in such a spin I hardly know which direction to take. I could get lost in the trees. Children will be crying for water. The dying grandmother will be parched. My baby will be awake and will have to be fed by one of the other mothers even though my own breasts are so full that they're stinging. Boiled head. Useless hua.'

The truth about stories is that they expose a full range of emotions for our examination or experience — of love, hate, anger, joy, jealousy — or of moods from ecstatic to despondent. They can make us laugh or cry, fill us with despair or hope, satisfaction or longing, and in doing so, help us to understand our inner selves:

> It would have been a vile enough invective even levelled at one's peers, but now here was this earthling foul-mouthing a most ancient and venerable ancestor who had been around even before the time of the separation of Earth and Sky. Rona, even in her dazed state would not have dreamed of disrespecting Earth in the same way, yet Moon is a close relative of Earth, indeed the very closest. Earth and Moon probably started out as conjoined twins. In fact they must still

be conjoined twins in some mysterious way as there is definitely a push-me pull-you relationship between them. There's some dance in which the two are forever coordinated and where one could not exist without the other.

The truth about stories is that they can stir the social conscience and consciousness and provoke thought. Or maybe they simply entertain or help while away a period of quiet time:

But in a way it was fortunate it was Moon she picked on otherwise it could have turned out much worse for her than it did for Rona.

If Rona had decided that it was the passing of the dog-shaped cloud that was the reason for the blackout, or that it was the fault of the whistling wind, and if she'd aimed invective at Dog-cloud or Wind instead of at Moon, it could have been the end of her.

Both Cloud and Wind are children of Tawhiri Matea who is the Great Coordinator of elements — wind, rain, storms, tornadoes, snowflakes, whirlwinds, thunder, sleet, hail — the whole orchestra. He too is a most ancient and venerable ancestor, though is of a later generation than Earth and Moon. He is subject to Moon's pull and has to mind his p's and q's when it comes to her.

... no one messes with TM. He can uproot whole forests, flatten houses, buildings, towns, cities and whip sea waves up to a fury. He's a scrapper from way back and you disrespect him or his offspring at your peril. Everyone knows that.

Anyway, no one with any sense vilifies those on whom their own existence depends.

If TM, being neither as austere or as composed and measured as Moon, had been the one on the end of Rona's vitriol he probably would have struck her down right there. Her relatives could soon have been handing her corpse up into the trees so that the birds could clean her bones. Lesser beings, such as chiefs, kings, bishops, lords and commanders, have dished out far more severe punishments than what Moon decided on for Rona.

Never in all her centuries had Moon been maligned in such a manner. She'd never been maligned in any way at all. On the contrary, she had grown accustomed to adulation and exultation by prophets and poets throughout the ages. Even when stars galloped by on fiery sky horses and called, 'Howdy, Paleface' in seductive voices she didn't take umbrage. She took it as a kind of homage to her candescent beauty. In fact she was pleased to have someone come by and call out to her. It was a solitary path she was on. Moon led a lonely existence.

It is often the case that conjoined twins are not equally endowed at birth, one being more favoured by circumstances than the other, and Earth had come out better off than Moon in many respects. Unlike Earth, Moon had no adornments to distract her, no offspring to amuse her, no light of her own, and she bathed only in reflected glory. But she had her own mana and didn't mind.

The truth about stories is that they can take up old themes of conflict, life, death, mystery, magic, in new and different ways to stimulate and give birth to new ideas:

Even so, Moon knew that she now had to be firm, that she would need to come down strongly and make an example of Rona so that a lesson could be learned for all time.

'You'll have to come here and say that,' said Moon, and Rona felt herself being lifted from the ground. When she realised what was happening, she grabbed hold of the tree she had been sitting against, hoping that it would anchor her. But the moon's pull was too great. The tree was uprooted and both woman and tree were taken on a journey skyward.

Early in the morning people came out of their sleeping houses wondering what had happened to Rona. Some had been waiting all night for water. They went off along the track to look for her, soon arriving at the place where she'd fallen. They found the broken calabashes and saw the disturbed soil where the tree had been uprooted. They saw the blood on the ground and thought at first that Rona had been killed and taken away by their enemy.

It was a child, calling and pointing, who drew their attention to Rona who was being drawn upwards clutching a tree, her cloak and her long hair spreading behind her, the two calabashes still tied at her waist. They watched throughout the whole day as she journeyed, and by the time the night came could see her caught up there in the centre of the moon.

The truth about stories is that they can be image producing, stirring the imagination and transforming thought:

At first they thought she had been swallowed and was being slowly digested by the moon. They were sorry about such a fate. But after several months, as they watched the moon diminish, hide itself for a time, then gradually reappear and grow again, they could see Rona hadn't been swallowed at all, and hoped that Moon would one day return her to them.

Rona soon came to understand that Moon would never release her and that she would never see her children or her people again, so she decided she would have to make the best of the situation. Her new home was roomy and comfortable and she became aware that anxiety and stress were unknown in this new place. She found she could relax there. She realised too, that war, though invented by the atua at the time of the separation of the Great Parents, war had since been taken on exclusively by earth beings, her own kin, as part of their identity. War was now executed only in the earthly panoramas. She was pleased to be above all that.

It was a long time before Rona's family accepted that she would never come back to them. They believed at first that she had become

Moon's servant. Some said they could see her sweeping Moon's floor or lighting her lamps and candles. Others said she was gathering Moon's firewood or shaking out bedclothes or shining the rings of the moon.

But after some generations the people decided that their ancestress, Rona, was not Moon's servant at all. They observed her seated at Moon's window. They saw her dancing in many rooms. They saw that her hair had been coiled up into a chiefly topknot and decorated with tall combs. They understood that Rona and Moon had become close companions, and become as one, as together they collated the seasons and rolled and unrolled the tides.

Generally, we can say that stories are important in all our lives. They are educating, affirming, enlivening, or we hope that they are. Every society and every age has, or should have, its own stories that reinforce who its people are, how they do things, how they say things, what is customary to them. They tell what the many aspects of their culture are, or we hope that they do.

Some time ago now, I think in the early eighties, I presented a paper at a NZATE conference, New Zealand Association of Teachers of English, which I titled, 'Books are Dangerous'. Because of the theme of this weekend's conference, 'The Truth About Stories', and because of the other Thomas King quote that's in the programme, that is, 'Stories are wondrous things. And they are dangerous.' I want to revisit that paper briefly because it takes up similar thoughts.

As a child I loved to read. I had a few books of my own and was well on the way to reading by the time I went to school. My parents were tellers of anecdotes. The stories they told were usually funny stories about our relatives or our ancestors. Sometimes the stories would exist in one memorable sentence only, such as, 'You know you had an uncle who rode on a whale', 'Your great-grandfather had two rows of teeth, which he used when he was climbing ropes and ship's masts', 'Auntie so-and-so was so big that when she died they had to take a window out of the house to pass her casket through'. The stories I shared with cousins were usually ghost stories, told in the dark, which we loved to scare ourselves with. Or it was with my brother that we made up our own stories, which usually set us in motion, swinging from tree to tree, usually in the living room. Or had us jumping from shed roofs, attempting to fly.

On the whole, the schools I went to were schools without books, or without extra books. At my school you didn't see books, you saw religious statues and holy pictures. We had our catechisms, our progressive primers, arithmetic textbooks, and little books of the lives of saints and martyrs that were meant to be edifying. Somewhere away in the cupboards were School Journals which were distributed at lesson time.

I had a few books of my own which I treasured, and we had a grandfather who provided us with weekly supplies of comics. I was about eight when I joined the Newtown Public Library. As a young teenager I was an avid reader of *The Schoolgirls' Own Libraries* until I grew tired of them. But the books, whether comics or *Girls' Own*, or classics, were always an exotic experience. Always the children in the books that I read in my early childhood lived in other lands, lands of snow and holly and cobblestones, where there were big bad wolves and woodcutters who lived on bread and cheese that they carried around in a handkerchief tied to a stick.

Children lived in cottages with roses around the door or in many-roomed houses with nurses to look after them, even though they didn't seem to be suffering from any illnesses. They went out to play in the garden, which I thought meant they were allowed to run all over the cabbages. They did not belong in extended families as I did. They did not look like me. They did not speak as I did. They arranged midnight feasts. They had terrible stepmothers. It was wrong to be poor. If you were poor you usually did some brave or clever deed — climbed a beanstalk, killed a giant, spun straw into gold, guessed a name — that made you rich and enabled you to marry a prince or a princess. Sometimes you could own half a kingdom. On the whole you lived happily ever afterwards. On the other hand, maybe you died in the snow selling matches.

In this paper I spoke of the reasons for reading, some of which have been mentioned. That is that we read or tell or enact for enjoyment, for relaxation, information, self-development. That there are social aspects to stories. Discussions take place, sharing and common interest and that stories reflect different societies and environments through characters, settings, themes, language etcetera. They help set and affirm the social and ethical values of the people that they are about, showing what is important about a particular group of people, explaining their world and defining relationships.

I was emphasising my belief that everyone needs their own stories for healthy growth and went on to talk about what I saw as the danger, or the harm that could be done, the danger that there was if there were no books, stories, dramas, movies to do these things for a particular group, where that group was not receiving legitimacy, where there were no mirrors, or none in the literary sense, to give affirmation, nothing to boost self-image; where people may see themselves negatively, or only in the distorted reflections of the lives of others, whether it be through oral stories, books, newspapers, advertising, art and symbols or screen media.

What I was attempting to say was that if there were no stories that told people about themselves and told only about others, the message was that they were unworthy of affirmation in the world of stories and books. Therefore, there was a likelihood that they were left unanchored, unsafe, and away in the margins of society. Or that if there were stories about them, but they were untrue or unenlightened and stereotyping, then that was dangerous too. For example if there was a bias in the way their histories were told and a negativity in the kind of language used in the telling.

Another point I thought important was that though there may be stories about a particular group or culture, they may be set mainly in a past age, or within a certain quaintness of genre, which denied existence of the true culture in the present time. For though mythologies, folklore, legends and oral histories are important, alongside them there must be contemporary stories or new versions that are positive, exciting and robust. Also on the danger-list were the types of books that negate a certain group. Where, for example, no-one in a book is ever brown or black unless there is something wrong with them.

From my childhood reading I can remember Epaminondas who didn't have the sense he was born with. There was Uncle Tom's Cabin and the original Uncle Tom with his servile manner. There was the primer book where I read the story of the kind teddy bear who didn't like being brown and cried because he wanted to be a white teddy bear. One day he came across little sugar doll crying because it was about to rain and she was going to get wet. He very kindly gave her his umbrella. She stayed dry but he got a soaking. Consequently, all of his colour washed away. He was overjoyed to find that he had become a little white teddy bear.

In my teaching days I particularly noticed stories like *Little Black Sambo* because no matter how interesting the stories themselves may have been, just think of those three words of the title. The tweeness of 'little', the redundancy of 'black', and the derogatory implications of 'Sambo'. Then there was the wolf who needed to dip his paws into flour to make them look safe and mother-like. I thought, how would it have come across if the Big Bad Wolf had been a white guy who had to dip his paws in soot to make them acceptable when he put them on the windowsill.

In 2002 I went to Zimbabwe to an international book fair and conference. While there I was taken to the rural area of Mudzi, where Aotearoa, as part of an aid program, had set up a very fine library and resource centre. I was sorry to see a copy of *Robinson Crusoe* on one of the shelves of the library, whose readers were all indigenous Africans. It was a simplified version, with a picture of the skinny little black man prancing along the beach looking terrified. He was saved by Robinson who, in true colonising spirit, renamed him. The man had his true name taken from him in the way that so many have had their names taken away during times of colonisation. The man became Crusoe's servant, not because he didn't have good survival skills, or for any other reason than that he was a black man.

I was very fortunate in my childhood that I had parents, a brother, cousins and relatives who gave me my own stories which defined and described me, letting me know who I was, where I came from and where I belonged. Because the truth about stories is that people of all ages, all places, all backgrounds, need their own stories for their health, growth and wellbeing.

And now we live in more enlightened times. I presume that books such as those mentioned no longer have a place in our institutions, or that if they do it is because they have become a resource for programmes on racism, sexism, or whatever other 'ism' there might be. I do hope that we live in more enlightened times. When I see some of what our children are viewing these days I do wonder about that.

The truth about stories is that they are peopled by a variety of characters, familiar and exotic, good and bad, strong and frail, true to life and larger than life, ordinary and extraordinary. The bad can become good, the good bad. The strong can become frail and vice versa. The ordinary can become extraordinary. As in the case of Rona. She started out as an ordinary wife and mum but through various happenings and circumstances was elevated to become the tide controller.

Finally, the truth about stories is that they can provide deep satisfaction, because maybe a mystery is solved or true love found, or because a twist in the tale is wonderful. Or maybe there is an open-endedness, providing an edge on which the reader or listener will linger for days or weeks, or forever because there is more food for thought, or there is ongoing emotion attaching itself to that particular story, long after the telling is done.

2007 TONY SIMPSON

Food for Thought

I always listen very carefully to how people introduce me, after I had a terrible experience once many years ago, introducing myself to some people. At that stage I was Secretary of Actors Equity, the national actors' union, and I was invited to go to the Soviet Union as it then was, as a guest of the Cultural Workers Union. One evening I found myself on a train from Moscow to Minsk — this is going to sound like one of those stories about an Englishman, an Irishman and a Scotsman — and the compartment I was in was occupied by a German who spoke no Russian and no English, a Russian who spoke no English and no German and myself who spoke no Russian, English of course, and a language similar to German called 'Extremely Bad German'.

I managed to work out that one guy, the German, was a theatre director from Dresden and was extremely drunk, and I thought I'd better introduce myself in Extremely Bad German. So I did, and he went and sat as far away from me as he possibly could, and he wouldn't speak to me for the rest of the twelve-hour journey. Some years later I was talking to a German friend of mine and I told him this story, and he said, 'Well what did you say to him?' And I told him, and he laughed, and said, 'I think it was a really bad idea to introduce yourself as the Secretary of the New Zealand Gigolos' Union.

Anyway, I'm going to outline for you today why it was that until the 1960s we in New Zealand largely ate meat and two vegetables for our main dish, with a stodgy pudding to follow. And if you don't think that's of any significance to a social historian, just consider this: eating is one of the very few things that we all do every day of our lives, if we can. That is to say, from the moment we're born 'til the moment we die. And something so utterly central to our existence is also absolutely central to our culture. It's important that we should be aware why we do what we do if we're going to understand that culture, and food is no exception to that rule.

But let me begin, not with cholesterol, but with raw data. Between 1861 and 1881 there were 556,156 immigrants recorded as entering New Zealand. Because of an accident of history, a very high proportion of those who came during that period were distressed rural labourers. That was because important changes in the British agricultural industry flowed from the internationalisation of food production and led to a large surplus of such workers in Britain and this, in an unregulated labour market, always leads to severely depressed wages. When their recourse to industrial action failed, they turned to other expedients, the most important of which was emigration.

So, many of those who came to New Zealand in our 'heroic' period of immigration were from an agricultural background; comprising the labourers themselves and of course their families. This meant that they brought a culture with them that enshrined an approach to food production and consumption, and this had a key influence on the nature of our local cuisine. In particular, it was an approach that focused on small-scale production for domestic consumption. We're talking here about what is loosely described as a market-garden culture, but it had a much broader influence on the nature of the culture that eventually emerged in this country because these agricultural workers also brought another cultural element with them. They were determined they were not going to allow the re-creation of the social relationships they'd suffered in Britain, which had led them to contemplate emigration in the first place.

As the historian James Belich has sagely remarked, 'No-one emigrated to New Zealand to be worse off.' And that included the impoverishment of their diet, which had been one of the consequences of the agricultural depression that drove them here in the first place. That included some significant notions of what their ordinary lives should have been if they hadn't been deprived. At least two of them were things they had experienced in an attenuated form and these things were the harvest home feast and the farmer's ordinary. Let's take those in turn.

The harvest home feast in nineteenth-century England was held by tradition any time between the end of August and the middle of October and, as its name suggests, it marked the completion for the harvest of the year. Its date reflected the area of the country and the state of the weather that year. If you're in the southern part of the country it's more likely to be later in the year. It's a very old festival dating at least from the Middle Ages and it was known as Lammas. As far as we can establish, it marked the first church communion service, using bread from the newly harvested corn, and so it may very well have been a pre-Christian festival — like Christmas itself, and a number of others — which was simply taken over by the early church and converted to Christianity, as it were.

In essence, the harvest home festival was a religious ceremony followed by a feast in celebration of the fact that with the harvest in, that community was going to survive for another year. Bear in mind that we're talking here about a Europe in which the threat of famine was ever present every year for centuries. So. it was a very important thing to mark, that you'd got the harvest in. These harvest home feasts were usually provided by the local landowners and could be quite lavish. But more to the point, they involved the consumption of quite a lot of meat, which these rural labourers never saw, by and large, at any other time of the year.

When I was making my notes for this talk, I came across a reminiscence from a place called Haddenham, in Buckinghamshire, which is worth quoting. The person said, 'No institution was more popular or more deeply rooted in our village sentiment than our annual feast, which fell on the first Sunday after the nineteenth of September. As the lack of enough to eat was the normal experience of the poor a century ago, so a day given to fill the belly with good food was a delight. The ancient celebration was really of that character — a literal feast of good food and drink, with the mirth that goes with these things.'

Well, as it happens, quite a lot of the mirth in question was fuelled by very large quantities of beer and cider in the nineteenth-century, and the local clergy sometimes tried to stamp it out for that reason but they were generally unsuccessful. I'm pleased to report the drinking remained one of its features. And so poor rural labourers who came to New Zealand were not entirely without experience in good eating. And they had something else to remind them of what that meant — the farmer's ordinary, the thing that I mentioned earlier and which forms part of the title of this talk.

Most rural areas had a local market town in which there was a weekly market to which the farmer and his labourers carted their produce for sale. The markets usually ended about midday and the farmer would go off to have his midday meal at a local inn. That meal was known as the 'ordinary'. It was essentially a fixed-price, standard dinner served to anyone who had the cash. It was usually quite heavy and consisted of thick soup, a pie or savoury pudding, and roast meat or poultry with vegetables and potatoes, and a sweet fruit pie and cheese. But mark that the labourers didn't get to eat in this fashion. They brought their own much more meagre lunch and usually ate it sitting under the farmer's dray or in the yard. But they were very well aware of what the farmers got that they didn't.

Well, once the rural poor had taken the long step to emigration, for those who left the British Isles not only were these contrasts fixed in their mind's eye, but the voyage to the 'new' land itself created a further opportunity for contrasts and comparisons. If they came to New Zealand in steerage, as most did, then they would have lived daily in very close proximity to their cabin-class fellow passengers. That would have been unusual because had they still been living in Britain, they would not have experienced that close living with any of their social betters — they were denied that by the concept of class separation — and they would certainly not have seen them eating their lunch.

In these circumstances they quickly became aware how much better the middle and upper classes fared than they did when it came to food. In fact, the contrast in the diets of steerage and cabin passengers on nineteenth-century immigrant ships is one of the most immediately apparent and notable features of the immigrant experience. Strictly speaking, the diet in steerage, where most of the people travelled— cattle class. you can call it if you like — was regulated, and a certain minimum of food had to be supplied as a condition of the sale of the ticket. In fact the food supplied to immigrants to New Zealand and Australia was probably better than most, partly because the journey was quite a long one and therefore had to be better conducted, but mainly because it was largely under the control of provincial or national governments or the New Zealand Company and its various offshoots, so they were therefore better conducted than the private business ventures which characterised, in particular, the American immigrant trade, which was really little more than an adjunct to the timber industry.

If you went to America you were carted there by people who wanted to fill the hold because they got a bit of money out of that, and then made their money by taking timber back the other way. You can imagine what that was like. The diet for steerage passengers on New Zealand Company vessels was largely set out in a schedule, which you can read in the company publications. And of course, they emphasised how generous it was and how well people were going to eat but it can't have been particularly exciting, even if it was adequate. It was then up to the passengers to prepare that food as best they could.

Three hundred or so passengers would cram the steerage compartment of the average immigrant ship. They were divided into messes of ten or a dozen people and they would choose one of their number, who was known as the mess captain, to collect the rations, and then another to undertake the cooking, or if there was a cook on the ship to oversee that activity, to make sure there was no theft or other monkey business. That responsibility could be onerous. As F.W. Leighton onboard the *Bloomer* in 1853 said, 'It was a task of no honour and very great difficulties from the various tempers you have to please.' The duties involved are described by an Edward Cuzens who travelled on the *Travancore* as a boy of ten. He said:

> The rations were served out once a week, and meat was twice a week by the Chief Officer. At this function the family was not a name but a number. In the mate's book was entered the quantity of each article to be supplied and when the number was called out some representative of the family was expected to step forward and take what was coming to them. [The meat was tagged for subsequent cooking.] The next step was to carry the meat to the galley, which was presided over by a big negro who threw them together into the boiler and left them to stew until dinner time. At about half past twelve forty or fifty people assembled at the galley, each with a tin dish for their dinner meat, when the cook also arrived with a big three-pronged fork thrust into the boiling mass, pulled out a joint, called out the number on the disc, which was quickly claimed, and so on until the boiler was empty.

The chaotic scenes that ensued when the rush to the galley occurred don't have to be imagined because they were described by John McKenzie, who travelled on the *Travancore* as a cabin passenger. He was a first-class man who observed the rush to get food from the poop deck, and described it as like, 'so many dogs let out of their kennel to get their food'.

In fact, the cooking facilities themselves could leave a great deal to be desired. Galleys, of necessity, were quite small and some cooks who didn't know much about cooking beyond the mass methods I described would sometimes demand additional payments from the passengers if they wanted to do any cooking on the side to supplement their diet.

On one ship, the *Anne Wilson*, on a voyage to New Zealand in 1857, the waiting time for the main meal of the day could be up to six hours. And by the way, in that particular ship there was a pigsty on the galley roof. The set scales of rations weren't very lavish, with a pound of ship's biscuits and three quarts of fresh water a day. On alternate days there was half a pound of salt beef or pork and small supplementary quantities of flour, raisins, suet and pulses with sometimes potatoes, rice, sugar, butter and pickled cabbage as a safeguard against scurvy, with small quantities of tea and coffee sometimes available.

That diet improved a bit as the century progressed, with some greater emphasis on fresh fruit and vegetables but not very much. In the many books published for would-be immigrants, passengers were advised to take their own supplementary rations, and most did. But the really interesting thing was the contrast between the messing arrangements for the steerage and those for the cabin passengers. Everything you read first-hand, any original source — and there are many — about nineteenth-century immigration to New Zealand, mentions that difference. And to say that the cabin ate lavishly is a considerable understatement.

In 1839, gentleman Alexander Marjoribanks made the long journey to New Zealand with about 150 other immigrants in the ship *Bengal Merchant*. He said:

> We, who are in the cabin, or the cuddy, as it is generally called at sea, consisting of nineteen individuals, fared sumptuously every day; a circumstance highly credible not only to the New Zealand Company, but to the liberal captain of the ship. (Marjoribanks worked for the New Zealand Company by the way, so he would say that.) In fact, it may be said that we did little else but eat, drink and sleep, during the whole voyage. We had four meals per day, and at dinner always had five or six dishes of fresh meat, with a carte blanche of claret and other wines, besides a dessert of fruit.

This fresh meat, on this particular voyage, was supplied by an astonishing 60 sheep, twenty-one pigs and 900 head of poultry, which were taken on board before the ship sailed. The noise of the hungry pigs demanding food was, he added, 'almost equal to that of a clap of thunder'. Presumably that sound got less and less as the voyage progressed.

Detail of this ongoing feast is supplied by the diary of Martha Adams, who travelled out to Canterbury in 1850 with 16 others and sat down at the first-class passengers' dining table. She said:

> We had roast beef, as good as if just fresh from the hands of a country butcher, and your own cook: mashed potatoes and carrots, stewed beef steak, boiled salmon, green gooseberries and damsons ... then we had every day four if not five dishes of meat at dinner including the above, with fresh pork and mutton on joints, meat pies, poultry and curry: and the plum pudding we had today weighed I should think six pounds. At tea we had fresh bread, for which the passengers find marmalade and preserves in preference to the salt butter; and our breakfasts are quite abundant in proportion to our dinners. In the way of drinkables water only is provided: but ale, and porter, wine and spirits are sold, and I find lime juice and a little sugar in my water the most agreeable beverage possible.

That's four substantial meals every day. Her final comment was, 'Altogether we lead a very comfortable existence.' It's interesting when you write books — I found her when I was first writing a book about immigration — and you read the original letters of these people and you almost come to live with the people concerned. And I came to thoroughly dislike Martha Adams. She was an appalling snob. There are numerous comments in the same vein that you can get from the literature available. The contrast between the messing arrangements of the steerage and of the cabin, as I said, is one of the central lasting impressions of the experience of nineteenth-century emigration to New Zealand recorded in many hundreds of letters and diaries.

When you put this together with another factor which impelled emigration not only to this country but also to Australia, the United States and Canada in the nineteenth-century, you discover a very distinctive outcome by way of the food cultures which developed as a result, in all of these lands. The other factor was land itself — who should own it and what they could do with it. If you study British politics in the nineteenth-century you almost immediately come to realise that the 'land question', as it was called, was central to almost everyone's political agenda, and that one of the main factors driving emigration was the desire on the part of both the poor and those with resources but landless to get their hands on some land of their own. There were various schemes to allow people in England to own small holdings, as was set in train by the political radical group the Chartists, the origin of the present-day allotment movement. It's still very active around the major cities in Britain as you'll have seen if you've been there.

But all that was never going to deliver land occupation to other than a tiny fraction of the landless poor, and emigration was a much more likely means of achieving it. The New Zealand social historian Miles Fairburn has explored what that meant in nineteenth-century New Zealand and the society that has subsequently emerged from it.

Fairburn cites quite a range of sources on the importance of getting hold of land in the new colony, not only for the gentleman investors who got a good deal of it by one means or another — some decidedly dodgy. He also explores, interestingly, the significance of land ownership to small landowners and proprietors. Among those he notes are I.R. Cooper, who in 1857 said:

> Those who arrive in the colony without capital will, if they enjoy good health, are sober and economical in their personal expenses, and able and willing to work at any one trade as farm servants, boatmen, shepherds, or house servants, soon realise sufficient capital to invest in land, cattle or sheep, and thus render themselves and their children independent.

Or similarly, Alexander Bathgate in 1874 in Dunedin, says, 'Very many working men live in their own freehold cottages and some of the suburbs are almost exclusively filled with neat little houses owned by working men.' Or the *New Zealand Handbook* 1888, which sagely remarks, 'though an immigrant might not be assured of a fortune, yet a comfortable living at home in healthy surroundings, a fair start for their children and reasonable provision for their own future are within the reach of immigrants if they are careful and industrious.'

Quite literally dozens of other writers could be cited on the same theme, on the ease of small land ownership and the comfortable subsistence of those in modest circumstances. By 1885, fully 60 percent, or two out of three, adult males in New Zealand owned their land freehold or Crown leasehold. That's an astonishing statistic. And in anecdotal form, it's one of the most generally encountered commonplaces of the writing of that time about nineteenth-century New Zealand and those who've written about it since. Letters and diaries and newspaper articles and memoirs are full of what can only be described as exclamations of astonishment by people comparing their situation in New Zealand with that which they had left behind by emigrating. Something which would have been impossible, absolutely impossible, in the old country — that's to say, a small holding of their own — was quite readily achievable in the 'new'.

Much of this land was available because it had been invaded or even simply stolen from the indigenous owners by all sorts of legal chicanery. It was not of course a public issue. Fairburn particularly, a very interesting historian, has interrogated the meanings of this pattern and, in particular, the use that small leaseholders put this land to once they got it. And that turned up something very interesting.

First and foremost, it was a hedge against the calamitous consequences of unemployment. In the England from which a great many of the settlers had come, your home went with your job. It was, and still is, called a tied cottage. Lose one, your job, you lost the other, your home. And quite a lot of those immigrants who came to New Zealand in that period had experienced that trauma. But if you owned or leased land and had built or owned the home on it, then that didn't happen.

Beyond that, of course, having your own land meant that you could grow your own food, more or less without restriction. Bear in mind that in nineteenth-century rural England, although you might occupy your farmer landlord's cottage, that didn't mean you could pick the fruit in the garden or keep a pig, or even plant potatoes. You had to get his permission. And sometimes he said no. In New Zealand you could do what you damn well pleased without anyone's permission. And people very quickly did.

In late nineteenth-century New Zealand almost everyone kept livestock, including those who lived in towns. This meant invariably chickens and a pig or two and, for the better off, a cow. This caused problems, of course. and the town ordinances of the period are full of regulations dealing with roosters crowing loudly in the morning, wandering stock, the effect on the water supply and the smells associated with keeping pigs in built-up areas.

New Zealand's nineteenth-century towns were actually very dirty and unsanitary places. There's been a whole book recently published about that and the struggles of our early research scientists, who were mostly doctors, to get the epidemics which resulted under some sort of control. If you go and look at a nineteenth-century cemetery you'll find whole families wiped out by diphtheria or scarlet fever, water-borne diseases which have now, more or less, disappeared. But of course it was going to take more than a few medical men to halt the enthusiasm of families to keep livestock and to garden without restraint to feed their families.

Sometimes, when you examine the social history of the period from the middle of the nineteenth-century until the First World War, it seems that the working families of that time spent every spare moment they had at their disposal working on their gardens. The men grew fruit and vegetables and the women, probably because most of them were at home during the day, looked after the livestock. The agitation during the nineteenth-century for a half holiday on Saturdays — not having to go to work on Saturday afternoon — was probably driven in large part because people needed the time to cultivate what were large gardens by our standards, when Sundays were more generally regarded as unavailable because of religious observances, and because they'd also been set aside, even in England, as a day of leisure. Gardening, as those of you who have done it will know, certainly is not.

This habit of cultivating large domestic gardens persisted well into my childhood after the Second World War and was a very important part of the household economy. A fascinating survey published by the New Zealand Department of Labour in 1892 explored the household expenditure of working people. Although the food they ate is covered in detail — it included, you'll be fascinated to hear, an average of two kilos of meat per person per day — it nowhere mentions eggs, fruit, vegetables, bacon, jam or pickles. Now that doesn't mean that people didn't eat them. They were dietary staples all right. The point is that people didn't buy them. They produced them for themselves.

This tells you, by the way, the origin of the quarter-acre section. It was enough land to contain a small cottage and a garden you could live off if you had to. It takes on even more significance if you're familiar with the nineteenth-century New Zealand labour market. Until the 1930s, about a third of all workers were employed in New Zealand in rural areas as rural labourers, and that meant that a great deal of the work was casual or seasonal. The same pattern, although not to the same extent, pertained in the towns. Many jobs that we would now regard as permanent or full time were casualised, some of them by the day. So, working families expected periods of unemployment, particularly at a time when there was no welfare state and when periodic economic downturns were regarded simply as acts of God and treated much more fatalistically than we would treat them post Keynes.

A large vegetable garden and some laying hens are important back-ups to the home economy. This is a fascinating example of a genetic cultural principle widely commented on, which is that if people are denied their culture, they will reinvent it in another form. For centuries the working people of Britain had relied upon a tradition of market gardening, which was central not only to their rural domestic economy, but to their culture. When the disruptions of first of all the industrialisation of Britain, and then the growth of international specialisation in food production, made that gardening culture untenable, they left in large numbers to escape the consequent impoverished hardship of their lives. And when they got to wherever they were going, in this case New Zealand, they re-created that culture as fast as they could. They did that from the very outset, the pre-Treaty settlers taking advantage of the abundant access they had to food resources.

Edward Jerningham Wakefield, son of the more famous Edward Gibbon Wakefield, in his racey, readable book *Adventure in New Zealand*, describes the interior of a shore whaling station, in which he draws particular attention to the number of hams smoking in the chimney. Clearly these working people enjoyed a much more comfortable life than they would ever have done in England. He subsequently described one of the working-class areas of town, in this case Wellington. He said the workers used to work at their little patches of ground after the labour of the day was over. 'Wadestown, denuded of timber and looking early on like a bleak hill of poor soil, soon boasted a population of 200 working people whose neat cottages and smiling cultivations peeked from every nook among the picturesque hills.'

I'm not sure how the present inhabitants of Wadestown would respond to a description of them as quaint and picturesque workers, but you get the picture. It was seconded by William Mein Smith, one of the New Zealand Company agents, who writing to his father in 1841 referred to the abundance of lettuces and endives, radishes, mustard and cress, potatoes and pumpkins. In fact, from the early 1840s in Wellington there was a nursery garden from which many of these plants were propagated, at the foot of Nairn Street, about 100 yards from where I live, in what is now central Wellington.

Some two decades later, Lady Anne Barker in her famous *Station Life in New Zealand*, an evocative memoir of life in early colonial New Zealand, described a typical day's eating by her shepherds and other farmhands:

> Porridge for breakfast with new milk and cream ... to follow — mutton chops, mutton ham or mutton curry or broiled mutton and mushrooms, not shabby little fragments of meat broiled, but beautiful tender steaks off the leg; tea or coffee and bread and butter, with as much new laid eggs as we choose to consume. Then, for dinner at half past one, we have soup, a joint, vegetables and a pudding; in summer we have fresh fruit stewed instead of a pudding, with whipped cream ... We have supper at about seven; but this is a movable feast consisting of tea again, mutton cooked in some form of entree, eggs, bread and butter, and a cake of my manufacture.

And she goes on to explain half apologetically that because her fruit trees and bushes are not yet fully grown, she can't yet do the jams and preserves that would probably also be served at some other farming stations.

  There are two immediately interesting things about that menu. First of all, it bears no relation to the steerage-class rations on the immigrant ships which these workers had come on, but it does bear a great similarity to the food eaten in first-class. Secondly, there's no class distinction: Lady Barker and her workers eat from the same menu. That same message comes through in the letters of the working-class settlers themselves writing home. For example, Grace Hurst, farming in the Taranaki in 1858, writes to her sister in England, 'We have almost everything within ourselves' (that is to say they provided their our own food) — milk, butter, eggs, flour, potatoes, ducks, fowls, vegetables and fruit.' Louisa Johnson, who landed at Dunedin in October 1874, wrote back to her friends at the village of Grandborough, 'I wish a lot ... would come. Joe says he will get you all a meal such as you never had at home.' Two years later, Michael Cook, a farm labourer who'd settled at Geraldine in Canterbury, wrote home to describe his new garden pigsty and said, 'You said I was to send you word if we kept Christmas up. Of course we do, and we had green peas, new potatoes and roast beef for dinner.' And one I particularly like, George Catley, a shoemaker, writes home, 'This is the place for beef steaks and mutton ... What with one good thing and another I'm getting quite stout, and have every reason to like this country.' But perhaps most tellingly of all we listen to the voice of George Tapp, writing home from the Taranaki, and previously an official of the Kent Agricultural Labourers Union. He said, 'Working people don't eat sheeps' and bullocks' heads or liver here. They have the best joints as well as the rich.'

Well, what you've been witnessing as I've progressed through my narrative is in fact the birth of the egalitarian society which has characterised this country, notwithstanding the efforts of the spiritual descendants of the likes of Martha Adams, to return the rest of us to metaphorical steerage. And what you've been seeing it through is, of course, the medium of food. Paradoxically, it has occurred through the conjunction of two contradictory processes which go to make up the overall process of change and adaptation. I said earlier that those who are denied their culture will sooner or later invent it in a new form. British immigrants who came to New Zealand in the nineteenth-century were suffering from a sense of loss. They felt strongly the prior existence of a land of content that someone had taken away from them. Whether it actually existed or not is neither here nor there.

It was the sense of unjust deprivation that something rightfully theirs had been stolen from them that induced the most aggressive and vigorous of them to get up and go in the first place. One of the things they recalled from the past was that they had had enough to eat. That may or may not have been true either, but it was remembered as something which was true, which comes down to the same thing in the end. This is the process we call immigration. It was one of the most significant defensive mechanisms the British working people, deprived of their culture, could find to reclaim it. Their rulers, by the way, knew this and hated it. And the story of immigration from Britain is literally full of tales of how those same rulers again literally chased after their workers who were planning to emigrate, and tried to stop them. Not always; one thinks of the Highland Clearances, for example, but often enough. Mostly, our forebears got away, and one of the things they were getting away from was hunger and malnutrition. When they arrived at a place where that need was no longer an issue, they stayed.

There was nowhere else to go, unless you had a taste for penguins, but here's the strange paradox. Once they had the abundance, what were they going to do with it? They'd been deprived of it long enough to have forgotten the immediate solution to that problem, but they knew or remembered enough of an abundance to know it as a rural tradition of butter and eggs and cream. These were mainly country people and thus culturally closer to Jane Austen than Charles Dickens; they'd seen for themselves what plenty meant when it came to eating at the harvest home feast, on market day when the farmer's ordinary was served for midday dinner, and what the cabin passengers ate on the voyage out.

So they didn't wait to be asked twice. They simply got on with inventing the pavlova and the lamington and eating meat three times a day and so invented a whole new culture of food which was to last in this country for over a hundred years and which, in many ways, is still with us. As I said at the outset, you can uncover the nature of a whole society through observing what it eats and the historical reasons why they do so.

And on that note, I rest my case.

THE
WRITING
IS
ON THE
AIR
HERE THE
WALL
ONCE
WAS

2008 CHRIS PRICE

Trouble with the Truth

Kia ora koutou, and thanks Murray. Murray Gray described this keynote address as an opportunity to rant, but as anyone who knows me will tell you, I'm far more disposed to fret than to rant, so let's call this a fret. Not an opinionated blast, but an attempt to find out what I *think* by seeing what I *say*. I'll preface it with a thank you to Auckland University and the Michael King Writers' Centre for providing the time and space to think, and to David Larsen for getting me started.

But I want to begin with a small experiment, one that involves turning you all into proof-readers for a moment. Take a look at the words in the photograph behind me — beautifully produced in letterpress type on a handcrafted paper banner by word artist Tara McLeod. Can you spot the typographical error?

The banner in the photograph declares in bold capitals, 'THE WRITING IS ON THE AIR **HERE** THE WALL ONCE WAS'. Now if you're thinking that sounds a bit odd syntactically speaking, then you'd be right. The banner shows a poem by my friend Gregory O'Brien, but this version enshrines a significant mistake. It should read, 'THE WRITING IS ON THE AIR **WHERE** THE WALL ONCE WAS'. Even so, this version still appears to make sense at first glance. I sometimes ask visitors to my office if they can spot the mistake and, unsurprisingly, they very seldom do.

So, this slightly wonky poem provides the title for my address because it encapsulates in its correct form, and its uncorrected one, an unease I've been feeling in the last two or three years about the increasingly fluid relationship between literature and the 'truth'. Tonight, I'm trying to work out, through a tour of some recently published books from New Zealand and elsewhere, whether it's still possible to talk about them in the same sentence.

Now I should immediately declare I'm not aiming for a rigorous, philosophically defensible notion of the truth, if there is such a thing. By truth, I will simply mean the common-sense version of the word we use when we ask questions about discernible reality that can be documented or verified through investigation, such as, 'Is it true that New Zealand First received a donation from Owen Glenn?' A question to which, unless you subscribe to a radically postmodern view of reality, or unless you're Winston Peters, which may amount to the same thing, there can be only one correct answer.

But I'll be using the same word to talk about literary truth, the kind we mean when we say a novel feels 'true to life'. If you've arrived here tonight already convinced that 'the author is dead', along with any hope of objectivity, you may find that the rest of this address takes place on a kind of theoretical flat earth whose inhabitants are creatures of primitive uninstructed habits, which need to be simplified, boiled down and reduced ultimately to theory. You should probably go and have a drink and return for Polynation [the next event]. But for those who remain, I'll begin this fret proper with one semi-scientific attempt to pin down literal rather than literary truth.

There's a new kind of lie detector in development, one that purports to be more reliable than the polygraph. And it's already licensed for commercial use. Using MRI brain-scanning technology, the California firm No Lie MRI claims it can see the difference between the way lies and truth light up the brain. Never mind that the neuroscientists who work with this technology are a lot more circumspect about what it actually shows. Before No Lie MRI had even begun advertising, people were lining up for its services. According to the company's founder, the questions of guilt or innocence they wanted answered all revolved around issues of sex, power and money.

I can't help but think of the late Grace Paley's advice to fiction writers that even the slightest story must contain the facts of money and blood in order to be interesting to adults. Lately, the 'facts' have acquired an aura of uncertainty, both in literature and in life. We're finding ourselves more and more in trouble with the truth.

In 2006, the *Merriam-Webster Dictionary*'s word of the year in the USA was 'truthiness'. Coined by the satirist Stephen Colbert, the word is defined by the American Dialect Society as 'the quality of preferring concepts or facts one wishes to be true, rather than concepts or facts known to be true'.

Colbert's own definition is 'truth that comes from the gut, not from books'. 'It was the truthiness of all those imminent mushroom clouds,' noted the *New York Times* journo Frank Rich, with reference to all those weapons of mass destruction that we heard so much about a few years ago, 'that sold the invasion of Iraq.' Hillary Clinton's 'mis-statement' earlier this year about having arrived in Sarajevo under sniper fire is another instance of truthiness. The great poet Homer — Homer J. Simpson that is — offered his own definition of truthiness when he said, 'I wasn't lying. I was just writing fiction with my mouth.'

The 2006 word of the year quickly jumped the tracks from the political world to the world of books when James Frey's bestselling memoir of addiction and recovery *A Million Little Pieces* was exposed as being riddled with invented experience. Frey's advocate, Oprah Winfrey, at first declared it didn't matter if some of the memoir was made up because it felt true. The subsequent pillorying of both Frey and Winfrey for their lax attitude to the facts doesn't seem to have deterred other exponents of truthiness from having their shot at fame, or, made editors more inclined towards fact checking. This March, 'Margaret B. Jones', a half-white, half-Native-American woman whose memoir vividly describes her foster-childhood selling drugs and running with the Bloods in South LA, was outed by her own sister as Margaret Seltzer, a nice white creative-writing student who grew up with her biological family in middle-class Sherman Oaks. Perhaps the most notorious fraudulent memoir in our corner of the world is Norma Khouri's *Forbidden Love*. Some of you may have sat in the audience at the Auckland Writers and Readers Festival a few years back, as I did, and been utterly persuaded by Khouri's tale of the honour killing of her Jordanian woman friend, even to the extent of handing over money for her support fund for other threatened women. Although *Forbidden Love* also turned out to be shot through with confabulation and good old-fashioned inaccuracies, its author continues to defend it, essentially on the grounds of its truthiness. What difference would it make if her friend hadn't been killed? Even if that were the case, the book would still be valid because some women are killed in this way, Khouri insists in the documentary *Forbidden Lie$*. She even submits to a lie detector test in the film, although in this case it's a notoriously unreliable polygraph.

In this context of truthiness, then, some of our most admired writers and editors have also begun to engage in a deliberate blurring of the line between genres and between the 'benevolent deception' of fiction (as author and *New Yorker* journalist Janet Malcolm calls it) and the once rigorous integrity of non-fiction. Short stories and poetry by Lydia Davis and Anne Carson have been reprinted in an anthology called *The Next American Essay*. Closer to home, Australian writer Helen Garner returned to fiction this year with *The Spare Room*, a story told by a narrator called Helen who shares not just her author's name, but many other recognisable facts of her life. Closer still, Damien Wilkins's 2007 story collection *For Everyone Concerned* includes more than one piece originally written as non-fiction.

When a journalist like the *New Republic*'s Stephen Glass is found to have manipulated the facts, fudged the truth, or, just plain lied, they lose their job. When politicians are found to have done so, they lose our mandate. When a novelist does it, it's called benevolent deception, or simply, craft.

And what of the writer of so-called creative non-fiction: memoir, travel, biography, essay, and their increasingly trans-genre offspring?

As children we often ask, 'Is it a true story?' But in our grown-up postmodern world, why do we still care if our novelists and autobiographers are serving us truth or mere truthiness? Why do we feel upset when we think a story, of whatever genre, has put one over on us? In the case of the fraudulent memoir, the most obvious answer is money. Frey had no luck selling his manuscript as a novel, but he earned $4.4 million in royalties exploiting readers' credulity and empathy after it was reclassified as a memoir. And, as somebody pointed out in *Forbidden Lie$*, Norma Khouri's *Forbidden Love* was not sufficiently well-written to have found success as a novel. It was the compelling nature of its 'true story' that guaranteed it an audience.

In the case of fiction, any justification for readerly discontent is less obvious, though. It's hardly news that novelists and short-story writers use material gathered from life, after all. In both cases, though, our response depends on our understanding of the unwritten contract between the writer and the reader. Helen Garner lays it out clearly: 'In non-fiction,' she says, 'the writer's obligation is to get as close to the truth as you can get and to have not passed off as true, things that you can only guess or speculate … Norma Khouri violated that contract and people were justifiably distressed and felt cheated.' Calling a piece of writing a novel is, to state the blindingly obvious, a declaration that it should not be read as literally true. 'Even though it may be close to real experience,' Garner insists, 'I have taken the liberties I am allowed to take if I am writing fiction.'

The fiction label, in other words, implies informed consent, *caveat emptor*. Yet in a 2001 essay, 'The Woman in the Green Mantle', Helen Garner had referred to 'the dangerous and exciting breakdown of the boundaries between fiction and non-fiction and the ethical and technical problems that are exploding out of the resulting gap.' This suggests an awareness that crossing the line is not an uncomplicated matter. As Lloyd Jones found out to his cost back in 1993 when he published *Biografi*, a work which the *Oxford Companion to New Zealand Literature* subsequently described as a 'semi-fictional travel book', and which the blurb on the newly released edition from Text Publishing calls part travel narrative, part fable, but which its 1993 UK dust jacket labelled a gripping true adventure story.

When the narrative engine of the book — a search for the body double of Albanian dictator Enver Hoxha — was revealed to be a fiction, readers who believed that the book had been offered to them under a non-fiction contract were aggrieved. Lloyd's defence of *Biografi*, published not long after things had blown up in his face, still steams with exasperation fifteen years on. '*Biografi* is a book,' it begins. 'This seems to me to be irrefutable. And there I would like to leave it, except for the fact that I have tried this line before and unfortunately it does not work.'

Lloyd was our canary in the creative non-fiction coal mine, or perhaps minefield if one can mix metaphors in that way. Back then he considered it neither necessary nor desirable to disclose the contents of his literary bag of tricks. But today writers are more inclined to declare their hand openly, or knowingly play with readers' expectations. In an interview on the ABC's *Book Show*, Damien Wilkins freely acknowledged 'shameless theft' of things that have happened to people he knows for use in his novels.

One of this year's Auckland Writers and Readers Festival guests, John Burnside, called his memoir *A Lie About My Father*. And just in case we'd missed the point, the first sentence reads, 'This book is best treated as a work of fiction.' There's your contract, signed with informed consent. So, are we readers naive to maintain an attachment to literal as well as literary truth? Some writers seem to think so. Where we see walls, they see only air. Like Lloyd back in 1993, Helen Garner this year declared herself surprised by the anxiety around the overlap between fiction and 'whatever the other thing is called', and claimed not to understand the concern about whether something is literally true. In her view the fiction contract absolves the novelist of any obligation to literal truth and licenses them to make free with it to suit their own formal and narrative purposes.

Each writer must negotiate this contract with the reader according to their own lights. In *Mr Pip*, Lloyd Jones 'invents the oral culture of Bougainville', as I once heard Damien Wilkins put it to him, but not the island's flora and fauna, on the grounds, he once told me, that the reader needs to be able to trust in the veracity of this fictional world.

Jim Crace, a writer who takes a mischievous delight in toying with readerly gullibility, invents flora and fauna so plausibly that readers are surprised to find he's made them up. Both writers are working at persuading us about the accuracy of their observations. If we believe them, one reason is that their writing has that crucial component of literary truth: authority. Literary authority is not a matter of expertise or moral authority, but of voice. Our most practised boundary blurrer, Martin Edmond, quotes Márquez on the subject: Márquez wrote that from Kafka he learned '*it was not necessary to demonstrate facts: it was enough for the author to have written something for it to be true, with no proof other than the power of his talent and the authority of his voice.*' Lloyd Jones has described learning a similar lesson from Calvino's story, *The Baron in the Trees*, in which a character steps out of the window onto a tree branch part way through the story and does not come down for the next 30 years. 'The important thing,' wrote Lloyd in his defence of *Biografi*, 'is literary truth.'

Fifteen years later, when debate briefly erupted over whether a Pākehā New Zealand male could authentically represent the experience of a Pacific Island woman in *Mr Pip*, he found himself obliged to add, 'literary truth is not the same thing as authenticity'. It's interesting to compare Lloyd's position as the author of *Mr Pip* with that of the artist Theo Schoon, who fell deeply in love with Māori rock drawings. Hamish Keith suggests that Schoon felt he had studied the drawings that he loved for so long and with such care, that in his imagination he had enrolled in their culture. 'Tragically,' writes Keith, 'he also believed by that he had a right to outline and improve the faded designs in order to photograph them.'

Hamish Keith concludes that, in a multicultural society like our own, cultural cross-dressing is not an option. It's a view that seems entirely reasonable when applied to the art world, but try applying it to literature, where cross-dressing of the cultural, historical and good old-fashioned gender varieties, is the stock-in-trade. Without it, we wouldn't have had *Mr Pip* or Emily Perkins's *Novel About my Wife*, or a great many of the world's great stories.

Lloyd insists that we must give complete sovereignty to the idea that you can imagine the other, otherwise literature goes down the drain. If that's so, what the cross-dressing novelist must pray for is not authenticity, but the grace of accuracy. And what he or she risks is being judged on their accuracy by those who consider themselves more expert than the author, perhaps on the grounds of their scholarship, or of their status as insiders in the area where the writer's imagination trespasses.

Mr Pip has received two differing report cards on the accuracy of its identification with its Bougainvillean protagonists. On one hand, Selina Tusitala Marsh — whom you'll see later tonight, and who doesn't, she says, oppose cultural cross-dressing in principle — has closely examined the text and concluded that it suffers from some significant failures of imaginative empathy or accuracy that render it unconvincing. On the other, the *Scoop Review of Books* reports that Agnes Titus, the first Bougainvillean to read *Mr Pip*, found it convincing. 'It actually brought memories back,' she said, 'because it seemed too true; it was quite painful. It was like re-living the situation again.' No two people read the same book, as any writer who reads their reviews will tell you.

The Australian historian Inga Clendinnen, however, does object to the notion that imaginative empathy is all the novelist needs to do a good job of rendering 'the other'. Tackling Kate Grenville on her assumptions about writing historical characters in *The Secret River*, Clendinnen suggests that 'an unexamined confidence in empathy tempts us to deny the possibility of significant difference.' And she quarrels with the idea that literary truth is as good as, or better than, the historian's — a notion that lies behind Andrew O'Hagan's assertion, 'Literature has the longest and purest memory of who we are.' Or Geoffrey Lehmann's conclusion that Garner's *The Spare Room* is truer than non-fiction.

Clendinnen notes, somewhat irritably, that while it is possible to disagree with the historian about what happened and what it means, the self-created world of the novelist cannot be contradicted. And while living people who find themselves as thinly disguised characters in a novel may sue, 'the dead can be traduced, parodied or exalted at will. They have no protections beyond what might be provided by their historian defenders. But should an historian protest, "He/she was not like that at all and I can prove it," the novelists — indeed the whole legion of litterateurs — will roar in chorus, "Irrelevant! This is a novel, stupid!"' She adds tartly, 'That practised slither between "this is a serious work of history" and "judge me only on my literary art" has always annoyed me.'

'The ideal thing for me would be to write and say, "Here's a book. It's a story. Read it anyway you would like,"' said Helen Garner earlier this year, again echoing Lloyd Jones. And in the aforementioned ABC interview, Damien Wilkins remarks, 'My mother says she reads my books twice — the first time for gossip about people she knows or people I know, and the second time, as a book.'

Of course, a novelist does not write primarily for his mother or even for an inner circle who may see his work as a *roman à clef* or wonder why he can't disguise his raw material more effectively. His ideal reader is the stranger who can't see the joins between fact and fiction, who can read his novel as 'a book'. What's interesting to the novelist, in Garner's words, is 'taking a chunk of experience and mushing it up together with other things that are inventable, remembered from some other time or stolen from other people's stories ... [to] see if I can make it into something that works, an object, a little machine that runs.' Or, as Wilkins puts it, 'There's this thing called form, you know?'

In the photoshop of memory and imagination, what happened is constantly, perhaps even instantly, being pruned and shaped into narrative. The writer's primary material is to be found in the foul rag and bone shop of the heart. And when we lie down there — as I think Martin Edmond slyly suggests in *Luca Antara*, when he portrays an affair between the first-person narrator named Martin and a married woman that's undertaken with her husband's active collusion — what harm is a little deception between consenting adults if it makes life more interesting?

On that score, it's easy enough to go along with Henry James's idea that 'the only obligation to which in advance we might hold a novel … is that it be interesting.' But it's in this territory of creative non-fiction that Martin Edmond navigates so deftly where things start to get really interesting. And when I hear literary theorist Stanley Fish claim that the death of objectivity relieves me of the obligation to be right, and demands only that I be interesting, I find myself wanting to take a step back and say, 'Hang on a minute, mate.'

The novelist Nicholson Baker's recent foray into non-fiction, *Human Smoke*, makes an interesting case study. *Human Smoke* is a collage of vignettes and quotations from newspapers and other documents that forms a picture of the thinking that led up to World War Two. It offers none of the context or analysis an historian would provide. Is that a problem? After all, Baker does not mix his history with imaginative elements. You might even say he pays his readers the compliment of crediting us with enough intelligence to draw our own conclusions rather than imposing his. The book applies the techniques of fiction seductively and has been praised by literary heavyweights. If you are an historian however, you may feel, as Anne Applebaum does, that Baker 'has used his license as a novelist to excuse himself from all of the tedious work of genuine knowledge.' That 'You cannot fault his scholarship, because no scholarship has been conducted.' And that 'You cannot disagree with Baker's argument, because … no argument has been made. Baker does not build a case,' Applebaum writes, 'he insinuates something, leaving the reader to guess what.'

In this case it seems that the practised slither of the historical novelist risks becoming the creative non-fiction writer's undignified slide down the pot-holed slopes of history, with fine writing providing camouflage for inadequate research, fudging of the facts or sloppy thinking. But here's the thing: a novel or a poem often begins in a moment of puzzlement, of not understanding, of *inexpertise*. Grace Paley once again nails it I think, when she writes:

> One of the reasons that writers are so much more interested in life than others who just go on living all the time is that what the writer doesn't understand the first thing about is just what he acts like such a specialist about — and that is life. And the reason he writes is to explain it all to himself, and the less he understands to begin with, the more he probably writes … In other words, the poor writer — presumably in an intellectual profession — really oughtn't to know what he's talking about.

In other words, most novelists and poets are amateurs who write to find out and whose work exists on a shifting continuum between observation and invention, and it's only when they cross the border into creative non-fiction that they risk attracting attention from the creative non-fiction police.

I speak as someone whose hands are not clean in this matter. My last book, *Brief Lives*, has the heart of a poet, the skeleton of a biographical dictionary and the flesh of prose fiction, biographical anecdote and personal essay and it remains cagey about which parts might be true and which invention. And this year, despite having no special expertise in nineteenth-century literature or history, let alone the history of medicine, I've embarked on a book-length work of creative non-fiction that will centre on the life of the nineteenth-century English poet, anatomist and suicide, Thomas Lovell Beddoes. The prospect of having my door kicked in by the creative non-fiction police is already making me anxious.

But I suspect this category anxiety I'm feeling also has to do with the wider continuum of uncertainty and mistrust in which we now read. The world of print journalism has been blurring the boundaries for some time now. A journalist writing a book about his experiences in a war zone creates a composite character out of the people he has met in order to offer a concentrated summary of their experience. Is he sparing us the tedium and shapelessness of the world as it is to bring us only the noteworthy parts? Or misrepresenting the world in order to make a better read and hence a more saleable product? One example from Farhad Manjoo's excellent and unsettlingly-titled book *True Enough: Learning to Live in a*

Post-fact Society will have to stand in for the many different ways in which the online world undermines our faith in the truth. In that realm, we're constantly being presented with pictures that aren't 'real', some harmless and amusing, others a little more sinister in intent.

'During the 2004 US presidential campaign,' Manjoo tells us, 'a skilled Photoshopper swiped a 1971 shot of John Kerry at an anti-war rally and stitched it seamlessly with a 1972 image of Jane Fonda at a rally in Miami Beach. The composite photo shows a thoughtful, appreciative Kerry next to an agitated Fonda. It was given a border, a headline, a caption and an Associated Press credit and was made to look like an authentic newspaper clipping that proved Kerry's close association with a reviled Hanoi Jane.' The photographer who took the original picture believes that 'the real danger of living in the age of Photoshop isn't the proliferation of fake photos, rather it's that the *true* photos will be ignored as phoneys. When every picture is suspect,' he says, 'all pictures are dismissible, and photography's unique power to criticise will decline.'

Indeed. This is the very conclusion that Lloyd Jones was forced to reach about *Biografi* fifteen years ago. While insisting that a book of this kind could legitimately contain imaginative elements, Lloyd also lamented the fact that the book was to be published as fiction in Germany, calling it 'cruelly ironic for those political victims who, after years of charade, thought they were getting their "true story" out in the world for the first time. Such is the risk of mixing the genres,' he wrote. 'Introduce an imaginative element and suddenly everything becomes questionable.'

Well, since then a virtual tidal wave of unreliable information and questionable expertise has swept over the web and seeped into the mainstream media. 'There's an arms race between truth and fiction,' as Farhad Manjoo puts it, 'and at the moment, the truth doesn't appear to be winning.' Reality TV, Second Life, YouTube and other social networking sites encourage us to fictionalise our identities, and because information lives forever on the web whether it's right or wrong, bad science and statistics, or political half-truths and outright fictions can maintain a hold on the public mind long after they have been conclusively disproved.

The blogosphere amplifies the ancient power of opinion and gossip to create as many closed communities of agreement as new openings for debate and dissent. Do you think the American Government was behind 9/11? Believe that AIDS isn't caused by HIV? You can now find a lot of 'information' to back up your beliefs and a virtual community of believers to cocoon in.

Anne Applebaum sees Nicholson Baker's *Human Smoke* as part of this Wikipedia world. For her, it's a manifestation of 'the contemporary cult of the anti-expert' and belongs not with works of serious history or literature, but with Dan Brown's *The Da Vinci Code*. 'The only difference,' she writes, 'is that instead of treating [his] "forgotten facts" novelistically, which is in a way more honest, Baker has chosen to present them as a collection of carefully dated and foot-noted anecdotes, which gives them a greater aura of truth ... And never mind that the facts have been chosen selectively, even randomly, by writers who do not understand the context in which they originally appeared and indeed, have deliberately tried not to understand it. Brown and Baker are not "experts" after all. They are, to put it politely, artistes.' *Ouch.*

You could see this as sabre rattling in defence of a narrow academic turf. Nonetheless, at a time when we appear to be hastening towards a collapse of the boundaries between fiction and the news, do we, the imaginative writers of fiction and 'whatever the other thing is called', want to capitulate uncritically to a kind of truthiness? Is it still benevolent deception we're practising here? Or are we amateurs and artistes just fooling ourselves?

Wearing her fiction writer's hat, Helen Garner asks us this question about the character she calls Narrating Helen in *The Spare Room*: 'What if it was me or wasn't me? What difference would it make to the meaning or worth of the story?' It took a while before I put my finger on what was troubling me about that question. *The Spare Room* — which incidentally is a terrific book — marks Garner's return to fiction after a long absence that began with a kind of crisis of faith in the novel, a feeling that it had perhaps become used up as a form. Disillusioned with fiction, she eventually came to feel that there was 'something honourable to offer in its place' — namely that 'dangerous and exciting breakdown of the old boundaries between fiction and non-fiction' mentioned earlier. And I realised that what was troubling me about Garner's decision to write *The Spare Room* as a novel was the sneaking suspicion that after fifteen years of writing books such as *The First Stone* and *Joe Cinque's Consolation* about people who might argue back or even sue, perhaps Garner wasn't making a wholehearted return to fiction after all, but more of a disingenuous sideways shuffle that would liberate her from the obligation to be faithful to the full range of other people's often inconvenient truths.

That thought bothered me. I'd always considered Helen Garner a writer of formidable integrity and here I was entertaining the idea that she too might be slithering. My trust in our contract had been undermined.

Now don't get me wrong, I find it dispiriting both as a writer and a reader to imagine living in a world where every book is prefaced, as are the later editions of James Frey's sequel to *A Million Little Pieces*, with a disclaimer outlining which parts of the book are real and which imagined. But I'm not sure about living in the world Garner longs for, where there are no categories but only books.

If all books are to some extent lies and if there is no 'truth' but only competing truths to choose from, is it not perfectly reasonable to say that truthiness is all there is? Or even, as George Orwell might have framed it, that lies are the new truth? When fiction behaves like fact and fact like fiction, it seems that the time is not far when a majority of us, like James Frey and Margaret B. Jones, may be neither willing nor able to distinguish between truth, that profoundly outdated concept, and fiction, or between life and art. And I'm not sure I want to live in a world where journalists have abandoned any attempt to be right but only aspire to be interesting, and where the authority of the writer's voice has become an acceptable substitute for expertise.

The cognitive scientist Steven Pinker has considered the adaptive value of fiction and believes it's not just a 'spandrel' or intellectual cheesecake — in other words a by-product of evolution with no practical use. Fiction, he says 'engages our emotions and our social psychology. It's often been noted that the goals of fictitious characters are at least indirectly related to the ultimate goals of evolution: survival and reproduction. This is not the red-in-tooth-and-claw struggle that we're familiar with from the animal world, but the struggle for survival and reproduction in a species that's intensely cognitive and social—a species that lives by its wits and its social coalitions.'

We're back among Grace Paley's facts of money and blood here. Her casual conjunction of facts, those verifiables and falsifiables that science can discuss, with money and blood, standing for the messy and unscientific domain of human relationships, suggests that she felt it not unreasonable to expect invention to offer news of reality. On some level to instruct as well as delight.

It could be argued that the degree to which fiction both fits with and — pleasurably, usefully — extends our social intelligence is one of the measures of its success. In the struggle for survival, it's helpful if we have a reasonable chance of telling the difference between truth and lies. And in the twenty-first-century version of that struggle we need to know that our sources of information about the world are capable of telling the difference too.

In fiction, there may be nothing at stake except delight, but history deals in matters of weightier consequence. In 2006, when James Frey's memoir was exposed, Michiko Kakutani contrasted the insistence of the author, his publishers and his 'cheerleader' Oprah Winfrey, that 'it didn't really matter if he'd taken liberties with the facts of his story' with the attitude to memory embodied in another memoir selected by Oprah, Elie Wiesel's *Night*, an account of his experience in Auschwitz and Buchenwald. She suggested that a 'truthy' Holocaust memoir would provide ammunition and succour to the Holocaust deniers. Earlier this year, as if to test Kakutani's thesis, the author of a bestselling Holocaust survivor memoir, Misha Defonseca, confessed that it was a fiction, and that she wasn't Jewish. So even this bastion of moral authority to bear witness has not emerged from the last two decades unscathed.

It seems that there is a crisis both of authority and authenticity in the autobiographical novel, the memoir, and in certain types of creative non-fiction. Now that fiction and non-fiction have proceeded from one-night stands and illicit affairs to de facto relationships and civil unions, both writers and readers may need reminders from the creative non-fiction police to keep the lie detector plugged in, alongside the credulity we need to appreciate great stories.

As readers, we still need to remember that, as Greg O'Brien so eloquently put it in his Janet Frame lecture a few weeks back, 'Literature is a prism through which we see the world and not a mirror held up to the world.'

But as writers we should think twice before jettisoning truth in favour of truthiness. 'This isn't just a slippery slope', as Frank Rich wrote back in 2006. 'It's a toboggan into chaos, or at least war.' Remember the truthiness of all those 'imminent mushroom clouds'?

The first casualty in war is truth, and in the contemporary arms race between truth and fiction, the first casualty is trust. Without trust, it's not just the contract with the reader that's undermined, it's the entire social contract that may be at risk of crumbling. An authoritative voice may be enough in a novel, but we also need our writers to be on intimate terms with journalistic, historical and scientific truths, even as we acknowledge that those truths are themselves necessarily imperfect, tentative and partial. And even as we defend the fiction writer's freedom to juggle with them. At the same time we want a literature in which 'beauty is truth, truth beauty', we also need our politicians, our corporations and their spin doctors to follow a higher literary and moral example than that of our friend Homer Simpson and not be writing fiction with their mouths. Whether we turn to fiction or non-fiction for our news of the world, the contract is signed in blood and money and we are all proof-readers.

Which brings me back to Gregory O'Brien's poem on the screen behind me. As with the fraudulent memoirs I mentioned, it's not easy to see what is wrong with this text. It appears to make sense and the error does not completely disable the poem. But like a piece of mutant DNA, the invisible defect does leech the poetic organism of its power, rendering its impact less delightful and less instructive. Close enough, in this case, isn't good enough. The words only regain their full charge when the missing piece of code, that letter 'w', is restored.

Today it really does seem that the more we try to pin down truth the more it shimmers and retreats, leaving the writing on the air where the wall once was. The notion of objectivity, if not dead, is certainly in a twilight zone. But I still believe that all our narratives operate at full power only when they're plugged in at the wall, connected with the verifiable truths of our world. Accuracy is still part of the contract, and for the proof-reader, close enough or true enough, isn't good enough.

Thank you.

2009 TE RADAR

By Buy Bye the Book

Haere mai te whānau. Haere mai, haere mai, haere mai. Kō Te Radar tāku ingoa. Kō Ngāti Pākehā ahau. Ka tū te ure. Kia ora.

Thank you. For those of you not so familiar with te reo, that's what's known as a mihi — an introduction or a greeting. The story behind that mihi in a way deals with what I'm going to talk about in the next little while. I put the mihi together several years ago when I was approaching Māori Television to ask for some funding, and one of the first things I learnt was that it was very important to know your language and your protocol. And I learnt that it was very important to have a mihi to introduce who you are and where you're from. And then I learnt that when putting your mihi together, it's very important to consult your local kaumātua or your local iwi.

Fortunately for me, my local kaumātua and my local iwi at the time were the same person: Mike King. I said to him, 'Mike, can you help me put this mihi together so I can go to Māori Television and get some funding?', and he said, 'Sure, Radar', and we put it together. I went and performed the mihi in front of a funding panel and I was met with absolute silence — just this big row of pūkana eyes staring at me, which I thought was their way of expressing their admiration for my knowledge of their language and protocol. An old kuia stood up and shuffled slowly forward and she said, 'Kia ora, Radar,' and I said, 'Kia ora, Kuia'. She said, 'Do you know what it was that you actually said?' I said, 'Yeah, Kō Te Radar takū ingoa, my name is Te Radar; Kō Ngāti Pākehā ahau, I'm of European extraction; Ka tū te ure, I stand before you proudly'. She said, 'No, dear. What you actually said is, "My name is Te Radar. I am a crazy white guy and my manhood is standing up".' I got the funding.

To me that says a lot about who we are, and I was thinking about it today because Murray had said he wanted me to do the keynote address and he wanted me to tie it into this theme: 'By Buy Bye the Book', and I couldn't figure out what to say. I was thinking about it and I thought, who are we as a people? What are we trying to discuss here? And I came to the conclusion that we're a lot of things, and so in many ways the conversation will deal with more than simply books, because I think we live in an age where we're transcending what we consider to be the notion of a book. And so the conversation will be broader, as I referred to before, because we live in a broadband world and we're at a crossroads. I was so concerned about this that I even wrote notes down. It harried me for days. I had to do an address this morning in Napier to the New Zealand Dieticians' Association on a subject about which I know absolutely nothing, and even that didn't have me as concerned as this did. So I think we should do fairly well.

I've broken it down into three sections. The first is to look at what it is to do things 'by the book'. We're a nation of people, I think, who don't do things by the book. We're descended from people who didn't do things by the book. They fled where they were. They got into their canoes, on to their vast winged waka, into the shiny waka of the sky, and they came to this land — that wasn't doing things by the book — to create this new nation, to create what I think is a new culture, discarding many of the old ways while keeping the parts they liked and adding new things to it.

In a way, it's that conversation that will happen over the next couple of days here, as we sit down and continue to discuss who we are, where we've come from and where we're going. And to discuss what I think is often not discussed enough, the concept of art and ideas. Discussing art — God bless it, finally art has made the headlines this week thanks to Hamilton, not boring. Listen to this: The Springboks were concerned that they were going to have to stay in the city that was boring. Clearly they'd never been to Hamilton — the last time the Springboks were there, 1981, I think it was, not boring.

And then we had the great and the learned minds of society trying to discuss in the media what art was, those wonderful intellectuals Leighton Smith and Paul Henry engaging the nation in a discourse about whether a pile of recycled materials that had packaged artworks put into a pile in the middle of a gallery by curators was art. 'No!' they said, 'The people have spoken'. Leighton Smith had thought long and hard about this, probably over a coffee, and they declared, 'This is not art!' And it made me think they had sort of missed the point, because there they were discussing it. In many ways it was excellent art — I've seen terrible art in my time. I remember the opening show I saw in the Auckland Festival this year was a piece of art, a piece of dance — if dance can be called art — that was so atrocious, so abysmal. I was so infuriated by this piece of work that I wanted to storm out of the theatre and go and find someone from the ACT Party and find out how to join so that I'd become influential in creating the policies of the ACT Party. One of the policies would be to cut all future funding of the arts so that no one would have to sit through what I had. In this state of anger, it struck me that what I had seen, as much as I hated it, had been a brilliant piece of art. It was the piece in many ways that took me through the rest of the festival, the benchmark upon which I weighed everything else; a fantastic thing.

Despite the likes of Paul Henry and Leighton Smith and various others opining this week about what I think was a brilliant piece of work, that of putting the wrapping of other bits of art into a pile in the centre — by an artist who never even left Germany to do it — it was fantastic! That's the world we're living in: minions! — it's good. It says a lot about the way ideas will be floated over the course of the weekend — that art is changing.

We live in a country where the last piece of art that made the news was et al.'s 'braying dunny', as it was christened. Again, a wonderful piece of art, interpreted in a completely innovative way by those in the media. The more you heard of it, the more fantastic you thought it was, this toilet they said brayed like a donkey. And when I gathered that the braying noise was a recording of the sound of the nuclear tests at Moruroa, and that this piece of art talked about the French coming here and polluting — shitting in — our Pacific, it struck me as a wonderful and provocative piece of art. Whether indeed it is that, I don't know, but to me it is wonderful. And yet it was dismissed out of hand in the media. That is the state of our art criticism.

I'm also going to talk a lot tonight about comedy, because it's a medium in which I work. Two weeks ago, comedy made a small headline. There was an article in one of the Sunday papers about the state of comedy — it was a review of Rhys Darby's reviews in Edinburgh. Rhys Darby, that is, one of our most successful comedians who had gone to Edinburgh and whose show had sold out before he even arrived; a magnificent achievement in any way, shape or form in one of the biggest platforms of comedy in the world. And what was reported in the Sunday News? They cherry-picked out the very worst of the lines they could find in his reviews and said, 'Conchord falls from his perch'. Outrageous! Did they pick up the fact that some of these reviews, the *Guardian*'s, had only given him a three-star review. The *Guardian* gave Ricky Gervais a two-star review. It did say, somewhere near the end, that some people in the crowd had thought it such a terrible show that they had stood and applauded it. But did they report that? No. They cherry-picked out these terrible things and you think, you know, we make fun of this Tall Poppy Syndrome and yet it seems to be more alive and more well than ever. And in fact, I think we shouldn't make fun of it, because it seems to be who we are.

I think you see it often in other kinds of things: literature, language. The celebration of language in this country is a terrible thing, when people want to have an informed debate about whether an 'h' should be added into a word to make it a word that has another meaning, whereas other people say, 'Well to us, the word without the 'h' is part of our legacy and our heritage.' Is there a rational and informed debate about it? No!

You know, I often think that if we spent as much time celebrating pride in the revival of language, our pride in our literature and our arts, as we did moaning and bitching about it, we would be a lot better off and probably a lot happier. So, do we do things by the book? No.

One hundred and sixty-eight million, one hundred and seventy-eight thousand, and seven hundred and nineteen books, as of last Friday, have been written, according to Google. They're attempting to scan all of them and put them onto a computer to do something with. What that is, I suspect, is to allow everyone to have access to them and to pay none of the writers. We're going to be discussing this, and this goes into this concept of 'to buy the book'. I wanted to address this in terms of not only who is buying the book, but a bigger question, who is buying the notion of what a book is and what it should say?

We often think, in terms of books, do they reflect our voice? I listened to Nicky Pellegrino at the last book festival I attended, in Taranaki. (I was there because I wrote a book, not because I had anything to say, but because I wanted to get on the book festival junket; it seemed to be fun. I get to speak at events like this.) Nicky Pellegrino writes bestselling books, for a publisher in England, set in Italy. She wanted to set them in New Zealand, but the English publisher didn't think that New Zealand was interesting enough. Clearly they have never been here and clearly they have never heard of Michael Laws. Although to be fair, after Rhys Darby, he was the next New Zealander to be mentioned in the *Guardian*, a triumph for comedy on many, many levels.

And so, when we're thinking about this notion of to buy the book, I'm thinking about what is it that we buy? What are we buying into with these books? Are they a reflection of ourselves in a wider sense? I'm thinking, where are the writers? What are they thinking about? This is a great funding question: Who are you writing for? And do the people you're writing for really want you to write at all? Important questions that funders want to ask — arts administrators! Hamish Keith, again at Taranaki, did a wonderful presentation. He put what I think is a very relevant question in this day and age: do we need full-time arts administrators working for organisations like Creative New Zealand, when all they really have to do is every so often get together and say we think you, you, you should have some of this money, and then they can go home again and let us get on with our work.

Nonetheless, my favourite moment of funder-based art was at a New Zealand on Air conference on the state of comedy. Because many people would have you believe we haven't had any decent comedy since Billy T. James and Creative New Zealand was concerned about this — TVNZ and various other people — Creative New Zealand turned up to this conference with a graph and onto this graph they had graphed where people thought comedy was. They had given it criteria such as 'blokeish comedy' and 'intellectual comedy' and they'd drawn some bars and they'd plotted on to the graph where they thought comedians were happening. They said, 'This is where Matthew Ridge and Mark Ellis are' (well-known New Zealand comedians, of course); 'this is where Billy T. is; this is where we think you are. We would like you, comedians of New Zealand, to make more comedy in this area here.' What they didn't realise was that if they'd simply brought a camera along and filmed their presentation and put it on TV, comedy would have risen exponentially in the minds of the New Zealand public.

It was a terrible thing; people cried at the meeting. For the Topp Twins, who I think had been named TV entertainers of the year more than a decade prior, it was another 14 years, I believe, before they were even seen on our screens again. Who was buying their work? We, the public were, but someone decided that we didn't want that and ergo they didn't put it on the screen. Television New Zealand, in terms of buying our stories and paying for them — somebody has to — have had their charter taken off them because they came to the conclusion that you couldn't make intelligent programmes about New Zealand that would rate well. My suggestion to them was, try! Just try!

Again, TVNZ, unwitting purveyors of comedy, announced about three or four months ago that they had to save $25 million in order to make a return to the Government of ten percent on their investment. They went, 'Oh my God, what are going to do?' They put out a press release that told us what they were going to do. They immediately summoned 50 of their senior managers to a crisis meeting — 50! I would have suggested that the crisis meeting should happen in the carpark, and they should say to them, 'It's a crisis. The first ten of you back in the building keep your jobs.'

They have since decided that the best way to save $25 million is to stop making programmes. Brilliant. Again, in the odd kind of thinking we live in, one of the biggest arts venues in the country, Aotea Square — they call it the heart of Auckland; I'd hate to see where the sphincter is if Aotea Square is the heart — managed to lose over the course of two productions a million dollars. I did the figures: they could have funded New Zealand productions, New Zealand writers, New Zealand folk, to the tune of $20,000 a week for a year on the money they lost on *My Fair Lady* and some Shakespeare performed by famous overseas actors that no one could afford $170 a ticket to go and see. It's astounding that that happens.

And when that was happening, what were the investigative and hard-hitting arts media in this country doing to figure out why it happened? Well, Russell Baillie, editor of the entertainment supplement of the biggest newspaper in the country, was moaning that he didn't really like March or April because it was the time of the year when comedians had the audacity, before the comedy festival, to send him press releases about their shows. How dare they do his job for him!

I thought to myself, you know, instead of complaining about that, why didn't he get out and investigate, and ask why these shows were brought over. What were The Edge doing funding these things? Of course they made a great deal of money from *Priscilla, Queen of the Desert*, it was a bloody good show. But *My Fair Lady*? Good God Almighty! And don't get me started on poetry — I'm going to in a minute.

There they were in Aotea Square imagining people would rush in and see these shows. Aotea Square, in terms of these notions of who we are and what we're doing, is awash with all the joy and life-fulfilling vitality of a nineteenth century prison exercise yard, and it's there we go to celebrate art and culture in this country. Bloody hell. I prefer rooms like this with good honest folk like you. [Audience responds.] Yeah, thank you; I'm not afraid to patronise you.

In terms of this funding thing I'm looking at, who was paying for and buying the work? Where was all of that money going? We're turning out journalists and writers and actors in enormous numbers; they're all going to these tertiary *institutions* — they are institutions, often. They're paying all their money to be trained in the arts, at a time when it's probably never been worse getting work as a journalist, or a writer, or an actor. Nonetheless, they're all out there investing their hard-earned money, and good for them.

So, as to who is buying these stories, I don't know. I go into bookshops, I look at all the books, and I often think to myself, 'Who buys these? There's an awful lot of them.' I hope someone does buy them because I want to keep writing them.

Not only do we have to buy them, we also have to read them. The most shocking thing I've seen recently was a school, I think it was in Wellington, bribing young boys to read books. They were offering a can of Coke or a meal at Subway or a ticket to a movie if they read a certain number of books in a certain time. And I thought to myself, 'Why don't they just give them more interesting books?' It's not rocket science. Maybe it should have been?

I used to write for the *New Zealand Herald*. I'm often heartened: even a couple of weeks ago, I was congratulated by someone in the street who said, 'I really love your column that you write in the *Herald*.' I didn't have the heart to tell them that they fired me five years ago. I don't know who they've been reading, but they must be excellent. The most letters I received at the *Herald*, other than when I wrote about the Destiny Church, was when I wrote a column about Cambridge High School, who had decided a building they had was filled with a whole lot of things they didn't really need, so they were going to close the library and sell their books. They were going to turn it into a remedial room for problem students, and they were going to hook up to the Internet there, because clearly any knowledge that anyone needs is now all available on a small terminal and they could use that room for a better purpose.

It struck me as absolutely astounding that this wasn't at least *near* the front page on the news — I mean, to get rid of books! From a school library! To me, libraries are summed up by a single photograph I saw in a mining museum in the north of England. It was a photograph of a group of miners in their Sunday best, standing outside the brand new building that was their library. They were so proud that their community had raised enough money so that on a Sunday or in the evenings these men who toiled away like underpaid moles under the earth could go up and read. They could have access to books and their children could have access to books. There was such pride and delight in these men's faces that the image is scorched into my mind every time I think of libraries.

Again, we're going to face this in the near future — the funding of libraries. A user-pays library system, they want. We do pay, through our rates, you know, and to take away the ability for people who can't afford to buy books to go to an institution that has books available free, and then charge them for it, seems to me to defeat the purpose.

Now the theme 'buy the book': when it comes to buying the book and buying these ideas, I think books are too expensive. And because they're too expensive, we get to the last word in this of trilogy of words, bye — goodbye — to the book. I think we're at the stage of seeing the end of the book as we know it — the book that is printed on the dead tree. It's a problematic form of translating a medium. It's ecologically unsound and relatively unsustainable to print books on dead bits of paper — you need to print it at a place, then transport the book all the way to where it's sold. Often — writers, you'll know this — your books are stored in an enormous warehouse, you don't know where, where you can't get access to them because the publisher wants to charge you too much to buy copies of your own books to sell to people to make a profit from it because you haven't bloody surpassed your royalties limit. Then they're put on shelves only in small numbers, because shelf space is limited, and then someone has to take them away. It's an enormous ordeal, the paper book, the dead tree.

Paper books are good, on paper. You can fan yourself and you can read them in the bath and you can use them as toilet paper — that can be useful. We're coming to an age now when that's going to change. Before we go into this new era, one of the greatest things I've seen for the book on paper (which we all love and we're all nostalgic for because that's probably the generation we are) is something called the Espresso Book Machine. It is essentially a glorified photocopier and you can say, 'I would like a copy of this book here.' They download it from their computer-based storage thing; it goes into the machine; it is printed into book form and cut and bound; and you're handed the book and you walk away.

What a wonderful amalgam of the future and the past that machine is for those of us who still want to have an actual book that we can use when the power goes off, as it will increasingly in the future. A synthesis of the past and the present, because we're now getting into an age where the transmission of books is becoming quite different. I think many of us love that notion of the book as the solid, paper-based object, but when we think about what a book really is, it's just the content, it's the ideas. And does it really matter in what form those ideas are transmitted, if people are interested in the ideas? It's great to have a library full of books, but if no one's going to use them, then those ideas just sit there. So if people are able to access those ideas at a reasonable price, by getting rid of carrying that paper book and being able to download it on their computer, I suspect we will all, as writers, begin to make a lot more money.

And Kindle is out! Kindle, for those of you who haven't heard of it, is essentially a little e-book reader. They ran into trouble the other day, because Kindle — the people who run it — reached into people's Kindles electronically and deleted a book. What was the book? It was *1984*; I suspect the irony wasn't lost on them. But they were books that people had and read in real time. There was a story of a student doing his essay on *1984*; he'd annotated it with various notes and things, as you can do on these books. He watched it all disappear as they reached in and they took the book out of his Kindle.

It was eventually discovered to have been done because of various copyright issues and things like that, but for these people to have the power to reach into your library and take your books away is a very scary thing about where that technology is going. It is probably the downside to the e-reader technology. There's a wonderful sculpture — an installation in Berlin, where all writers at book festivals have to mention having been to at least once. In Berlin, in the big square where they burnt the books there is a glass plate in the middle of the floor. You can stand on that thick glass plate and look down into a white room with empty bookshelves. It's beautiful. And that's what came to mind when I thought of these people reaching into the Kindle and taking books out.

So obviously we need to get over that issue, but the other problem that we're facing is an information overload. We're living in an era where there is so much information that we don't know what to do with it. I went to the Digital Futures Conference in Wellington, which was talking about the future in a digital world, and they were excited that every film ever made, every television programme ever recorded, would be available to us to be streamed down the copper wires of our telephones. We would have access to everything, but what they never mentioned was where we would get the time to watch it all.

To me it spoke also of the tyranny of choice. When you have too much choice, you often don't choose anything. With three television channels there might be nothing on, but you'll find something to watch. With 96 television channels, there's still nothing on and you can't figure out what to watch and, good for us — I hope people will go and pick up a book. And I think e-books are going to be the same. When you go on holiday you often end up reading a book you might not otherwise have read, because there aren't really any books there. At someone's holiday house you pull a book off the shelf; it looks to be the best of a bad bunch and you read it — you're almost forced to experience something you wouldn't otherwise have. If you take your Kindle with you, with 700 books downloaded, are you ever going to actually read an entire book? Or are you going to flick all the way through that Kindle, read a few pages here and there and just skim? We're creating this enormous pond of knowledge that I think is going to end up being very, very shallow. That is the future for us.

Another thing worries me. This concept of having exposure to the ideas is all well and good, but at the end of the day we do love books in their traditional form and we have to ask, are a lot of things about them going to disappear? What will happen to the cover art of a book if you're downloading it? Will we no longer be able to judge a book by its cover? If it's downloaded onto our Kindle without any other form of things, where will we, as authors, write autographs on books? Where, when you're giving a book to a loved one or a colleague, will you write an inscription that in years to come someone who buys that book in a second-hand bookstore will look at and think, 'I wonder who that was? I wonder what they did to earn this lovely little inscription and have that book passed on to them?'

The other thing is that I wonder if computers and Kindles in all their various forms are going to become the hieroglyphics of the future; undecipherable objects that people will scratch their heads and look at and think, 'Geez, I wish we could understand what that was. If only we could plug them into something; if only we could turn the power on and decipher what is stored in these memory boxes, because we know it's something'. And it goes further than books: How many of you have digital cameras? How many of you put your photographs only onto your computer? And when that computer disappears, where are those photographs? Where are those musty smelling boxes of old photographs that you pick out of your grandparents' drawers and look at and wonder who those people were?' Those little dog-eared photographs, water-stained and watermarked, but at least a tangible thing. Yes, they too can be destroyed, by water or fire, but to have things locked away in ones and zeros on a box makes me think that we're going to be in danger of losing them.

You can have a ratty dog-eared copy of *1984*, and you can hide it under your bed with all of the other things that you don't want people to know you read. But to be in an era where something can be taken away from us, either by our inability to turn on a machine, or by some higher force reaching in from some never-never world and taking it away, I think is a very dangerous thing.

I left a large page of notes at home — I hope this has been making sense. [Audience responds.] It hasn't made any sense? Good. It didn't make any sense to me when I was writing it, so you know, really, you could just call this poetry. Sorry, Wystan. [Wystan Curnow is in the audience.] You know, I had a bloody good talk about funding. I remember when I proposed to Emily Perkins ... that we could solve the funding problem for novelists and whatnot by stopping funding poetry, an art form that I rank just above dance, and the two of them somewhere below macramé and slightly above making motorcycles out of recycled sodapop cans. I am happy to discuss this; everyone has their own favourite art forms. God, she was aghast — couldn't believe that I'd even mooted it. It made for a very interesting conversation, one, nonetheless, that we can continue to have.

I guess we're living in a brave new world where the nature of books is changing. I urge you all to come to the wonderful sessions over the next few days. I'm really looking forward to the one on the electronic notion of what the book will be, because while I'm saying it's vulnerable, it's also going to be massively enriching to look through a book — to wonder what that means and to be able to click on a couple of buttons and go further and further into the sources of this knowledge; to be able to access photographs and video clips of things in books that you're reading about right there. If you want to know about certain things in the book, you'll be able to Google them up from the book.

I remember Gordon McLauchlan's wonderful history of Auckland, *The Life and Times of Auckland: the colourful story of a city*. I said to him, 'Why didn't you put in any maps or any pictures?' He said, 'Well it was a bit too expensive. We couldn't really afford it'. Again, something that we really need to address in this country is the cost of accessing our heritage from the archive libraries. I asked them the other day how much it would cost to use some images, and I was staggered. There is no way I could give up all of my royalties on my potential book to have ten photographs in it. We own those archives; they're ours. While it's good that there are these repositories, that need to earn some kind of money to keep them there, we need to question how we can access them to tell, and to continue to tell, our stories. The same with video footage: at the archive it was $20 a second. Twenty dollars a second! I said, 'For God's sake, I'm in the theatre. Twenty dollars a second — I'll have to spend the next 15 years touring the bloody show in order to get a couple of minutes worth of footage.'

As we look at the world of these e-books, to be able to access footage on those books, to enrich what we're reading about, to go and search through and find photographs of authors and places and times and things, I think it is going to be wonderful.

While all of these things happen, we are living in a brave new world of publishing. It's never, never been easier to be published. You've only got to get a Twitter account and you're a published author, almost — blogs and things like that. You can develop an audience for your work online. Some books have already had massive pre-sales because people started blogging about the nature of the book, and communities have formed. Really, that's one of the great things about it, to be able to put literature out there and to have ideas come back from our audience, to be in touch with people and to discuss the nature of our work. It is great to have this, but not everyone can. If you can talk to fans and critics and writers in Japan or Australia or Papua New Guinea — wherever they have better access to broadband than we do — it's going to make for a wonderful new world of literature: the sharing of ideas and the celebrating of concepts, which in many ways is what this weekend is all about.

And so, while we can discuss whether we go by the book, while we can go out and buy books, while we're contemplating saying goodbye to the traditional form of the book, the ideas in books are going to stay with us. A kiss will still be a kiss. And a tear will still be a tear. And laughter will still sound like laughter. Regardless of the form books take, the ideas will still be there. We'll still be able to share them, and so long as we can do all of that, we're living in a great world.

I don't know if this has been the most coherent keynote address you've ever had, but then you did hire a comedian. I generally don't tell people

I'm a comedian because to say you're a comedian makes you about as popular as a pervert at a PTA meeting. Under 'occupation' I've put a lot of things in the past: 'hedonist' was one, and the woman at the thing said, 'Is that a medical thing?' I said, 'In a way — it's quite hands on.'

And as to that concept of what we are as writers, I generally classify myself simply as an opinionist, but going into Australia recently I didn't want to cause any trouble, and so on my Customs form where they asked my occupation, for the very first time I put 'writer'. It was a wonderful moment. I went through Customs and the guy said, 'Ooh you're a writer?' I said, 'Yes, I am.' He said, 'What do you write?' I said, 'Wrongs!' To me, that's what we do.

Enjoy the weekend. Thank you so very much for having us. Buy a book.

2010 DAME ANNE SALMOND

Right Word, Right Place, Right Time

Ko te wai a hora nei, ko te marae e takoto nei, ko koutou āku rangatira kua pae nei. Tēnā koutou, tēnā koutou, tēnā koutou katoa.

It is such an honour to be here tonight, to be part of this festival and to see and to join in the plaudits for Mayor Bob Harvey. Bob and I had a period together as fellow trustees on the Parks and Wilderness Trust; we're both passionate about restoring the environment and making sure that our children — and great-grandchildren — have beautiful places to play in and to enjoy. And there's a mayor, a philosopher mayor, a surfie mayor and a visionary mayor. Bob, I'll never forget the time we went out to see you and Barbara and you showed us crop circles just behind the beach. I just thought that was absolutely fantastic. So the spirit of Waitākere and the spirit of the West — that's the wonderful thing — cannot possibly be lost and this festival will carry on I'm sure.

I thought I'd talk tonight about the joy of writing. Why? Because it's one of the great pleasures in my life. Not the only one, luckily, but a very intense and powerful one all the same. And I thought I might add a small item to that illustrious genre of writings entitled, 'The Joy of …', because we've got a couple of those volumes at home.

The joy of writing is intimately bound up with the pleasure of reading. Ever since I was young, I've loved to read books. I can still remember the sense of freedom and discovery I felt when I got my first library card and found I could take out any book I wanted from the public library in Gisborne. I didn't have to wait for someone to give it to me as a Christmas present, or a birthday present, or to sneak into my brother's room to pinch one of his books about World War Two — he had this very large collection: *Dam Busters*; *The Colditz Story*; *The Wooden Horse*. I'm famous in our family for reading almost anything. I loved the library in Gisborne. There's something entrancing about rows and stacks of books: the smell of print and paper; the kaleidoscope of colours; the certainty that there are worlds to explore inside their covers just waiting to be opened. It's unpredictable and tantalising. When you pull a book off a shelf, you never know what you're going to find, who you might meet, what new kinds of experience you might encounter.

As the eldest girl in a family of eight, time to myself was rare and very difficult to come by. When I found a good book, I had to climb up the big walnut tree in our back garden and hide amongst its leaves in summer, and hope that no one would find me. Sometimes I'd hear my mother calling and feel bad, but at the same time absolutely thrilled that I'd managed to disappear for a while. And while I was reading the world around me seemed to vanish, and it still does, and I'd be off in someone else's reality.

Some books are comforting and inspire delight. Others are frightening, sometimes depressing. I soon found that reading enlarges your life through the alchemy of imagination. It has a strange, sometimes intimidating power.

About the same time too, I discovered the joy of telling stories. There were three little boys in our family (later four) and at night I used to cuddle up with them and tell them stories to put them to sleep. My brothers were always the heroes in these adventures, which went on for months. I remember one saga, the story of Pumblechook, a bumbling Brit who lived in the heart of the African jungle in a cottage surrounded by a garden full of flowers, which I think I made up out of a combination of my grandmother's beautiful scented garden, crossed with the Dr Dolittle books that I was getting out of the library. And there was another endless serial that went on with the boys exploring a bizarre variety of planets, enduring all kinds of dangers and performing marvellous feats of bravery and endurance. And if they were being a pain, these little boys, a hint that they might not get a story that night would work like a charm. This is probably why I now write quite long books about exploration and discovery. It goes back to those nights tucked up with my little brothers and the thrill of keeping them quiet, even entranced sometimes, on those imaginary journeys.

It wasn't until I was sent to a girls' boarding school in Masterton in the Wairarapa that I began to write. I absolutely hated being torn away from my family and at school we would write letters home every week. (One of the worst things actually is that teachers sometimes used to read them before they posted them). Later, I kept a diary for a while. We had a superb English teacher called Mr Bird, a tall, rugged man, who introduced us to English literature. He encouraged me to write short stories, and some of these were published in the school magazine. There was a school library, though I don't think we had much time at boarding school for reading, apart from our homework.

In the morning you'd get up at 6.30 for a run around the block, splintering icy puddles in winter, and then there was breakfast, lessons, lunch, lessons again, sports in the afternoon, dinner, homework and then bedtime. And it was, again, really hard to find time for yourself on your own, let alone to read, although there were a few quiet places in the school grounds. I remember a grassy clearing surrounded by trees with a little gravelly stream running through it, inhabited by koura, translucent freshwater crayfish.

When I arrived at the University of Auckland after a brief sojourn in the States as an American Field Scholar in Ohio, I studied English as well as anthropology and Māori Studies. We had some fantastic lecturers: Prof. Musgrave (Judith Binney's father); John Reid; M.K. Joseph;

Professor Forrest Scott (who taught us about the Angles, the Saxons and the Jutes). The poet Kendrick Smithyman, I remember, was my tutor. Witi Ihimaera was in the same class and we became very good friends. At that time there were no courses in creative writing, otherwise I might have majored in English. And it was then, that I rediscovered the joy of reading and the thrill of good writing.

But it wasn't until I had something that I was dying to share with other people, that a desire to write picked me up by the scruff of the neck and shook me. Inspired by a fascination with Māori language and culture, I decided to major in anthropology because that's where you could study those things in those days, especially linguistics. But when I wrote my Masters thesis, after a riveting stay with a community of people from the Polynesian atoll of Luangiua, who lived just outside of Honiara, the capital of the Solomon Islands, it was a frustrating experience. At that time, linguistics was captured by the generative theories of Noam Chomsky, a brilliant linguist at the Massachusetts Institute of Technology, who devised quasi-mathematical ways for describing linguistic pattern. Our professor, Bruce Biggs, had initiated a major project to describe and compare all of the Polynesian languages, and the languages of the Polynesian outliers of Luangiua and Sikaiana, two atolls off the Northern coast of the Solomons, had not yet been studied. And so Peter Sharples and I, Masters students in linguistics, were dispatched to describe these languages for our theses and sent off to Honiara.

It was the most extraordinary experience. At the ripe old age of 20, I found myself living in a racially divided community. The Luangiua people lived in a little village on the beach, just outside of Chinatown, not far from the village of the Sikaiana people, where Peter was working. I'd been studying the Luangiua language in Auckland with a young woman called Noella Kakapenga, who'd been sent to study at Queen Victoria School for Māori Girls in Auckland. The idea was that over the summer we would travel together to the Solomons, catch a boat and go to the atoll, and I would study the language. But when we got there and went to go on board this boat, it turned out to be a missionary ship. The missionaries took one look at me and said it would be far too dangerous for me to go and live on the atoll, and they wouldn't let me go. So I stood on the wharf waving goodbye to Noella and crying my eyes out. And some of the people from Luangiua who lived in Honiara saw me and came to talk to me. They said, 'She's crying for Kakapenga,' so they came and embraced me and invited me to their village. Most of those people were just visiting Honiara for schooling or for medical treatment and they knew almost nothing about White people, whom they found quite bizarre, but fascinating.

So over the next few months I biked to the village every day, and on my way through Chinatown picked up a big tuna and put it over the handlebars of the bike, or a string of pineapples or coconuts, and then sat with people in their houses or on the beach studying the language.

One family took me into their home, and I guess their hearts, and taught me to speak Luangiua and guided me through the intricacies of local kinship and hospitality and exchange. These people were not much influenced by European life or customs — the women were bare-breasted, had tattoos on their wrists and thighs which were sacred, especially those on their thighs, and practised love magic; the men used a form of Polynesian judo to fight the Melanesian guys in the pub, went fishing in canoes and performed shark magic.

On rare occasions there were feasts on the beach at night, lit by kerosene lanterns, with fish and pork and beautiful baked puddings that I loved, cooked in earth ovens. We'd dance to the thud of giant bamboo canes banged on the beach. And they told fantastic stories and found me endlessly funny. It was a very interesting experience, at 20, being this kind of standing entertainment for a whole village of Polynesian people. When I washed my teeth, for example, the kids would come and watch and then run back into the village and describe this weird performance. Or when I tried to explain why European women covered their breasts, that seemed so ludicrous to them. Or about Christmas and Santa Claus coming down the chimney. Chimney? What's that? Very entertaining.

At the same time I liked these people so much more than the White people that I was meeting in Honiara, who often seemed arrogant and were sometimes extremely rude to my friends from Luangiua, and also to me when I was in their company. There was a kind of apartheid that operated in the town — I got thrown off beaches when I was there with my Luangiua friends, getting the names of shellfish, and all this kind of thing. Very illuminating to be on the receiving end of racist behaviour.

Despite a few nasty experiences with these escapees from the Raj or British Africa, I had a fantastic time in Honiara, and when I left, my Luangiua 'mother' gave me a necklace plaited from her own hair. I did write my generative grammar of Luangiua, but it seemed an impoverished way of responding to those experiences. While the grammar was published by a prestigious press in the Netherlands, I knew that hardly anybody would ever read it, and certainly nobody from Luangiua, certainly not in that generation. And after that I decided that I would write books that people would want to read and, I hoped would enjoy.

I spent a year at training college after that, because I was pretty sure I was going to be an academic, and so I thought I should learn to teach. After that I went to the University of Pennsylvania in Philadelphia where I studied language and culture. I'd met Jeremy [Salmond], my husband, who's here tonight, just before leaving New Zealand and so I finished my PhD papers in record time so I could get home again. Eruera Stirling, the distinguished Whānau-ā-Apanui elder, whom I'd met during my first year at the University, suggested that for my thesis I should study hui, or gatherings, on marae, and when the time came and I got ready to do the field work, he and his wife Amiria offered to take me on those excursions. A number of you will know about Eruera, a well-known orator, an authority on tribal history, and Amiria who was one of the best storytellers I've ever known.

I came back home to New Zealand, now a junior lecturer in anthropology at Auckland. I bought a little blue VW Beetle and we set off on these odysseys to marae that lasted for almost two years, visiting places that loom large in the Māori topography of New Zealand. Places like Waiomatatini on the East Coast, Tūrangawaewae in the heart of Waikato, Maungapōhatu in the Ureweras, Parihaka in Taranaki. Sleeping on marae, listening to speeches and waiata during the day; tribal stories, jokes and debates at night. In a curious way it was quite like my time with the Luangiua people, a sojourn in a strange land, half familiar and yet at the same time exotic and entrancing. Jeremy quite often came with us, and while I'd tape the proceedings he would take photographs, capturing the essence of marae in a wonderful series of photographs that are there in the book that I eventually wrote about these visits.

Now I had something I was dying to write about and share with other people. It seemed bizarre that in my own country I could walk into another world with its own language, its own rhythms of time, its own types of food, sense of humour, system of knowledge, art forms, history and protocols. It was in a way like that wonderful book, *The Lion, the Witch and the Wardrobe*, except without a wardrobe, just a little blue VW, and two extraordinary guides in Eruera and Amiria Stirling. We were very privileged I realise now, because in those years, few Pākehā really were interested in te ao Māori, the Māori world. Partly for that reason, and also because Eruera and Amiria were with us, Jeremy and I were made very welcome on marae all over the country. In those long meandering journeys that we took across and around the North Island in particular, we went to visit places you would only visit if you were going to a hui, or if you were brought up there. Places like Marokopa, Tikitiki, Ahipara, Te Teko, Omaio, Omaahu. And for me there was this sense of discovery, of amazement because each region, each place, had its own history, its own marae protocol, its very distinctive qualities. The people were different.

I realised then, and I'm glad this happened to me right at the beginning, that if I wanted to learn about te ao Māori, a lifetime was not going to be long enough. So when I wrote my first book — I don't really count the *Generative Syntax of Luangiua* — when I wrote my first book, *Hui: a study of Maori ceremonial gatherings*, it was my PhD thesis. I was really fortunate that my supervisor or mentor in the States, Ward Goodenough, an eminent Pacific anthropologist, understood and sympathised with my desire to write about marae in a way that would be accessible to a wide range of readers, especially Māori, and true to the patterns of those gatherings. As my supervisor, he could easily have destroyed all of that if he had wanted. But he didn't.

So the theme of the festival this year, 'Right Word, Right Place, Right Time', captures so much of what I was trying to achieve in that first book, and still drives me as a writer today. This was a time when marae protocols were largely hidden away from other New Zealanders, except for the rather lame version of the haka that the All Blacks used to perform in those years. When you look back at videos of it now, it's embarrassing. The All Blacks do a fantastic haka today, but then it was not great.

These marae stood in nooks and crannies in the countryside, often along a gravel road, way out 'in the sticks'. The very first urban marae were being built at that time to meet the needs of Māori who'd migrated to the cities. There was no Lottery Grants Board funding for marae buildings, no dawn ceremonies to open new buildings, no pōwhiri on public occasions, like tonight. No kapa haka competitions of the kind we see today. No Māori TV. How the world has changed since the early 1970s, and changed for the better. Back then, it was a matter of trying to find the right words to share my sense of wonder at what I was discovering on marae with other New Zealanders, who at that time were often quite dismissive of tikanga Māori; of Māori ways of doing things and being.

 I suppose it worked, because *Hui* is still in print and when I was thinking about this I realised it was written 40 years ago. Gosh, that gave me a shock. I wrote it as a tribute to those marvellous gatherings. I loved being on marae. You enter another time-space dimension, when you go into a hui. When I see that book in Māori households or I see a young kid holding it wrapped up in plastic, or an orator, as has happened on occasion, tells me they used it when they were preparing for their first venture at speaking on a marae, it makes me gulp. Ah! But none of that would have been possible without Eruera and Amiria. No way I could have gone into that world without them and without their guidance and their advice, and their protection for that matter.

And out of that experience tumbled two other books, the life stories and reflections of Eruera and Amiria themselves, and here the writing challenge was very different. It was a matter of sitting down and listening to each of them in sequence. One or two long sessions a week, over a year or so in each case, using a neck microphone. I remember Amiria, she'd forget that we were taping; she would think that the mike was her tiki Mahu-tai-te-rangi and start playing with it, so the tapes have these kind of rattling noises on them. And I'd drape a cardigan over the tape recorder so she wasn't distracted by the whirling reels, because we used reels in those years. Then transcribing the tapes, putting the stories into roughly chronological order because these were to be life stories, and then trying to find a way of capturing their voices in writing; ways of thinking and speaking that I had come to know so well because we spent a lot of time together in those years. We didn't start writing together until we had been together for about a decade, maybe more. With *Amiria: the life story of a Māori Woman*, it was pure fun for me. I loved it. Our own daughter Amiria was just a baby, and she would sit on my lap as we taped, and in the tapes you can hear her gurgling and sometimes crying a bit. *Amiria* is a women's book about growing up on the East Coast. The shock and drama of a taumau arranged marriage, as Amiria experienced it. Family life on the farm, the triumphs and tragedies of raising children, life in the country, and the tragic circumstances of their shift from the East Coast to Auckland.

Amiria used to tell her stories to me in English and so when I picked up the transcripts, and started working with them, it was a matter of editing them to ensure that the final version did her justice, captured the charm and riveting quality of her stories — while editing out the repetitions and the places where the differences between Māori-English and standard English jarred a bit, while keeping the rhythms and flavour of her speech.

When her family said to me that the book sounded just like her, I was absolutely thrilled. A lot of women got in touch with her and me when it was published, finding in *Amiria*, a comfort and a reflection of some of their own lives. I don't quite know what happens when you take a transcript like that, you think of the voice and the person you know so well and then try and transmute that voice onto a written page. But oral language and writing are very different forms of speech. I've noticed sometimes that journalists today sit you down, turn on the tape recorder, and what comes out the other end when it's published is the raw transcript. I find that really disappointing, because for me, the difference between raw speech and written media should be acknowledged, understood and respected.

With *Eruera: the teachings of a Māori elder*, it was even more challenging to write because Eruera would always switch into Māori when he wanted to talk about tribal history, for example, or traditional matters. So not only did I have to try and capture the quality of his English, which was different from Amiria's, in the edited text, but I also had to try and translate his Māori into that idiom. Also, as a leading elder he sometimes ventured into areas where I didn't feel comfortable as a young Pākehā woman with three small children. He lived habitually in a zone where ancestors would speak to him, he'd see signs around him. He lived habitually in a tapu zone. And I felt that my own expertise and my own experience and knowledge weren't adequate to the task of translation at times. So Eruera ensured that we conducted our sessions under tapu conditions: we stayed away from food; we talked in seclusion; we had karakia; we had incantations at the beginning and end of each session.

Like Amiria, he wanted his book to be written, even though by that time I had three children under five. You can imagine what that was like, trying to write a book of that kind under those conditions. But he wasn't well. He was getting on in years and feared that he might not survive to pass on his knowledge and the things he wanted to say to a younger generation of Māori, his main intended audience for that book. By the time it was published, Jeremy and I and the children had gone to England. I was on leave at the University of Cambridge. But Eruera was absolutely thrilled by the way it was received and when it won the joint first prize in the Wattie Book Awards that year, he was elated. Although in the meantime Amiria had died, leaving him desolate.

I'll never forget the award ceremony that year. It was right in the middle of the 1981 Springbok Tour. The country was in ferment. I remember Geoff

Chapple making a passionate speech. He got, I think, the third prize on that occasion, but took the opportunity to make a powerful speech about the Tour in the opening part of the Awards. Then when the University of Auckland awarded Eruera an Honorary Degree in Literature for his wisdom and insights that we'd captured together, and Ngāti Porou raised the roof of the Town Hall with a haka at the graduation ceremony, it was absolutely unforgettable. Afterwards at their house in Amiria Street, Eruera played the piano and sang love songs in his soft, slightly hoarse voice. He and Amiria had a bit of a sparring relationship at times, they sparked off each other, but he missed her terribly and before long, he also died.

So with Eruera and Amiria both gone, I had to try and find my own feet as a writer. I didn't realise how much they'd shaped and guided, not just my career as an academic and a writer, but also my life and our family; they were godparents to our children. We saw a lot of them. After their deaths for the first time I didn't know what my next book would be about long before the last was finished. When the idea for a new book had come, it tumbled out of our experiences together, especially on marae with Eruera and Amiria.

While I was on leave at the University of Cambridge in 1980-1981, I had a degree of temporary distance from my own country. I could see the way that I was approaching anthropology, that task of exploring the worlds of other people, was very different to my peers in Cambridge. I could also see that New Zealand was somehow different from other settler societies. For all of our flaws, at that time in the late seventies and the early eighties, we were beginning to struggle with the reality and consequences of our shared history with Māori. My collaborative style of anthropology, wanting to make sure that the voices that spoke out of the books of Eruera and Amiria were their own voices, I think grew out of those struggles.

When Eruera and Amiria both died, I was lost for a time. After a while, I found that I wanted to go back to the beginning and try and trace how the relationships between Māori and Europeans had evolved, and write a history of those very first encounters, that saw the people on the beaches and behind the palisades as just as human as those on board the ships. It seems obvious, but then it was a huge intellectual effort to grasp how such a two-sided history might be written. The old unilateral ways of understanding and describing the past in the Pacific — they're still all around us, I would say — as a triumphal progress of European expansion, were so deeply ingrained, not just in scholarship but in our culture in general, and in Britain and those heartlands of Europe. It was extremely difficult to imagine an alternative. It took me a long time to try and wrap my head around it. It wasn't just a matter of the right time or the right place or the right words then, but the right thinking. At the same time, I was trying to learn a brand new discipline, which was that of working with documents instead of with living people.

Because I had no historical training, I invented some research methods of my own. For example I took a Xerox machine [photocopier] and copied the logs and journals to a standard size. Then I cut up these Xeroxes into accounts of a particular day or an episode and pasted them onto A3 sheets, with three columns on each sheet, one for each log, and lined up the account of each episode and each day side by side. I might have perhaps ten or twelve accounts of the same episode or the same day, lined up on these sheets along the floor or the kitchen table. It worked brilliantly. That's still the way I work when I'm working with this kind of material, because I can read right across and get a sense of each of the writers of those manuscripts. I can compare them with each other, and pick up the details and in my mind enrich the event from all these different accounts told from different perspectives. Then it was a matter of trying to distil this into a narrative. I also kept meticulous archive books, which have been invaluable in letting me retrace my footsteps through archives around the world, and make sure that I have found every surviving document from a particular voyage. And that's probably why the books are quite detailed, and the ones on voyaging and exploration are fairly long. Einstein once said, 'A little knowledge is a dangerous thing.' And so is a lot — I think Geoff Walker, my publisher, would agree with that at times!

At the same time, I was looking for images from the voyages. If you spend a lot of time on marae, you get used to being surrounded by visual richness, by the carvings of ancestors, their graphic presence, and I wanted to have that sense of visual immediacy in my books if I could. I've been very lucky that publishers have always let me put lots of pictures in the books. One of the surprising things that happened was that I started getting vivid and marvellous reactions from artists, especially New Zealand and Pacific artists, to these books. So, I was often (and I still am, which is wonderful) invited to exhibitions by artists who have read one of my books, looked at the pictures and been inspired to create a series of works. People like John Pule, Michael Tuffery, Peter Ireland, Marion McGuire, quite a few over the years have got in touch with me. I'm always amazed at what they've done with the material that was there in the book. If you didn't know, you would find it difficult to retrace their imaginary footsteps back to that particular book.

And so, I think that readers should not underestimate how important their feedback is to writers. During those long hours in front of a pile of manuscripts, or these days the computer screen, or out in the field, or trudging through documents and archives, you always have in mind that your aim is to reach out to other people. When a reader gets in touch and you realise that a book has entertained or moved them, or made some kind of difference in their lives, it's incredibly rewarding and very encouraging.

So, the line of enquiry that began with my first book about the meetings of Māori and Europeans proved to be very fertile, like a kind of gold seam, running deep into the ground. I've written a number of books now in that vein, attempts to realise two-sided histories of voyaging and discovery: *Two Worlds*, and *Between Worlds*, about the first encounters between Māori and Europeans in New Zealand; *The Trial of the Cannibal Dog* about Captain Cook's Pacific adventures and the people he met and who shaped him in the Pacific; and recently *Aphrodite's Island*, about the European discovery of Tahiti, and in which Tahiti itself and the people are the heroes; and most recently *Bligh*, about William Bligh, and his Pacific excursions, including the mutiny on the *Bounty*, which is being edited as we speak.

I think I've just about finished that 'two-worlds' saga. I have the sense that this particular line of enquiry is ready to be set aside, but it's been such an adventure writing those books, visiting the places that the explorers went to, getting out on the water wherever possible, photographing, meeting the descendants, time travelling, sitting on Taputapuatea Marae, wishing I could talk to Tupaia, the high priest navigator, going out in a crayfishing boat in Tolaga Bay/Uawa, coming ashore, and thinking of the Te Rawheoro school of learning, just up the hill, going out in a small boat with one of my brothers in 2000 when the tall ships came into Gisborne and hearing them all creaking and flapping around us, just to get that sense of what it was like to be amongst them out in the water.

When I started writing *The Trial of the Cannibal Dog*, I discovered the novels of Patrick O'Brian about the eighteenth-century Royal Navy, and since then I've been trying to use novelistic techniques in writing history, although constrained by the evidence. O'Brian was a fantasist — I've read biographies about him — but his grasp of life on board those ships is fantastic and meticulously researched, and he knows how to spin a great yarn.

And so, all through my writing career, I now see, I've continued to read voraciously, trying to learn from other people who know how to conjure up a world on a page. Like many other writers, I'm sure — like many of my fellow writers here, all tribute to you — I polish and polish. I've learned that if you want to write books you have to be disciplined and you have to be patient. There is inspiration, but you also have to nail your feet to the floor sometimes. It takes time, it takes space, so that you can free yourself from everyday life for a while. And I always think of Virginia Woolf, *A Room of One's Own*, and think how lucky I've been in my life because Jeremy and the kids have been extraordinarily patient with me over the years. It can be lonely writing books, and it can be frustrating. It's easy to get lost in the middle of all those pages, and you don't always know how other people are going to read what you've written. So I try to get people whose opinions I respect to read my manuscripts long before they go off to the publisher, and to give me honest feedback, about both content and style. I just say, 'I want you to give me a really tough read. Have I got it right? Where did you get bored? Where's it wrong? Does it jar? How can I make it better?' I think all writers need that feedback before they encounter the wider world of readers. It's good having a bit of warning in advance from people who you know and trust and who will be relatively kind.

For my next venture I'm attempting a 'one-world saga' of Māori life just before European arrival, I'm part of an expert team and some members of the team are here tonight. It will be based on all the surviving evidence about life in Aotearoa New Zealand and it will be a new kind of challenge. Werner von Braun, a scientist, said something that I rather like: 'Basic research is what I'm doing when I don't know what I'm doing.' And that sense of jumping off into something new is brilliant. So, I love writing. And it's an enduring art form, which is fortunate.

As I said at the beginning, I love books. The texture and weight of them, their portability, the fact that you can read them in the bath. You can even drop them in the water then dry them in the airing cupboard, which happens to some of my books sometimes. I like being able to annotate them in pencil. I'm afraid a bibliophile would be horrified by the state of my library. I'm not sure that ebooks will ever have quite the same sensuous qualities. I'm sure if you drop your ebook reader in the bath, there will be a different kind of outcome. The Internet has transformed research almost entirely for the better, making it so much easier to talk with colleagues around the world, find documents and images, and enrich the story. And for me, I'm looking forward to what might come next, and the only thing I'm sure about is that it's going to be a total surprise.

Nā reira i āku rangatira, ka nui āku mihi aroha ki a koutou katoa. Tēnā koutou, tēnā koutou, tēnā tātou katoa.

2011 ALLEN CURNOW

Landfall in Unknown Seas

The 2011 festival theme was 'Landfall in Unknown Seas', in honour of poet Allen Curnow. This year there was no keynote address, but an extended session on poetry and a panel discussion on New Zealand's longest lasting and most respected literary journal *Landfall*, started in 1947, and named after Curnow's well-loved and well-known poem.

'Landfall in Unknown Seas', commissioned in 1942, was extraordinary for its time, addressing nationalism from the perspective of a first encounter culture clash, challenging the memory of the past, and taking a swipe at the smug colonial who pinned on the past like a self-congratulatory decoration.

Many lines from Curnow's poems have entered the New Zealand lexicon, including, 'Not I, some child, born in a marvellous year, / Will learn the trick of standing upright here.'

At Allen's last public performance at Going West in 2001 poet Glenn Colquhoun said, 'Allen Curnow is a man who holds within his arm-span the history of modern New Zealand poetry'.

Robyn Mason, Going West Festival

LANDFALL IN UNKNOWN SEAS

The 300th Anniversary of the Discovery of New Zealand
by Abel Tasman, 13 December 1642

I

Simply by sailing in a new direction
You could enlarge the world.
                              You picked your captain,
Keen on discoveries, tough enough to make them,
Whatever vessels could be spared from other
More urgent service for a year's adventure;
Took stock of the more probable conjectures
About the Unknown to be traversed, all
Guesses at golden coasts and tales of monsters
To be digested into plain instructions
For likely and unlikely situations.

All this resolved and done, you launched the whole
On a fine morning, the best time of year,
Skies widening and the oceanic furies
Subdued by summer illumination; time
To go and to be gazed at going
On a fine morning, in the Name of God
Into the nameless waters of the world.

O you had estimated all the chances
Of business in those waters, the world's waters
Yet unexploited.
                  But more than the sea-empire's
Cannon, the dogs of bronze and iron barking
From Timor to the Straits, backed up the challenge.

Between you and the South an older enmity
Lodged in the searching mind, that would not tolerate
So huge a hegemony of ignorance.
There, where your Indies had already sprinkled
Their tribes like ocean rains, you aimed your voyage;
Like them invoked your God, gave seas to history
And islands to new hazardous tomorrows.

II

Suddenly exhilaration
Went off like a gun, the whole
Horizon, the long chase done,
Hove to. There was the seascape
Crammed with coast, surprising
As new lands will, the sailor
Moving on the face of the waters,
Watching the earth take shape
Round the unearthly summits, brighter
Than its emerging colour.

Yet this, no far fool's errand,
Was less than the heart desired,
In its old Indian dream
The glittering gulfs ascending
Past palaces and mountains
Making one architecture.
Here the uplifted structure,
Peak and pillar of cloud—
O splendour of desolation—reared
Tall from the pit of the swell,
With a shadow, a finger of wind, forbade
Hopes of a lucky landing.

Always to islanders danger
Is what comes over the sea;
Over the yellow sands and the clear
Shallows, the dull filament
Flickers, the blood of strangers:
Death discovered the Sailor
O in a flash, in a flat calm,
A clash of boats in the bay
And the day marred with murder.
The dead required no further
Warning to keep their distance;
The rest, noting the failure,
Pushed on with a reconnaissance
To the north; and sailed away.

III

Well, home is the Sailor, and that is a chapter
In a schoolbook, a relevant yesterday
We thought we knew all about, being much apter
    To profit, sure of our ground,
No murderers mooring in our Golden Bay.

But now there are no more islands to be found
And the eye scans risky horizons of its own
In unsettled weather, and murmurs of the drowned
    Haunt their familiar beaches—
Who navigates us towards what unknown

But not improbable provinces? Who reaches
A future down for us from the high shelf
Of spiritual daring? Not those speeches
    Pinning on the Past like a decoration

For merit that congratulates itself,

O not the self-important celebration
Or most painstaking history, can release
The current of a discoverer's elation
      And silence the voices saying,
'Here is the world's end where wonders cease.'

Only by a more faithful memory, laying
On him the half-light of a diffident glory,
The Sailor lives, and stands beside us, paying
      Out into our time's wave
The stain of blood that writes an island story.

Allen Curnow

Permission to reproduce 'Landfall in Unknown Seas' by Allen Curnow, courtesy of the Copyright owner Tim Curnow, Sydney, and Auckland University Press

2012 PETER WELLS

Almost Always: Never Quite

Almost always, never quite. I was sitting in the New Zealand room of the Tauranga Library last week and I was looking through some missionary correspondence, all handwritten, since it came from the 1830s through to the 1860s. I was given the benefit of being an accredited researcher, in that I could look at the letters themselves and not the nightmare of microfilm — one of those supposedly modern interventions of the 1970s, which almost always was going to improve things, but never quite actually did.

In the 1980s, libraries all over the world cut newspapers up so they could be microfilmed, but the fact is newspapers show more signs of lasting longer than microfilm, which is problematic, and that's by way of an irony on how things improve by going backwards — the universal law of almost always, not quite.

Sitting in the library, I became aware of the endless pilgrims coming in seeking genealogical information. I couldn't help but overhear and be amazed at the almost saintly patience of the librarians, as they coaxed the shreds of information into a deeper reality. For example, I overheard someone say they were looking for a great-grandfather, 'What's his surname?' 'Smith' said the person, 'he lived in London'. Not to be put off, the librarian went off to find some information. Behind all of this is the global search for roots, from the popular television series *Who Do You Think You Are?* through to the Waitangi Tribunal researchers. The quest to find a track back into the past seems universal.

In New Zealand's case, and in the case with Pākehā, the research has a certain poignancy because of the huge fracture line, which is migration. This fracture line is so acute, so severe, and so deep that for many people it is a difficult act jumping back over time to reconnect with a past in a 'Motherland' which is now a foreign country.

There are many reasons for this difficulty. Those who left were often poor, they didn't necessarily write letters — those beautiful bounties from the past — but maybe even more so, the sheer effort in creating infrastructure once you arrived on these islands spectacularly lacking in industrial and Pākehā material culture: no chairs, no windows, no chimneys, no trains, little meat, no liquor and no opiates. The sheer grinding effort in making a living in such a tough environment meant you always looked forward, not back.

There were also the psychological difficulties in encountering another culture so rooted here and with an extraordinarily different understanding of just about everything. Migration wasn't easy. It was incredibly tough. You could say, for probably two to three generations, Pākehā suffered a profound culture shock. So now, so many generations later, the trail has essentially gone cold. Staying in touch with the past for Pākehā, has been problematic. Memory has not been valued. At most it is meant to be consigned to a symbolic handshake.

Then there are the winds of change — the cultural revolution of the last 40 years has reframed the past as we once understood it. Today all nineteenth century Pākehā are considered criminal racists and all nineteenth-century Māori wonderful freedom fighters, whereas, of course, history is more smudged, there are no straight lines. Which is where 'almost always, never quite' comes in useful with its sense of equivocation and uncertainty.

This evening I'd like to look at this sense of 'almost always, never quite' through the lens of Pākehā migration, beginning with my own from Auckland where I was born — I grew up in Point Chevalier — to Napier where my mother's family came from.

Almost always when I come back to Napier, I feel I've come home, but never, quite—I'm never quite a local. I'm almost always someone who blew into town. Most people know me down there not as an author who writes obsessively about Napier in book after book, or who went on a very long and enjoyable walk with William Colenso in *The Hungry Heart*, wherein I sat down and talked with the ghost of a giant with fascinating things to say to us today about the shaping of our shared past, but — in the only town on Earth that gave Maurice Gee the sack when he was town librarian — as something a little weird: a tour guide of the bone yard.

The Old Napier Cemetery is in a beautiful position, high on the highest hill, so it would be closer to heaven. William Colenso is buried near its gates. The cemetery is right beside the Botanical Gardens and is alive with tūī and wood pigeon. I started taking tours about four years ago to go with a museum exhibition which proved enormously popular. And ever since then every time we advertise a tour they fill up quickly. As I look at the faces on the tour, I sense their yearning to know a past which their ancestors were almost always a part of, but now they can never quite squeeze through the narrow politically correct keyhole of the present.

What is a graveyard but a library of stories — each headstone hiding or illustrating the drama of a human life? I tell them how hard colonial life was. There was no social security; if you lost your job, your family went hungry. If the breadwinner died, often the family faced poverty. The paupers' part of the cemetery is where people were buried without headstones or any markers. There was no penicillin. Many people died astonishingly young, or they just vanished to another town, leaving loved ones behind, while they went off in search of work.

My own New Zealand ancestors on my mother's side lie in this cemetery. The man who made the jump from Cornwall (thank you), his son, my great-grandfather — who made the family money and then blew himself up as a thank-you note — and other skeletal connections: two children dead from typhoid; a death working on a ship; a premature baby, and all their silent dreams and aspirations; enfolded lies and lives lived, as Thoreau said, 'with quiet desperation', all silent now.

Evidence is here in the graveyard of the major catastrophe which shaped my mother's family's life, the quake, the shake. In in the mosaic of shattered headstones lie parts of the past, shards recollected or left in the lurch; silent reminders of a violent past. And sometimes you need to remember that more people died in the 1931 Hawke's Bay earthquake, in a much smaller community, than in the recent disaster in Christchurch.

This brings me to the core of my talk, which is catastrophe, being an eyewitness to it and what that does to you, how you remember it, and how catastrophes like quakes, floods and terrible wars have shaped the New Zealand character, or perhaps the character created by their sheer hard graft conditioned them to 'almost always' cope with catastrophe, but 'not quite'.

What I am going to be talking about is a flood which occurred in 1897 in Hawke's Bay. On the evening of Friday April 18th 1897, when the Ebbett family sat down to tea they heard a low but pronounced rumble. It was the Hastings train, they thought, and went back to eating their meal. But when they glanced out the window of their house, they saw an astonishing sight. As far as they could see there was water. Water covered everything and it entirely surrounded their house. What was more, it was rising with remarkable speed; one foot became three in a matter of seconds. It had been raining now for over 24 hours, the long drought of 1896 had at last broken, and from Thursday midnight the incessant rain begun falling, accompanied by gale-force westerlies.

Floods had been a regular occurrence over the past decade, 'crippling industry and thoroughly disheartening settlers,' wrote the *Hawke's Bay Herald*. 'The latter have no sooner had an opportunity of recovering from one flood, than they are visited by another.' Geoff Park could have provided the reason why the floods were worsening in changing wetlands into pastureland. A whole ecosystem was abruptly altered. The slower filtration of multi-threaded streams and rivers, surrounded by wetlands full of vast toetoe, had helped slow down the coursing water and mop up the excess. But by the end of the century, much of the wetlands of Hawke's Bay had vanished.

Now the rivers, once they became flooded and broke their banks, could pour with astonishing speed across a flat landscape of pasture. And this is what happened on the evening of Friday the 18th of April, ironically, Good Friday. All over the province that Friday people recorded hearing a frightening *boom*. 'At first it was thought to be a roll of thunder, but the sound gradually approached,' wrote Napier's *Daily Telegraph*. 'Increasing in intensity until with a mighty gush, an immense body of water surged across an already swollen river, clearly indicating that the protective bank at Meeanee had given way.'

In little more time than it takes to relate, the turbulent waters swept into the township of Napier, filling up the department store of Neil and Close, ruining their fresh shipment of tobacco; into the cellars of Robert Holt's timber mill to the depth of six feet; rushing into the shop of Mrs Sutton, milliner, and ruining all her stock. Shop after shop along the main street was invaded by water. 'It seemed but a moment,' the *Hawke's Bay Herald* wrote, 'and the whole of the locality was submerged. Articles of furniture were floating about the rooms of residents. In many cases children and women mounted chairs on tables, while the male members of the family sought means to rescue them from their perilous position.'

Out at Clive, the small township closest to the river mouth, the situation was acute. Clive was as flat as a pancake and people began climbing onto roofs. 'We never had the slightest idea that we were in danger,' said one woman, 'the thing happened so suddenly, and the waters came upon us with such a roar and a rush that all we could do was climb onto tables.'

In another house, an elderly man fought to push and pull his paralysed wife into the roof space as the waters came closer and closer.

Soon the whole of Clive was submerged to the depth of nine feet, about three metres, and all over Clive families began abandoning their houses. The only place of refuge was a raised wooden bridge, spanning one of the rivers. They made their way in the storm, amid floating furniture and frightened animals, to the bridge. The rain was gathering in intensity, along with the wind. Waitangi, next to Clive, and where William Colenso's mission station had been, was ground zero of the disaster. All the rivers came together with astonishing force. Nearby was a whare in which an elderly man, a Pākehā, called James Broadbent lived. He was asked to 'leave his position to occupy a point of greater safety,' but he shouted back that he preferred to stay where he was. Shortly after the sea swept over the place and must have carried the whare and Mr Broadbent out into the ocean. For 'not a vestige of the whare or of Mr Broadbent has been seen since', the *Hawke's Bay Herald* reported.

The express train from Palmerston North, with 150 passengers aboard, stopped on the Takapau Plains as the waters rose all around it. Passengers prepared to bunk down for the night, some simply abandoned the train and began the trudge through the storm, along the tracks to the nearest township. The express from Napier got as far as Pakipaki, on the outskirts of Hastings. Onboard was the Wanderers' Bicycle Club, bound for the Whanganui Athletic meet on Easter Monday. When they passed over the bridge across the Waitangi River, they noticed 'the river was running very high while the low-lying lands were rapidly assuming the aspect of inland lakes … it was not 'til a sudden jar through the train when about a mile and a half beyond Pakipaki told that the brakes were applied, that any uneasiness was felt. The train came to an abrupt halt, and it was seen that the rails were covered for a distance of two-hundred yards with water. The situation was freely discussed, and … It was therefore deemed not advisable to proceed.'

Two men on a trolley went back to Hastings for instructions and, 'Hour after hour passed away and no news came, while the water deepened in front and the situation became more serious.' At last, at half-past five the train slowly began to proceed back to Hastings, 'Many stops had to be made on account of the critical condition of the rails.' Once back to safety, a rush was made for the hotels. The cycling team, turning their competitive streak to advantage, 'managed to obtain a sitting room with a piano, and a lengthy programme of songs made the evening pass pleasantly away.'

Not so for the men, women and children huddled miserably together on the Clive bridge, 'with water to the right and left of them and with no means of escape', the women drenched to the skin, the children crying and the water surging as it dashed under the bridge. The entire riverine basin of 100 square miles, over 25,000 hectares, had become a raging torrent, 60-square-miles wide, and roaring along at vast speed, removing anything in its path. Fifty-thousand sheep were drowned, caught against fences and trees or simply swamped and pushed and pulled with enormous force out into the ocean.

Meanwhile, the last wire came out of Clive on the Friday evening: 'For God's sake send us some help' And, 'that was the last telegraphic news received from Clive,' said the Hawke's Bay Herald. In Napier, the mayor, Mr G.H. Swan, asked for the train to get its steam up. By now it was near evening and he quickly gathered together a rescue party of ten men. Two boats were put on the train and the train steamed slowly out towards the epicentre of the disaster: the Waitangi rivermouth.

When the train from Napier got out to Waitangi however, the river had become an unrecognisable universe. 'For miles around, as far as the eye could see in all directions, was a huge expanse of water. The river waters met the sea at the breach, and the thunderous roar of the breakers as they dashed through the opening will never be forgotten.' The boats were lowered, and the train returned to Napier, picking up further boats and returned to the scene with further help. An hour had passed but everything had changed beyond recognition.

On arriving back there, the men on the train found that the final stopbanks had collapsed, and it was surmised that with the first burst of the floodwaters, the rescue boats, 'they together with their unfortunate occupants were swept out to sea, beyond the reach of human aid. Only those who have visited the scene of the disaster can realise the extent of the washout, and the certainty of the fate of the men comes home with force.'

The men and women and children on the Clive bridge meanwhile, had been rescued by other men in boats and ferried away to safety. But as for the missing men, 'Intense anxiety reigned throughout the town on Saturday night concerning the fate of the rescue party who were reported to be missing. A rumour gained currency during the evening that they had reached Clive and were all safe ... however, this proved false.'

On the 20th of April, two days later, a sombre announcement was made in the newspaper:

> There is now no shadow of a doubt as to the drowning of the two boats' crews who went to the relief of the settlers. There is not even a vestige anywhere of any portion of the boats, nor had any body been washed up. A lookout has been kept in all directions but we regret to relate without any result. The names of the drowned men are as follows:
>
> **NO 1 BOAT**
>
> Mr A. McCartney, licensee of the Albion Hotel, wife and four children.
> Mr F. Ansell, carpenter at Mr R. Holt's mill, wife and six children.
> Mr H. Brierly, wheelright at Mr G. Faulknor's factory, married, no family.
> Mr F. Cassin, clerk at Mr M. Lascelles's auction mart, wife and four children.
> Mr John Rose, commercial traveller ... family unknown.
>
> **NO 2 BOAT**
>
> Sergeant O'Donovan, four motherless children.

Constable Stephenson, wife and four young children.
Mr J. Prebble, son of Mr W. Prebble, fruiterer, married, no family.
Mr H. G. Oborn, employed by Messrs Kirkcaldie and Stains ... single.
Mr G. Chambers, blacksmith, at Gleeson's, single.

Only four bodies were ever recovered. Two were found out by the Pania Reef ten days later, floating among animal carcasses and presenting 'a shockingly mutilated sight'. Days later a further two bodies were recovered from the sea. The town, the region and the country went through a convulsion of grief. The Honourable James Carroll, the acting Postmaster General, noted that of the ten men who drowned, 'most of them left widows and children entirely without support and funds are urgently needed to meet their pressing necessities.'

The day after the discovery of the first two bodies, funerals were held. These were enormous and elaborate Victorian affairs full of pomp and ritual. Two brass bands played at the front of the funeral procession and 3000 people lined the streets — everyone wore black. Hats were taken off as a sign of respect as the cortège passed along, and vast crowds walked up the steep hill to the colonial cemetery and surrounded the graves where with a final emotional ceremony, a farewell was held.

The deaths seemed to touch a raw nerve, for in the deaths lay the valour of colonial existence, of a people dwarfed by landscape, by forces so much stronger than them. But how to formalise, make sense of, pay homage to, and recall, the bravery and loss of life? These were men who had of their own volition offered to help. How? Why? Whether they thought seriously about it, or whether in the moment of need they simply laid everything aside, we do not know. But for those left behind came the need above all to concretise, to make palpable, to show the world and to themselves that they would never forget and so, most human of all, validate the urge that they would never be forgotten; and the silent whisper within, that memory never lasts. This led to the creation of a magnificent monument on the Parade in Napier: the Clive Flood Memorial.

So, jump cut to 2012 and a weird wanderer, me, a visitor from another time and place, comes to Napier and finds this remarkable thing on the Parade. What is it? How did it come to be there? I love monuments. They're like frozen emotions coming from another age. Unfreeze them and within them lies something very real. And if we look at the ceremony surrounding the opening of this grand memorial, a monument vast in scale at 36 feet high (11 metres), it tells us how these immigrants, newcomers to the landscape, evoked their own gods and history and tried to make sense of what had happened to them.

When the Clive Flood Memorial was unveiled on Thursday the 26th of September 1900, that is three years later, the speaker strained to evoke the overpowering scale of that sad, fatal and fateful day. As the Dean of Waiapu, the Very Rev. De Berdt Hovell said, 'As the dense darkness came down, all the waters, sorrow, affliction and distress invaded every soul.'

It was the speed with which vast volumes of water raced over the plains that gave a sense of the overpowering force of nature. As lines from a contemporary ode said about the disaster:

> The waters racing wildly o'er the fen,
> Resistless on their raging course to sea,
> The flood defied obstruction, and these men
> Were launched into the great Eternity.

It was this 'howling waste of water', its blind anarchic force, which people talked about again and again. 'The majority of our drowned brethren were never seen again,' the Dean said at the unveiling. 'The sea gave us back some few of them, but the greater number lie there,' and here the Dean pointed to the sea. 'The ocean is their vast and wandering grave.'

What about the ceremony? What does this tell us about how these immigrants saw life? If it were a ceremony today, this event would have been preceded by Māori ritual with its own curious mixture of indigenous and migrant Christian culture.

They were memorialising too an event in which these immigrants had to come to terms with the power of local landscape and weather. Hence the rituals employed symbols drawn from the rich European culture these migrants had left behind or rather had brought with them as important tools of cultural survival. The music performed by the City Band, one of several local brass bands, was based on a magnificent piece of Handel's operatic music from Saul, the 'Dead March', used in the funerals of British monarchs. When the mayor's wife, in a traditional division of gender roles, 'turned on the water' of the fountain, since the monument had a practical use, the Band played Harwood's *Vital Spark*, that was based on an Alexander Pope poem, *The Dying Christian to His Soul*, and this in turn was based on a poem which the Roman Emperor Hadrian wrote when he was dying in 138 A.D. In English:

>Roving amiable little soul,
>Body's companion and guest,
>Now descending for parts
>Colourless, unbending, and bare
>Your usual distractions no more shall be there

In essence then, on the Napier foreshore one has elements of a rich thread which fingered its way back through the magnificent baroque of Handel to an ancient Judeo-Christian tradition, Saul and David, and then back to the lyric skills of a bisexual Roman emperor, who had lived in Britain at one point and was instrumental in promoting Hellenic civilisation in Rome.

There was also a nod to the local, the limestone for the monument. It was a local manufacture, or local mining, and the rituals involved local greenery too. The greenery tells its own strange story of mixed metaphor and place, for it included *Camphora officiallis* from Japan, weeping willow from Great Britain, cabbage trees from New Zealand and greenery from trees from California, Portugal and Labrador, all tied together with New Zealand flax.

And why a monument? As the Dean explained, 'In all ages and amongst all nations it has been the custom to commemorate in some permanent way the illustrious dead.' And the Very Rev. Dean Grogan added, 'If you go into the great cities of other countries' — and here one feels he is addressing the children of immigrants, people so divorced from their parent culture they no longer know how things are correctly done — 'you will find monuments in all the public places. They are there as teachers, educators, in a certain sense schoolmasters ... And this monument has its lesson — and what does it teach?' The message is simple: self-sacrifice, 'Greater love hath no man than this, that a man lay down his life for his friends.'

But was there a strangely mixed message in creating this monument as a fountain? That is, we remember men who drowned by drinking water. Or is it that the best way to recall ten good Samaritans is to put some cool water in your mouth on a blazing Hawke's Bay summer day? — the architect of the fountain must have been a dog lover, as he also created a small area for thirsty dogs. In this it represented immigrant values, Victorian civic values, an ideal of improvement, but inside the fountain lay a document, like its secret heart; and this was a time capsule.

So, what was the message to everyone in the future? One was a narrative of what had happened on that terrible evening of Friday, April 18th, when the ten good Samaritans laid down their lives for the greater good in an abstract ideal as old as Homer. But there was another document and this document interested me. This was, 'The balance sheet of a Hawke's Bay flood fund and other articles', the other articles are left enigmatic, but I'd like to think of humans of the future nodding and tutting at who in Hawke's Bay gave money, and in what amounts, and who didn't. There was an unsubtle air here of small-town retribution, which is entirely recognisable. The bottle was 'chemically prepared', we are told, so as to 'prevent water entering it, which would render the documents worthless'. Quite.

The Clive Flood Memorial in all its glory is still an imposing monument today. But then we come to a complete disjuncture or fracture line in the story, because up at the colonial cemetery are the actual graves of the four found drowned men. The headstones are budget, there is no swagger; no words even saying who they are beyond their names and the dates of their deaths; almost an anonymity. Did the money run out? Was so much spent on the splendiferous monument down the road that there was nothing left over? For the reality of where their battered bodies lay — almost always visitors, never quite at home — there's a kind of pathos to me in these humble graves. One in particular piques my sense of never quite-ness, of almost always being a stranger here, for John Rose didn't live in Napier. He was a commercial traveller, resident in Melbourne, travelling for a Sydney company which sold furs. He just happened to be in Napier on the night of the flood, a stranger in a strange land, as he was called. He's the one person not in any of the local photographs. He's the tenth person.

But he, staying at the Albion Hotel, heeded the call for volunteers. Was he in the bar? Had he had a few? Or was he a stranger in town dangling before his own irrelevance, and in a chance moment — alerted to danger — he came into his own, inhabited his skin, found an errand which expressed his essence, and so joined the ghostly crew? How brave, foolhardy — or is this what we call courage? First out of the bunker up on the hill, standing upright saying, 'I am human, too.' Then, the roaring rage of a taniwha, snapping and snarling and demanding its own — so the commercial traveller infers, and lowers himself into the broiling mass and disappears. His wife changed in an instant into his widow. Two children turned orphan and forever the silence, and the asking of a question, 'Why? Why you? Why there? Why then?'

The fountain no longer weeps, its waters no longer flow, and people forget, can no longer carry the burden of remembering. While up the Hill, his bones lie forgotten except by me and now all of you sitting in this room in a penumbra of remembering; and so, memory lives on. What is a graveyard but a library of stories and this is one of them: migrant, foreigner; colonial, first-generation jumper of the space who never quite made it home, almost always, never quite. But at home here now.

Almost always, never quite. Almost quite, never always. Home.

2013 CHARLOTTE GRIMSHAW

In Conversation On Conversation

Thank you very much. Thank you, it's great to be here. My mother is a Westie and I feel that I'm a Westie too and I love coming out here. I was told that my talk tonight should address the topic, 'In Conversation On Conversation' and I've taken that to mean that I can pretty much cover whatever I like. I'm going to start by mentioning some of the subjects that I've been interested in as a writer, but although I'm starting with my own preoccupations, this isn't going to be a talk all about me because my intention is really to talk about broader topics, and some of the issues I think we should all be concerned about as writers and readers.

I'm going to string a lot of subjects together. And I think I'll start by listing the ideas that have preoccupied me as a fiction writer, so this might seem quite a random collection.

How do I write novels about contemporary New Zealand, for example, while at the same time indulging my horrified fascination with Nazis? And how does an interest in the meaning of buildings find its way into my short story collections? I feel that there's a logic and an order and a sort of connectedness to my fixations, and yet they're disparate enough to allow me to start their inventory with a sewer pipe and end with the whistleblower Edward Snowden. So how do these things fit together? I can only hope that this will all make sense. Let's begin with the sewer pipe.

When I was a child growing up in Auckland, one of my favourite places was the sewer pipe that ran for half a mile from the bottom of our street across Hobson Bay — some of you may remember it. And if you asked me to list the things I loved as a child, near the top would be the sewer pipe. It was only when I recently contemplated calling a new novel *The Sewer Pipe*, that I was forced to consider what the words actually meant. You can imagine the worried faces in the marketing department. How are we going to sell this and what are we going to put on the cover? It had barely occurred to me that sewer pipe would have a negative connotation because the words had lost their literal meaning, and the pipe didn't represent to me what it actually was, which was a conduit for storm water and sewage. Instead it was a loved place, it was rich in memories. And this sewer pipe, or the pipe, as we called it, was part of my childhood world in Parnell, that included Hobson Bay and Tohunga Crescent.

Hobson Bay had the magical quality of being two places at once. At high tide we could canoe and fish, and we made rafts and floated them and sailed them, and at low tide it became an expansive exposed mudflat that we could walk out on. The pipe was a drain encased in concrete with a flat top, and it was mounted high on legs so that it made a narrow causeway on which you could walk, or even ride a bike. It crossed from Parnell all the way to Orakei. It didn't leak, as far as I know; the water was clean and at high tide it was fringed with pōhutukawa and was very beautiful. The bay was described by Allen Curnow, who lived in our street and who used to swim there and walk his dogs there. One of my favourite Allen Curnow poems, 'Spectacular Blossom', describes the kind of flowering pōhutukawa tree you would see at the bay in summer (although the poem pre-dates his life at Tohunga Crescent) and here are some lines:

> ... So many suns she harbours
> And keeps them jigging, her puppet suns,
> All over the dead hot calm impure
> Blood noon tide of the breathless bay.

In my high school years, I walked across the pipe every morning to go to school at Selwyn College; it was an endlessly visual presence for me. When a person walked along the pipe and you were looking from a distance, the seagulls would rise in front of the person and fly overhead and then settle behind, making a wave. The pipe has gone now, it's buried underground, but it's still very vivid to me and I see it as an example of the way the physical landscape imprints itself on the mind, and also the way that landmarks can transcend their everyday meaning, and become an amalgam of associations and memories, just as words and names can.

My earliest perception that structures can be symbols, that they can stand for something else, was based on my consciousness of the emotional evocative significance of the pipe. When I was a teenager and I used to walk across the pipe every day — I was also in the eccentric habit of going for long walks around the city. I used to walk from Parnell to Avondale if I was bored. And I liked to play with the idea of the city as simply topography, to imagine that the buildings no longer carried meaning as buildings, that they were just bits of landscape like hills and mountains and valleys. I liked the idea of divorcing buildings from their meaning because I was preoccupied with what their meaning actually was, and with what our physical landscape means to us and shapes our psychological terrain.

I had a number of other central preoccupations. I wanted to write fiction and experiment with plot — I was interested in politics and I was preoccupied by the way people in society related to each other. And in the same way that I imagined divorcing buildings from their identity, I thought about social relationships and imagined divorcing them from their traditional mores and expectations and values. I imagined deconstructing them as a part of trying to understand their construction. It makes me sound slightly autistic, doesn't it?

I can't remember exactly when it was, but one day someone in our family brought home a book by Albert Speer and it was called *Spandau: The Secret Diaries*. It was Speer's account of the 20 years he spent locked in Spandau Prison, and I found the book fascinating. I began to look for everything that I could find about him. I didn't quite understand at first why I found him so compelling. But I think somehow it was because the elements that shaped his extraordinary life seemed closely related to my own sort of strange preoccupations.

Speer was the German architect who, through a series of chance encounters, fell into company with Adolf Hitler when Hitler was about to become the Chancellor of Germany. Speer was eventually given the task of designing Hitler's dream city, which was to be the world capital, Germania, and the seat of power for the thousand-year Reich. Speer was captivated by Hitler. He was one of the few people who could be said to have been the Führer's close friend and it was even remarked that Speer was Hitler's unrequited love. Hitler eventually made Speer his wartime Minister of Armaments and, for a time during the war, he was arguably the second most powerful man in the Nazi regime.

As Hitler's architect designing for the new Nazi capital, Speer produced plans that would have shaped — had they been carried out — the city of Berlin into a material expression of the social landscape, a manifestation effectively of the tyrannical collective will of the time. He believed that he was an artist and, because of this, that he was above politics. And so he was a man who rose to vast power. He was called a genius and of course he ended up disgraced, a war criminal, a prison inmate, a failed artist but a talented writer. He was interested in everything that I was interested in: art, politics, criminality, free will, great historical events and possibly, I felt, clues to the mysteries that I was trying to unravel about the connections between planes: the physical and psychological, the social and individual, man made and natural.

The deeper question in all this, the question I think I've always been asking, is about liberty. To what extent on each of these planes are we free? At the Nuremberg trial, Speer successfully defended himself against the death penalty by arguing that he hadn't known about the systematic murder of the Jews. He engaged in what has subsequently been recognised as the reprehensibly cunning tactical manoeuvre of condemning instead of defending the Nazi regime and admitting a generalised complicity in atrocities, while at the same time neatly removing himself from specific complicity in genocide.

When the War was coming to an end, Speer had defied Hitler's scorched earth policy. Hitler's reasoning was that if the German people had lost the war, then they didn't deserve to live. And therefore he decided that the country's infrastructure should be destroyed and ordered his generals to blow up bridges and burn cities, to destroy power and transport networks with absolutely no mercy for ordinary German civilians. Speer defied Hitler's orders, covertly at first and then as the regime began to crumble, more overtly.

So he risked his own life to save Aryan Germans. The fact that he defied Hitler was a significant factor in persuading the court at Nuremberg to spare him the death penalty. Speer's mind, what you could call his internal landscape, inevitably became the subject of study. What was the real extent of his complicity in the crimes of the Nazi regime?

He set about answering the question in his own way. After being arrested and convicted at Nuremberg, and during his 20 year imprisonment in Spandau Prison, he began to write books. The first manuscript was written on scraps of toilet paper and smuggled out of the prison. He recorded how he rose to the position of Reich Minister in the Nazi regime and gave detailed accounts of life among the top echelon of the Party. He also wrote a vivid and often quite moving diary of the years in Spandau, during which he kept himself sane with, among other things, an imaginary project where he measured what was there — a large prison garden, then set himself the task of 'walking around the world'. He planned an imaginary route across the world and calculated the distances he would need to walk across each country. During his daily circumnavigations of the prison garden, he intensely imagined that he was crossing a particular country. He used maps and atlases to help him and he recorded the distances that he'd walked each day — his equivalent of walking around the world. His mind became the whole world and within it he could be free.

When he finally got out after 20 years in prison, he'd walked a distance of 24,000 kilometres. It was an extraordinary feat of imagination and mental and physical survival. In the course of describing in his books how he became this shameful thing, a top Nazi, he gave full attention to his guilt, or he *purported* to. There's a significant degree of subtlety in Speer's representation of his guilt, because beginning at Nuremberg his confessions were also his life-long statement of defence. Reading his mea culpa over a number of books the reader can witness and assess the force of his survival instinct; his desire to admit only so much; his ability to spin in his favour; his brilliance, his charm, his smoothness, his careful evasiveness, sometimes — often, actually — his raw honesty. And over the top of that his dishonesty, his 'big lie', because in the end it has to be the case that he knew about the murder of the Jews and didn't do nearly enough about it. The books are an inspection of the mind of the worst kind of criminal.

His great talent was his imaginative skill in conveying his story to the reader. He was a natural writer. He had the ability to draw the reader right inside his experience and to make it real, to convey his emotions and fears, and his doubts, and weaknesses. Because of that skill, and because of his strange and unique combinations of honesty, self-justification and self-preservation he has in his books — despite his attempts to evade — he's laid bare. Other people have written books about him as well of course, so he is laid bare. How many people who have risen to the top in a totalitarian regime have actually written about how it happened? It's pretty extraordinary.

His books constitute this fascinating human study and like everything to do with the Nazis, it's a horrible warning. Because Speer was given the commission to re-design the whole of Berlin and the world capital, Germania, his story involves the relationship between our inner selves and our environment, between our psyches and our cities, because he set out to express in architectural terms the ethos of the Nazi regime. To shape the crazy megalomania of Hitler into tangible materials, the designs for Germania were everything that you'd expect of buildings that were designed for a totalitarian regime. They were despotic, militaristic, cold and intimidating. In fact, Speer's father was shown the models for the city and said to Speer, 'You've all gone completely mad.' There was overblown grandeur, gigantism. There were avenues lined with tanks and guns. There was a dome so vast that it would have dwarfed St Peter's Basilica in Rome. Speer designed an office for Hitler that was so enormous that Hitler said, rubbing his hands together, 'By the time the visitor has crossed such a vast expansive of floor he'd be terrified.' Significantly Speer actually realised much later, that he had actually failed to take human scale into account. The enormous dome would have been too large to be used for any kind of meaningful gathering or audience. They *had* all gone mad.

In my fiction I've always tried to explore the link between physical and psychological terrain. So, if the humble sewer pipe was a totem for me as a child, then the terrible city of Germania stands as a dark fantasy. It's a menacing symbol of the link between material and psychological buildings as a metaphor for the mind. In the title story of my collection, *Singularity*, I quoted a piece from Lampedusa's classic novel, *The Leopard*, in which there's a vast palace of abandoned rooms, 'dark and sunny rooms, apartments sumptuous or squalid', into which two of the characters venture further and further until they risk being lost, and in there they find what the writer calls, 'the sensual cyclone'.

I think this is a powerful image, going deep into a man made structure that holds secrets, that hides things long forgotten. The idea of going so far into a building that you're lost, could be a metaphor for madness. And there's a recurring image in my story, 'Plain Sailing', and also throughout my collection *Opportunity*, of a house being carried through the night-time streets on the back of a truck — we know that Aucklanders are famously obsessed with houses — and I think houses are naturally linked to a sense of security. I didn't think about this so clearly until after I'd written it, but perhaps the image of a dwelling completely divorced from its moorings and towed through the streets represents the flimsiness of our hold on the natural landscape all the way out here in New Zealand, and our sense of living in a small remote place.

In my novel *Soon* the state of mind of one of the characters is revealed in her dreams about houses. When her position is insecure, she dreams about broken-down, ruined houses and when her marriage breaks up she dreams of a beautiful house that she can't enter. When her life gets back on track she dreams of the most splendid, beautiful mansion, a paradise.

In a *Metro* column recently, I noted the monumental size of John Key's house in Parnell and wondered what it said about his psyche. He grew up in social housing, but look at the shape of his dreams. So, my novel *Soon* is about the close relationship between my character Simon Lampton, who thinks of himself as apolitical, and a National Party politician David Hallwright, and the emotional bond between the pair. When I wrote the book I had in mind the relationship between Hitler and Speer because I was fascinated with the relationship from Speer's point of view given Hitler turned out to be insane. Speer was a complex case, so how can a man with Speer's talents have been mesmerised by a person like Hitler? Power must have been the main attraction, but other elements came into play.

Speer seems to have entered into the friendship with Hitler in a particular spirit, a frame of mind that reflected the mood in Germany when a generation was captivated less by political argument and more by a patriotic ideal embodied in a charismatic dictator. Speer thought of himself as an artist and a technocrat and believed that he was above politics. Hitler also subscribed to the idea that Speer was separate from politics and it was this notion, ironically, that allowed Speer, the 'simple artist', to bypass a lot of political manoeuvring and move into the top ranks of the regime, eventually to take on a role that was political — the Minister of Armaments.

On the question of the artist, I'll read a quote from a book by Joachim Fest on Speer:

Speer felt that his moral indifference was justified by the prevailing image of the artist. The idea of the artist as standing outside society, not subject to any norm and moral law, had become accepted ever since the romantic movement. Although Hitler developed his programme after entering politics to fit the circumstances, he took the moral authority for disregarding any human rights to justice, freedom or happiness and for establishing a new world order from the image of the artist. By calling Speer a genius, he elevated him to the altars of art, in a way, and freed him from the bourgeois values he might have clung to because of his background.

Speer's appointment as Armaments Minister did nothing to alter his sense of privilege; it mentally moved it to another plane. Nor did people believe at the time that technology was subject to any moral standards. The technical genius was regarded as a kind of half-brother of the artist. At Nuremberg, Speer recognised that he made himself guilty by his mere proximity to politics, that was why both he, and his lawyer in particular, insisted that as an artist and as a technician he had belonged to another 'innocent' world.

Fest goes on to say in a wider context that this defence originates from the century's ideology of the special privilege of the intellectual and his supposed right not only to impose laws on reality, but also to punish it for any deviation from the ideal. This notion contributed hugely to the atrocities of the age.

When Simon Lampton, who's a character who appears in four of my books, becomes a friend of my fictional prime minister, he suppresses his natural political leanings and takes refuge in the idea of himself as an apolitical technocrat. His attitude fits with the popular mood in the New Zealand society that I've portrayed in the novel — a general turning away from politics. There's a Twitter-age devaluing of intellectual argument and a belief that pragmatism has a greater value than politics. Simon Lampton's friend, Prime Minister David Hallwright, has a special skill in particular, and that is to pretend not to be a politician. Hallwright also presents himself as a kind of technocrat and pragmatist who will solve each problem as it comes along on its own merits, and without ideology. This persona actually masks the fact that politics is alive and well in Hallwright's Government and it's an especially right-wing agenda that he's presiding over. But the images of simple, straightforward, practical commonsense, coupled with a sort of cheerful nationalism and a tyrannical relaxedness, stifles political discussion and engagement. Hallwright is permanently pretending to be relaxed about issues while at the same time making sure that he gets his own way. And there are other factors there that stifle political engagement. There's the commercialisation of the media, which causes public discourse to become increasingly superficial and fractured. There's the demise of investigative journalism in the age of the Internet and there's the rise of celebrity culture. This state of intellectual shallowness is part of the general atmosphere of the novels *The Night Book* and *Soon*.

I read Speer's accounts of the repressive banality of the conversation in Hitler's court, where an evening with Hitler involved talking about dog training, vegetarianism and movies. In my novel, Simon Lampton's brother Ford is a character who does engage in politics and he criticises apolitical Simon for his detachment. Ford's continued mantra is, 'It is not intellectually good enough to be apolitical.' This introduces a debate into the novel. One brother is hanging on to the idea that he can be above politics and the other is asserting that an apolitical stance is not enough. But it's a debate, it's not a definitive answer because it may not be intellectually good enough to be apolitical, and as a citizen I agree with Ford's statement, but at the same time I don't think it's the role of the artist — the fiction writer — to write politically. It's not the role of the artist to create a work that demonstrates a particular political line. There's a useful Chekov quote on this. Chekov was writing about Tolstoy's *Anna Karenina* and he said, 'The correct way of putting the question is the artist's duty'. He singled out *Anna Karenina* because, as he put it, 'The novel solves no problem, but it's deeply satisfying because all the questions are put correctly.'

So, the fiction writer's primary aim I think is to write rich, entertaining, page-turning stories. Good fiction can also illuminate the problems that we face and ask the correct questions. As Chekov went on to say, 'A court must put the questions correctly but it is up to the members of the jury to decide each according to his own taste.' And he meant the reader, because he was talking about the novel. He meant the reader becomes the jury. The writer presents the questions to the reader and the reader decides. The reader obviously doesn't want the court — the novel — to present him or her with the verdict because that would be a meaningless exercise.

But Speer used the role of the artist as an excuse for turning away. His lack of politics was really indifference and his art, ironically, became suffused with politics, the politics of the Nazi regime. To me his life story characterises the tension between the physical and psychological, the social and individual, and between politics and art. He was operating in a society that had severely restricted individual freedom and he designed a representation of that repressive environment, so his conformity meant that he became an oppressor. His architectural designs allowed no choice. He presented his audience with a horrible fait accompli. His creation — the city of Germania — expresses without reservation a pure and completely repulsive ideology. His mistake was to fail to question, to fail to raise questions. Instead, he forced the verdict upon his audience. His city failed as art and he failed as an artist.

His life was full of twists. Later there was art in the way that he laid bare his psychological landscape, because in his books he purported to be telling the truth about himself, but I think what he was doing was telling a story about himself. It's one in which the reader does become the jury. The reader absorbs his testimony at face value but then looks beyond it, hears false notes, notices inconsistencies; you read between the lines and ultimately you deliver a verdict on Speer, and it has to be damning.

And so Speer became an artist as a writer by attempting at least a version of the truth or by engaging with varying levels of sincerity in the questions that he'd avoided when he was hiding behind this distorted perception of the artist's role. And because he was the cleverest, most educated, most psychologically 'normal' — because most of them were really, really 'not normal'— of the Nazi elite, Speer was described by one historian, Hugh Trevor-Roper, as being possibly the greatest criminal of them all.

He was no doubt more culpable than his escape from the death penalty at Nuremberg suggested, but his progress at least towards redemption lay in this willingness, after his arrest and imprisonment, to use those talents, to use his intelligence to describe how he went wrong. And the fact that he was in part defending his position as well as admitting guilt in his books, doesn't make them any less valuable as insights into history and into the protean nature of human beings. As a human being, as an artist, Speer was a failure: he was amoral, he was a war criminal, he was also repentant, tortured, charming and a good writer. He was an example of human complexity. No-one is entirely good; few are entirely bad.

This is not to say that anything that the Nazis did was forgivable, I mean they were *unforgivable*. But I'm just saying that we can acknowledge and explore human complexity as writers, as readers, as citizens and as voters.

I mentioned at the beginning that my preoccupations as a writer have revolved around the question of freedom. I'm interested in crime because I'm interested in free will. I'm interested in politics because politics involves questions of liberty and justice, and I've always been engaged in trying to work out how these interests can be used in fiction, while keeping fiction true to itself as art. True fiction not only entertains, but it gives us insights into our lives and into the lives of others, and it should encourage empathy and understanding. But its driver has to be the imagination. Not didacticism, which would render it dead on the page, and for me, not satire because that just caricatures and mocks.

I'm writing another novel at the moment and my main hope, as it was with *Soon*, is that it will be a colourful page turner, that it will be a barrel of laughs, bursting with interesting characters and a terrific piece of entertainment. That's the hope and the aim but I also hope that down in its engine room, as it were, that it will be powered by some serious ideas. And as I said, I've always been interested in the question of freedom and free will, and I've gone on thinking about that in the novel that I'm currently writing. So that being the case, I will finish on the subject of freedom in the present day.

As we all know, the Nazi era is one of history's cautionary tales and so of course Speer's observations are relevant today. He commented at Nuremberg early on: 'Earlier dictatorships needed followers who thought and acted independently at all levels. A mechanised age however, only required and produced the type of person who took orders uncritically.'

When the accused Nazi leaders were given the opportunity to make a final address to the Nuremberg court, Speer chose not to make any further statements in his defence, but he decided to deliver a warning. It was strikingly relevant to the questions that we face today in relation to the Edward Snowden affair and the GCSB issue here in New Zealand. Just before I quote what Speer said, I read a *Listener* column recently by Bill Ralston, which was headlined, 'The GCSB bill. Yawn.' So, to answer Bill Ralston's yawn or maybe to wake dopey Bill up, here is Speer in prescient form at Nuremberg:

> As the most important representative of a technocracy which had shown no compunction in applying all its know-how against humanity, I tried not only to confess, but also to understand what had happened. The nightmare of many a man, that one day nations could be dominated by technical means was all but realised in Hitler's totalitarian system. Today, the danger of being terrorised by technocracy threatens every country in the world. In modern dictatorships this appears to be inevitable, therefore the more technical the world becomes the more necessary is the promotion of individual freedom and the individual's awareness of himself as a counter-balance.

Speer's warning was given 67 years ago and it comes from one of those periods in history that have demonstrated the meaninglessness of the mantra, 'If you're doing nothing wrong, you have nothing to fear.' Europe's Jews were doing nothing wrong and their only hope for survival was to hide or flee from a government that had been democratically elected by the German people. Speer partook of that time; he foresaw the problem of increasingly invasive state surveillance in the future and he didn't call it a yawn. He called it a nightmare. Edward Snowden, who blew the whistle on the much higher level of electronic spying that we're being subjected to now, said in his *Guardian* interview that it should be the people who decide whether they want this degree of government intrusion into their privacy.

Speer sounded the warning and now Edward Snowden has repeated it and he's drawn attention to another plane where oppression potentially affects us, the virtual. I think the question has been put to us correctly, as Chekhov would have said, it's part of that same question of human liberty that I've always had in mind in my fiction. It's one of the big issues of our time: do we want a faceless technocracy to dictate the amount of privacy and freedom in our lives? I'll continue to think about this in my fiction — it's a really important question. We are the citizens of democracies and we are the jury on this one. I think we just have to hope that it's not too late for us to decide.

Thank you very much.

2014 ROBERT SULLIVAN

'small islands of meaning'

Te Kawerau ā Maki, tēnā koutou. E te rangatira, Fred tēnā koe. E ngā mana, e ngā reo, e ngā karanga maha, e huihui mai nei. Tēnā koutou katoa.

Thanks again, Murray, for this very kind invitation to be the first Sir Graeme Douglas Orator and to Sir Graeme for this opportunity to share my thoughts. As you know, the theme for Going West this year is Charles Brasch's 'small islands of meaning'. I'm going to talk about islands and the moana or ocean, and what it means for writers from all walks, and waka and the West.

Let's start here in the wonderful West, Te Waonui-a-Tiriwa, the great forests of Tiriwa, which is one of the Māori names for the Waitākere forest here. Save for kauri dieback disease, the bush is reviving, the air is sweeter here than anywhere else in Auckland. Instead of motorways and the urban jungle, we've got bush tracks and a real forest, and the soundtrack is driven by singing birds, chirrups and water. Instead of high-rises here, we've got bush-covered ranges and views of Lion Rock or the Cascades. The Waitākeres are one of Auckland's great cathedrals, an aspirational oasis of good living, a haven for Aucklanders' hearts and souls, as much as the islands of the Gulf. Do we know this? Or is it just there, a small island of meaning? this great, green sliver from a sylvan past, where the Manukau Harbour had firm white sand on its shoreline.

When I was a kid, every Sunday Mum and Dad would drive me, my brother and sister, in our Mark II Ford Zephyr called Galloping Gertie, to Cornwallis, where we'd get enough pipis for lunch. We'd fish off the wharf sometimes, but I only remember catching sprats. We only ever caught fish in our dinghy, the *Queen Mary*. I guess these memories are small islands of meaning too, standing out in a sea of news reports and other people's memories reshaped as fiction. Before my parents bought a house in Onehunga, I remember the long drives we'd take with us kids in the back, as my parents would look at suburb after suburb, imagining where we'd all live once we moved out from our flat in Grafton. Mum and Dad were dreaming out loud.

Some of the homes were way out West, on the way to Cornwallis with our pipi bucket in the boot, the house with the walls and roof made of the same wooden tiles — it's a brown one, it's still there, I think — which was a never-ending source of wonder as it slowly went up over the years, until we finally had moved to Onehunga. We lived in Grafton first, until I was seven. I painted the footpath with my feet with the hippies on Boyle Crescent. I'd like to think those hippies spent time at James K. Baxter's Jerusalem as well. The Med School was still being built with its new concrete valleys. In the School of Life building, I remember being amazed at what an echo was, and the hieroglyphics on the new Med School doors that must have said 'push' or 'pull'. I use that memory of seeing letters in a writing exercise — write a poem based on your earliest reading experience.

The Domain was our playground. There were great trees to climb and the old elevators in the Auckland Museum with their cages were good fun, too. When we went to Onehunga, it was the Jellicoe Pools just up the road, near the war memorial arch, and a little later, the public library that became the centre of my childhood.

What's the role of fiction in our collective memories? Does it work like memory or myth? I can remember when *The Bone People* won the Booker Prize. I would say that a sense of cultural tangata whenua-based memory imbues that work, especially the God canoe at the spiritual heart of the novel, whose green-pool resting place resembles īnanga, greenstone. In our second Booker Prize winning novel, *The Luminaries*, we have an echo of mauri in the idea of greenstone being collected by Te Rau Tauwhare, on the West Coast. More importantly, there's a sense of collective history here, where we've been in the nineteenth century and where we're going. Both novels are influencing, even mythologising, our sense of collective self without announcing themselves. Both novels asserted a different indigenous presence from a settler presence. In *The Bone People*, the God canoe is buried in an earthquake, except for the little God which Joe carries away, while in *The Luminaries* it is the character Te Rau who names a difference without defining it, between the nature of greenstone and the nature of gold. Each novel references real suffering of the life-sapping colonial connection. The Chinese gold miner Ah Sook is an indentured refugee of the British Opium Wars. Anna Wetherell is a local victim of the opium trade, while in *The Bone People*, the illness of Kerewin is aligned with poor ecology and deforestation.

The Northern Irish poet Seamus Heaney wrote a book called *The Government of the Tongue*. In his Northern Irish context, to name one's politics would have been a risky business, yet of course his work can be read that way. Neither *The Bone People* nor *The Luminaries* names its political perspective, but it's there in each, under their well-governed sentences.

Janet Frame's writing could rise up out of the sea here too. So too could Anne Kennedy's wonderful poem, 'Northness', which refers to Heaney's lamenting poem 'North'. Are islands openings of meaning in a turbulent sea? Are they is-lands, to borrow Janet Frame's idea? Do they rest on cardinal points? By the way, I hope you're going to vote next week.

Is an author a small island of meaning? Roland Barthes famously talked about the death of the author, but he also wrote a follow-up, lesser-known essay, called *The Friendly Return of the Author*. 'No man is an island,' says

John Donne. We must always have connections and affinities. To bring it back to the poet and editor Charles Brasch's 'small islands of meaning', he himself has travelled the great moana and he wrote this poem set on the south coast of the Big Island of Hawai'i. It's called, 'Great Sea':

Speak for us, great sea.

Speak in the night, compelling
The frozen heart to hear,
The memoried to forget.
Oh speak, until your voice
Possess the night, and bless
The separate and fearful;
Under folded darkness
All the lost unite -
Each to each discovered,
Vowed and wrought by your voice
And in your life, that holds
And penetrates our life:
You from whom we rose,
In whom our power lives on.

All night, all night till dawn
Speak for us, great sea.

In Brasch's poem we rise from the sea like islands, yet its setting — on the Big Island of Hawai'i — is far from small, as it's possibly the tallest mountain in the world, rising directly from the floor of the Pacific, 33,100 feet — more than 3000 feet higher than Everest. Less than half of Mauna Kea rises above sea level. It's a strange thing to see snow in the tropics, but that's how the volcanic peak of Mauna Kea is covered and depicted by Hawai'ians: as the Goddess wearing a white lei of flowers on her head. Yet, we know that the island is part of a chain resting on volcanic seamounts, stretching from the far north to the yet-to-surface Lōʻihi Seamount, south of the island, slowly rising over eons. It's expected to surface in 10 to 100,000 years. This pace is a planet's rhythm, not a human one.

Perhaps we are more like snowballs than islands. In 2008, not long before our family returned to Aotearoa, we visited Kalapana at dusk, where you could see a river of lava hit the sea. We were kept a kilometre away, but the ribbon of light was incredible. Now the crater inside the National Park is filled with glowing lava again, and a subdivision is threatened. When you experience stone as liquid, this notion that islands are solid things comes into question. We know this in the Shaky Isles.

Our voyaging ancestors knew this too. Micronesian star navigators continue to use 'etak', or moving islands, and 'pookof', the travel habits of sea creatures and signs of nature, as forms of navigation. With etak, the person in the voyaging canoe imagines that the islands are moving, rather than the vessel moving. It's a strategy that reminds us that the ocean's moving. Ben Finney, in an article in the *Journal of the Polynesian Society*, says, 'Without charts or instruments, the palu, or Micronesian [master] navigator uses a mental plotting system called etak.' He envisions the island of departure and the target islands moving, unseen, beneath the horizon. A third island or reef off to one side of the course becomes his reference point. Imaginary paths radiate from the canoe through the reference point to the stars beyond, dividing the voyage into segments or what they call etak. By visualising the reference island moving under a succession of stars, the navigator mentally structures his voyage.

Knowing the stars ain't easy. If your culture is without writing, such feats of memory learning are a matter of life and death. The Caroline Islanders for instance, had a 32-point star compass, which was the most elaborate recorded in the Pacific. It was aligned on the star Altair, at 81.5°. Which means it looks slightly off to Westerners used to true east.

The great Micronesian star navigator Mau Piailug taught these positional stars to the Hawaiʻian navigator Nainoa Thompson, and guided him on the journey of the deep ocean waka or what they call vaʻa, *Hōkūleʻa* from Hawaiʻi to Tahiti in 1980. Thompson merged Papa Mau's techniques with some of his own to read the stars. By moving his forefinger and thumb, he could work out his latitude by aligning his knuckles with the star Polaris. If Polaris has an angular height of 10° from the northern horizon, then the observer knows that they're 10°north. Thompson would also make observations in nature. One of these was in Tahiti, where he discovered paired stars set simultaneously, only at particular latitudes. Part of Thompson's brilliance is that he received traditional training by Papa Mau, and he then went on to memorise hundreds of rising and setting star positions using the Bishop Museum planetarium in Honolulu, spending all night in the planetarium, and also out in the night sky. *Hōkūle'a* is in Samoa at the moment; the ambition is to circumnavigate the globe.

According to the anthropologist Ben Finney, these oral feats of memory are even being replaced in the Caroline Islands by note-taking on paper rather than circling 32 pieces of coral in a canoe house. I've visited the atoll Chuuk in the Caroline Islands, about 2000 miles north of Queensland. It's a beautiful place. I was there with an election observation team from the East-West Centre in Hawai'i. What struck me about some of the islands fringing the lagoon, apart from the World War Two wreckage, are hundreds of curious kids in the families living without electricity. Everywhere was the ocean. You had to use a boat or you couldn't get anywhere. I also remember drinking kava from Palau and 'talking story' with the other observers: Americans; Koreans; Fijians and other Micronesians. It's the expanse of the ancestral achievement that stuns. It inspired me to write my poetry collection *Star Waka*.

The great navigator, James Cook, remarked that the spread of Polynesians from Hawai'i to New Zealand was the achievement of a nation. Epeli Hau'ofa, the pioneering anthropologist, described the Pacific as a sea of islands, and that rather than belittling islanders as tiny, that islanders traversed the ocean as traders and families. These small islands of meaning, were joined to many others and it was the sea that enabled the journeys. To quote Hau'ofa's seminal essay 'Our Sea of Islands';

... if we look at the myths, legends and oral traditions, and the cosmologies of the peoples of Oceania, it will become evident that they did not conceive of their world in such microscopic proportions. Their universe comprised not only land surfaces, but the surrounding ocean as far as they could traverse and exploit it, the underworld with its fire-controlling and earth-shaking denizens, and the heavens above with their hierarchies of powerful Gods and named stars and constellations that people could count on to guide their ways across the seas. Their world was anything but tiny. They thought big and recounted their deeds in epic proportions ... Islanders today still relish exaggerating things out of all proportions. Smallness is a state of mind.

To return to Nainoa Thompson, in 1984 he decided to voyage to New Zealand. Since the guiding stars in the far south were much harder to track than in the tropics as they hugged the horizon, he asked for help from New Zealand's own star navigator and master waka builder, Hekenukumai Busby, or Hector. Hector helped him memorise the stars in the far north of Aotearoa. He would drive Nainoa up to the lighthouse at Cape Reinga, from his home in Mangonui. He'd sleep in the car while Nainoa studied the stars there, and then Nainoa would sleep in the car at dawn while Hector drove back to Mangonui. At Cape Reinga he said he could see the east, the west and the northern horizons. Nainoa also learnt some of the myths and legends of Kupe, such as to steer to the left of the setting sun from Hawaiki when the pohutukawa blooms.

Nainoa first navigated *Hōkūle'a* to New Zealand in 1986. The name of that vessel, by the way, is the zenith star sitting above Hawai'i, called Arcturus. According to Nainoa Thompson's account on the Polynesian Voyaging Society website, the plan was to sail from Hawai'i, via Tahiti, to Rarotonga, then to the Kermadecs and then from there to Aotearoa.

On the journey from Rarotonga they spotted Alpha and Beta Centauri on the horizon, which they thought was the right latitude for the Kermadecs, and started moving to the west, when they sailed into a pod of whales. One whale surfaced and nudged them to the south with its tail, luckily without damaging *Hōkūle'a*.

A squall rose up in the north with thick cloud down to the water, so they gave up looking for the Kermadecs and headed south. They sailed into a thin layer of mist, so they couldn't see the stars, except for Jupiter and Venus, with lightning all around them. At dawn there were shouts from the crew. They had reached the Kermadecs. These islands had meaning for the crew. It meant 450 miles to reach Aotearoa. But it also meant for Nainoa that ancestral connections were being reforged, and he felt pride in the achievement of hardy Polynesians, who went as far as the Auckland Islands at 50° south without heavy weather gear. It also found meaning in the guiding myths of an ancestor, Kupe, who also relied on whales to guide his journey a millennium ago.

After finishing his study of the stars, and before Nainoa's ocean journey here, Hector Busby drove Nainoa Thompson back from the Far North to the Bay of Islands airport at Kerikeri. He wept when he farewelled Nainoa's family.

Not long afterwards Hector built the great voyaging waka *Te Aurere*, inspired by the feat of the Hawaiians and a call from Sir James Hēnare, who was also inspired by them. And not long after that, many of the Polynesian nations assembled their voyaging waka at the great Tahitian marae temple, Taputapuatea, on our ancient Hawaiki, the island of Raiatea, known as Laniakea in Hawai'i, and Rangiātea in New Zealand.

Is that what an island of meaning is? A point of land with a zenith star? A whale and a legend for encouragement? An ancestral home? Are islands of meaning beyond the colonial realm? Are they posters for the posts of post-colonials? Do islands of meaning write back? What would Kerewin Holmes or Alistair Lauderback say? 'Dew, bubbles, dreams, lightning and clouds', says the Dalai Lama. A leap from dew to bubbles to clouds and lightning is a poetic leap. It's how a poem moves, the same way a heart does. Part of the success of a poem is the pace of crossing between images. A short poem is a threshold to be crossed by a reader or a listener. As with a threshold, one does not know before the crossing what lies on the other side, or as Allen Curnow says in his poem, set here on the West Coast, 'You Will Know When You Get There':

> ... A door
> slams, a heavy wave, a door, the sea-floor shudders.
> Down you go alone, so late, into the surge-black fissure.

Or in Curnow's tercentenary poem on Tasman's 1642 discovery — and it's also a threshold poem, 'Landfall in Unknown Seas':

> Always to Islanders danger
> Is what comes over the sea

Or in the same poem:

> Simply by sailing in a new direction
> You could enlarge the world.

Meaning takes time, just like love. Islands of meaning are time-saturated, like names. The ocean that washes up on its shore has been doing so for aeons. When a beach is called Karekare, we know there is the heart's wild surf. The trees thrusting up into the interior have names like father, Te Matua te Ngahere. The birds nesting there, the bull kelp on the shoreline, these have meanings far beyond the names of our species.

Keri Hulme's Moeraki poems remind us that humans are not the only important beings, and that these islands of meaning rise up for midges and whales alike. Going west, like the Southern Cross hugging the horizon, is the gift of a forest, the sound of pounding Karekare Beach, or Galloping Gertie shifting down a gear going up a hill.

Hulme's poetry is also full of spirits, ghost-riddled middens and cemeteries. Perhaps it's in these edgy coasts where we can relate to the spiritual, as these leaping places lead to the beyond. Another ghost poem, Hone Tuwhare's 'Pupurangi', is written from the point of view of a deceased kauri snail. It's a very grand account of the snail's existence, full of swish and élan, as it travels through the forest with its conical house on its back. We discover that the snail no longer breathes because the kauri giants on which it depends have disappeared. Is Tuwhare's snail an island of meaning? This creature is as vulnerable as the tree in his iconic poem 'No Ordinary Sun', filled with post-nuclear blast imagery. A threshold we thankfully haven't crossed. In his poem there are no more islands because the ocean has disappeared, revealing a drab seafloor where the tree of life's end at last is written. The poem reminds us of the holiness of poetry, that our holy books are composed in verse and that the nature of our feelings held up in poems have the quality of greenstone, life force, of our better selves. It's also the perfect moment for a reality check from T.S. Eliot, 'Do I part my hair behind? Do I dare to eat a peach?'

Reina Whaitiri and I have just finished editing *Puna Wai Kōrero: an anthology of Māori poetry in English*. It's the third poetry anthology we've worked on together, beginning with the Polynesian poetry collections, *Whetu Moana* and *Mauri Ola*, which we co-edited with Albert Wendt, published by the wonderful Auckland University Press. We dedicated this first historical and contemporary anthology of Māori poetry in English to Hone Tuwhare, who did more than any other poet to champion the cause of Māori writing and to open many doors for others after him. Tuwhare's great friend, the artist Selwyn Muru, gifted us the title of the anthology, which roughly means 'the wellspring of speech'. Wai means water, but it also refers to the 'wai' in waiata, which means song-poetry, or reflecting water, or wairua or spirit.

The cover art comes from the artist Reuben Paterson, who's known for his glitter kowhaiwhai, and whose murals are in the Auckland Art Gallery. Selwyn Muru's title also reminds me of Tuwhare's title *Deep River Talk*. Unlike the first two anthologies from Polynesia, for this Māori anthology Reina and I decided to go deeper than the contemporary poetry. We went back as far as we could to find poets writing in English who had Māori whakapapa. So far the earliest one happens to be the most prominent scholar and leader of modern times in Māori life, Sir Āpirana Ngata, whose, 'A Scene from the Past' appeared in the *Auckland Star* in 1894. It describes a mighty gathering and the passionate welcome expressed through the haka pōwhiri. It was obvious to us that Ngata's poem should be first, given his status and his own anthologies which collect the sung and chanted poetry in te reo Maori, *Ngā Mōteatea*. His voice connected the traditions in Māori with those in English. To quote from 'A Scene from the Past':

> Ha! your blood is coursing now!
> Ha! your spirit's roused at last!
> Ha! the welcome rings out clear!
> Powhiritia atu! Haere mai! Haere mai!

In this poem Ngata brings the past into the present. He quotes from haka, describes the vigour of action songs, and in the celebration raises our awareness of the lifegiving value of such assertive expression repeated through the term, 'ha', or breath. He urges the ceremonial welcome of pōwhiri to continue and calls out the welcomes, and this revival continues today in the Māori language and cultural programming of Māori Television. Ha! It's all about connection, the ritual of pōwhiri makes social connection an easier thing. Ha! We hongi and share breath.

Many poets since Ngata have written in English while incorporating elements of te reo Māori and culture in their work. For instance, Arapera Blank, one of the Māori writers published in the 1950s by Erik Schwimmer's Māori Affair's magazine *Te Ao Hou*, writes in her 1986 poem, 'Rangitukia soul place':

> Home-made bread in the *Gisborne Herald*
> pork-fat mixed with golden syrup
> kānga waru pudding with clotted cream
> grandma saying, Ka mau te wehi!

And further on in this poem:

We are inheritors
of interwoven dreams
whose pāua-shimmering music ever
echoes on the wind.

The image of shimmering pāua reminds me of a fishing lure. I'm no great fisherman. My proudest feat was in the Scouts when I speared the only legal-size flounder one evening by lamplight, a complete fluke. And here I am still boasting about it more than 30 years later. Yet this pāua-shimmering music is the stuff of memory and of beauty and connection and contentment. The shimmering pāua is happiness. We have a saying, 'Kia hora te marino, kia whakapapa pounamu te moana, kia tere te kārohirohi,' which is just an excerpt from the beautiful whakataukī our Kaumātua Fred Holloway shared with us today. The anthology represents great and small memories, all of our possible feelings. This anthology is a vehicle traversing and diving and skipping inner and outer waves. Ngā kare a roto me ngā karekare o te moana. We wanted to bring out the connections between us as we do when we bring our memories of our families crossing the marae ātea/threshold into the meeting house. We wanted you to see us in our complexity, with all our love.

Islands of meaning are ones where other people matter. They are where the home fires burn. Charles Brasch began our beloved journal *Landfall*, where so many writers found their voices and the gathering tides of a New Zealand literature. I say this in gratitude: after *Craccum*, *Landfall* was where my work first appeared. Thanks to Michele Leggott, who is guest-editing Issue 161, and now our students at Manukau Institute of Technology are reaching that milestone. To borrow an idea from Rilke, *Landfall* is part of the design of every New Zealand writer's life, along with [the literary magazine] *Sport*, somewhere to seriously consider sending work, and because of that seriousness it turns on a writer's soul.

The Going West Festival is a personal milestone too, another '*Landfall*' for New Zealand writers. For a young writer Going West is a pōwhiri into the community of writers that we have. It brings us together. We're made to feel we belong here, with all those luminaries that we'd followed from afar, and we cherish those memories. I got to say thank you to Michael King here at Going West. Back in 1984 he spent two whole weeks with some Māori sixth formers interested in journalism. He was really keen to see us succeed. It was my first foray into the writing world, or rather, the reading world. I read *Being Pakeha* that year, along with *Potiki* and *The Bone People*. If there's a thread among the three books, it's that we belong here. You belong and I belong. That's part of what makes those books interesting to us.

A few years ago I visited Anzac Cove and the Somme, and then this year, just a few weeks ago, I visited Auckland Museum's Hall of Memories. And as usual, like many here, I looked for the names of my relatives, my grandfather's older brothers, and found meaning there. As a Scout the Anzac Parade was a big deal. We'd march with the veterans up the mall, along Grey Street, into Jellicoe Park, past the war memorial arch to the honour roll outside the pools. Wreaths would be laid. The *Last Post* would be played. Families would line the street, watching. I remember the parades as happy. I remember the community and how we made that our main value. A hundred years after the first Great War, and still too many wars after that one, we honour those men and women who died so we could raise our questions and make these islands meaningful.

And finally, here is a poem I wrote, called 'Arohanui':

Big love, that's what it means.
Aroha Nunui means huge love.
Aroha Nunui Rawa means very huge love.
Aroha Nunui Rawa Ake means bigger very huge love.
Aroha Nunui Rawa Ake Tonu
     means bigger enduring very huge love.
Aroha Nunui Rawa Ake Tonu Atu
     means biggest enduring hugest love,
which are some of the lengths and times of our longing.

Ngā mihi.

2015 STEPHANIE JOHNSON

Holding the Line

Kia ora everyone. My topic for this evening is 'Holding the Line'. In her most recent novel, *The Wolf Border*, the British writer Sarah Hall has a character think to herself, 'No-one is without choice. No-one is condemned to be changeless.' This sentiment is pertinent to our theme, Holding the Line, because the thing about lines is that they change: lines of war; lines of argument; lines for actors; lines in the sand; lines of cocaine — all are mutable.

And one line we all know that has not changed, that is held out here in West Auckland, is by one Murray Gray, who has manned the ramparts of Going West for 20 years. His continued devotion to this festival has enriched and delighted thousands of readers and offered support and nourishment to hundreds of writers. To you Murray, with gratitude. And on behalf of us bookish people, I'd also like to thank Naomi McCleary, Anna Fomison, Robyn Mason, Penny Hartill and all the Going West team, including those who volunteer their time and effort, for what is the oldest writers' festival in Auckland.

In 1996, when I was in my mid-thirties, with my second novel *The Heart's Wild Surf* clasped under one arm, I ventured out to the Corban's

Estate to attend what was the inaugural festival. I remember an enthusiastic pōwhiri, a large, dark cavernous space and lots of discussion and laughter. It was mid-winter and outside our breath frosted but it was warm and welcoming inside. I was on a panel with the famous Westie, Debra Daley and the soon-to-be famous Emily Perkins, who was there with her first book *Not Her Real Name.*

At question time, Emily fielded a question from a young man who asked her if she took a tape recorder to parties since her recall of conversations seemed so alarmingly precise. Since then I have attended this festival, both as an audience member and a guest. On one memorable occasion I was on one of the famous Going West trains stopping for readings at various locations along the way: a lady poet, newly in love with an historian, read a poem about how her discarded bra lay on the floor while they made passionate love; a prominent Aucklander of 'Scoots' descent, whose ancestors had lost their land in the Highland Clearances, thought he might return, and make a land claim; the artist and potter Barry Brickell inspected the structure of a restaurant, while we ate at a table below, he prowled the beams above our heads — I treasure a vase he gave me as a present that evening. All of us have anecdotes to share.

At Going West we are fed not only with words, but with beautiful food, much appreciated by half-starved writers. I applaud the current Going West exhibition, and I think it's high time that the memories of Going West were collected and published before they fade with time.

Lines then, the holding on to them, and the letting go. In New Zealand we have public figures such as politicians Richard Prebble, Paula Bennett and the current [2015] prime minister [John Key], who were nurtured by our once highly regarded cradle-to-the-grave social welfare system. We can all presume, as writers and readers, and students of the human heart, that at one stage of their lives they were glad of their warm beds, free schooling and healthcare. Let us imagine for a moment we are writing a novel about such a person and lines are appearing in front of us as we type or wield a pen.

Here is our character. John is a common enough name, so let's call him that. Here is John as a small boy in 1968, in his grey school shorts and jersey, his scuffed brown Roman sandals, with his lunchbox and bottle of bright orange Quench, busy trying to stuff his New Zealand made rugby boots into his cardboard school bag. Here is his mother at the kitchen sink, washing the Creamoata pot and telling him how lucky he is that the line extends from the soft sand to the hard and encircles him, that his health and success at school will be taken care of by the State, his teeth filled and his vaccinations given. Or perhaps the scene is different. Perhaps little Johnny's mother is grubbing potatoes from the frozen soil and warning him not to end up like her, dependant on the State. Perhaps she is sad and a little embittered, lonely and trapped and she tells him he must work hard, make lots of money and not be foolish enough to share it with malingerers. Whatever, she gives him a political line to follow. For our purpose, let it be the first mother with the porridge pot, who cautioned gratitude and generosity.

What happened to make him change his mind? Why did his line change? As writers we must give him a scene or scenes where that motivation is given, where we give the character the necessary stimulus to think another way and force the line on the graph to the right. Did he sit beside a smelly, unloved and homeless man on the bus and think, 'I won't end up like you.' Did he visit the warm, loving home of a school friend whose much older father had come back from the War too damaged to work and sponged off the State thereafter, or so his uncle possibly told him, as he worked a 40-hour week in a badly paid menial job.

Or is our character a child called Paula, young enough to grow up after the introduction in 1973 of the solo parent's benefit? This little girl is a flappy ears, hanging around the grown-ups. She hears a conversation about a woman with children to more than one man, who drinks too much, who smokes pot, who is on the benefit and she thinks how wrong that is! She listens to talk about how welfarism has damaged Māori, how people must be taught to shift for themselves and, in the absolutist mindset of some children — there really is a monster under the bed — she decides that if she ever has the opportunity, she'll pull the ladder up after her.

Or should we meet instead a fully-grown man called Richard, sitting at his desk and contemplating the carefully accrued wealth of the nation — the railways, printing offices, mines, dairy factories and forests — and thinking of the short-term gains and selling it all. What punitive delight rises in his heart as he begins to disperse our carefully shepherded wealth to the four corners of the globe. Such a reversal in his political line would have to have deep roots, or what they call in writing formulae, foreshadowing, which good writers do anyway without knowing the word for it. Let's say Richard is a deceptive person who has only ever paid lip service to the policies of his party. He forgets for a moment, as many governments have since, that he is our servant and not the other way round. He sees the hard work of our ancestors and the sense of community that they hold dear as something to be dispensed with. Perhaps he is sitting by the fire reading *Atlas Shrugged*, one of the most dangerous novels of the last century. Or did he change his politics for love, let a blue seep into the pink, merging his colours, entangling his lines and confusing my metaphor?

Let us abandon for a moment our confused characters, who were mostly born in the mid twentieth century, and leap ahead to our future, where today's preschoolers are in their thirties, say 2045. It is interesting to speculate whether or not the spectrum of left and right still exists, or whether it has been discarded in favour of corporate governance, following on from the neo-liberal, so-called transitional governance of today. Are they reading books, this generation? Do they find pleasure in absorbing themselves in lengthy narratives? Where do they go when they want to escape? Do they regard book-length works as TLDR (Too Long Didn't Read) because after all, YOLO (You Only Live Once) and linear stories are boring. What is fiction if it isn't linear? Now and again reviewers and publicists extol a novel for its revolutionary form, for its challenging of all the accepted forms: anti-narrative; interactive; but on inspection sometimes disappointingly these novels are still what they have always been: lines on a page, with intersecting webs of meaning and connection running in the subtext.

In a scene in my novel, *The Writers' Festival*, a five-year-old girl swipes the window of the car with one finger, as her mother drives along, as if she's flicking through Tumblr, as if the window is a screen and she's shifting the image. It was something my daughter observed on trams in Melbourne more than once and since the publication of the book, I have heard of other children doing the same thing. Is it just play? Or is there in fact a major revolution taking place in the way human beings perceive the world?

We hear often that the market is apparently demanding seamless transition from cyberspace to the real world, that we want the line blurred by wearable technology in the form of smart watches, or tiny mind-reading devices inserted in the ear that advertise products or forge connections based on existing personal data, or cyber-spectacles controlled by movements of the eyeball. Is it a deep-seated human desire for indolence that is powering these developments? Or is it more a deep-seated loneliness that has us crave constant communication with others, instant and easy?

When I was a teenager in the seventies, as labour and commerce underwent increasing mechanisation, there was a momentary prediction that we would eventually evolve to have tiny little wasted bodies and giant heads. Now it seems even our giant heads will not be necessary, not to serve our memory, since we no longer need to commit anything to them. In previous centuries we would be in awe of the work of certain writers, marvel at the breadth of their knowledge and understanding. Now we have the Google-novel, where it is sometimes apparent that the writer's knowledge of his or her period is only skin deep, where facts have been sourced as needed, the lengthy reading of tangential research material that yields a richer comprehension of how folk lived is not in evidence.

The World Wide Web brings with it far-reaching changes, not only to our traditional understanding and respect for good memories, but also to our notions of privacy, courtesy and identity. The nature of conversation has changed. No longer do we need to argue about a date or who said what or sang which song. Go online and you'll know in a jiffy. It is no longer considered rude to send a text or scan or email or Twitter while we're in flesh and blood company. Whole families sit about texting. Cafés are silent. Recently I went to a noisy cafe in Byron Bay Australia, which had a sign on the wall, 'No we don't have WiFi. Talk to each other.' Hopefully this will catch on.

What about those intersecting lines of communication about what these intersecting lines of communication are doing to our own computers, the ones that we are born with in our brains? Around the world neuroscientists are beginning to send out warnings. Last year the British neuroscientist, Dame Susan Greenfield published her book, *Mind Change*. In it she maintains that she and other neuroscientists are seeing physiological changes in the brains of children and young people, changes that she directly associates with frequent use of social media. Just as London cabbies with the knowledge, famously, had swollen parts of the brain that hold working memory, the hippocampus, neuroscientists are seeing larger amygdala in the brains of young people who spend hours of every day online. The amygdala is the part of the brain usually linked to emotionally charged memory, emotional behaviour and motivation. She writes, 'Research has found that the grey matter density of one particular brain region, the amygdala, was linked to social network size in the real world and also correlated with the subject's online social network size.' We know that the brain is plastic that it will adapt to any given environment, real or cyber. And what is this rapid, shallow engagement doing to our thought processes? Greenfield talks of thought having a beginning, a middle and an end in a specified linear sequence in a cause-effect chain. To quote:

> All thought, be it fantasy, memory, logical argument, business plan, hope or grievance, shares this basic common characteristic of a fixed sequence. And since there is clearly a defined beginning, middle, and end ... there has to be a timeframe. As I see it, this idea of sequence is the very quintessence of a thought, and it is the mental steps needed that will distinguish a line or train of thought from a one-off instantaneous emotion captured in a shriek of laughter or a

scream … if you place a human brain, with its evolutionary mandate to adapt to its environment, in an environment where there is no obvious linear sequence, where facts can be accessed at random, where everything is reversible, where the gap between stimulus and response is minimal, and above all where time is short, then the train of thought can be derailed.

Needless to say Greenfield's book is controversial and not least so with the industries now clustering around the high-tech honeypot. There are vast sums of money to be made from every stage of human life, iPads that attach to the cot, through to gadgets that record geriatric heartbeat and urine flow and lodge the data in the Cloud.

I don't want to get too side-tracked into talking about the Web, because like most of you I have welcomed it into my life and revel in the beauties it affords us. Apart from my own entertainment and research, I'm grateful for the emergence of online pressure groups like Avaaz, Action Stations, SomeOfUs and Getup! These are the protest lines we will increasingly march behind. When millions of signatures worldwide can force a corporation to delay or even halt some planet-destroying activity, when governments can be pushed into not signing deals with Shell, and Monsanto can be shamed, these are wonderful expressions of democracy at its best. No wonder many commentators suspect that the top-secret TPPA [Trans-Pacific Partnership Agreement] includes a section on regulating online protest.

What does little Johnny carry in his schoolbag now he's all grown up? Where he once carried a crayon picture of Captain Cook or a hunter shooting a lion, does he now have files of legal advice on dismantling indigenous and environmental law? On how to untangle the Treaty, how to outlaw protest? Off he goes with Timmy Groser, playing at big boys to sign us all away.

Now I'm sure that amongst you all there are some National Party voters and I don't want you to feel out of place, and so to that end I've invited along my fellow writer, Amanda Tauiwi Reinhardt Carlton, who is the inaugural National Party Poet, not to be confused with C.K. Stead, the Poet Laureate.

Some of you might have seen her on Facebook or heard her read before. Amanda has the health and wellbeing of the current government close to her heart and she's going to read two poems. Only two. So just wait one moment while I go and find her.

[Stephanie Johnson dons the persona and voice of Amanda Tauiwi Reinhardt Carlton with wig and accessories]

Good evening everybody. I am Amanda Tauiwi Reinhardt Carlton and I am the inaugural National Party Poet. I was selected by Julie Christie. I'm sure a lot of you are very jealous because I get rather a lot of money. And since we are in a reflective mood this evening, I'm going to read two poems from early in my career as National Party Poet and this is a poem I wrote out of love for the party in the last elections:

Elegy for What We Were
When I was a gel Holyoake was PM
and I loved him. How I loved him for his name
Holy Oak — the lovely way he spoke,
his funky platform shoes.
For the first twelve years of my life
the tiny kindly King of the land was Holyoake.

In Remuera and Fendalton and Kelburn and Maori Hill
summer lawns were mowed, there was tennis
in the afternoons, gin and tonic on the terrace.
Around the Sunday table the middle classes debated
care for the sick, the poor, the elderly, the necessity
of education for all, the 'socialist' ideal.

How strange to find us now, led by a man called Key
who would unlock it all, let it ebb away.
Just lately, when among the Party faithful, I see the ghost
of Kiwi Keith, red-faced, choked
on Slater's slime, sickened by Whale Oil's
hacker pals, the lies, corruption, deceit.

Oh spread your boughs over our shamed heads
Holy Oak, though you were not so perfect yourself.
You did send our boys to Nam, old man, caused a riot.
Still... this is something new, is it not?
The elevation of cruelty, celebration of mendacity.
Let us grieve for the lost heart of the National Party.

You may clap. Of course, this hasn't always been this bad. In 2013, our Prime Minister made a glorious visit to Buckingham Palace and the resulting photograph, which I saw was in the *Herald* again this morning, was beamed all round the world. And this is a poem that I wrote. Like Harry was asked to write a poem when his friends were getting married, I was asked to write a poem about John's visit to the Queen, September 2013:

I was nervous John, I admit
about your visit to The Queen.
I thought you might embarrass us all
but not at all it seems — not at all!
She's my cousin, of course, very distant,
so I wrote to her, Dear Lizzy,
Please excuse our Prime Minister's exuberance.
Dear lad's so excited you may register a protuberance!
Power delights him no matter how nominal.
Control by the rich – delicious idea!
Such sweet mediaeval laws he's been passing!

No protest at sea to stop the drilling
and the Trans Pacific Trade Agreement will shortly end
Protest on *lend*.

I'm blue, Lizzy, as Tory as you
but still it worrits me, it looks sick.
National to Nationalist
is only a little slip.

Bother the Chinese Lizzy, the Australians,
and the boys from Brazil with their giant drill.
Remember when Mother England put us to the breast –
and Enzed was a happy child sated, at rest
not a fretful babe, listless, apathetic?

I wrote to John too – a personal friend.
Dear John, Stop now dear. No more
selling us down the street
no more pretending at Balmoral
that all is well, all is well.

Most plainly it is not.
The youth are fleeing
there are no jobs
sea levels are rising
casinos are protected for aeons
and in the houses of the poor
the children… the children…

Will Liz give you a corgi to cuddle?
Will she sympathise with your lot?

> Oh – here's my breast John – take it
> Though it's droopy and long.
> I'll rock you to sleep
> And sing you a song.

[Stephanie Johnson ends persona as Amanda Tauiwi Reinhardt Carlton]

I think you'll agree that Amanda Tauiwi Reinhardt Carlton is someone you really only want in short doses. How are you all going listening? You've all been sitting there for a long time and I thought I'd just share this little beautiful quote with you, which is from David Lodge's 2008 novel *Deaf Sentence,* and he writes that, 'experiments have demonstrated that the average span for receiving continuous speech from one speaker is 20 minutes, and that it diminishes the more closely the discourse resembles written prose with its greater density of information and reduced redundancy.' I just thought you'd like to know that, and it may come in handy next time you're at a writer's festival such as this one, and you find your concentration wavering.

Earlier this year I interviewed Chinese writer Xinran for that other certain festival that happens down there [the Auckland Writers Festival]. Her book, *Buy Me the Sky*, about the effects of the one-child policy on Chinese society, returns us in many ways to Greenfield's book, *Mind Change.* In China the one-child policy has coincided with the advent of modern technologies, so that the more recent generations are called the three-screens generations, growing up with the mobile phone, the computer and the television. Many of them are at once overconnected with the outside world and totally isolated in their home life, which Xinran believes has created a kind of cold-hearted immorality. These generations bear all the hopes and ambitions of six adults: Mum and Dad and both sets of grandparents being their only family. They are so closeted and spoilt that many of them are almost unable to function in the real world.

It's my contention that if the situation in China is deep purple, then in the West it's lilac. Many of us know young people whose social lives take place almost entirely online. Parents of even very young children, where there are frequent stressful blow-ups over excessive screen time. We witness children in pushchairs oblivious to the passing street, their entire consciousness hooked into smeary iPads. Hospitality workers will tell you how for about two years now, children no longer run about and get under foot in restaurants, because they're intent on their devices, neither conversing with the adults nor getting into trouble, nor meeting the eye of the waiter when he takes their order.

As Xinran and I were chatting in the green room, she passed on to that 'certain other festival' her husband Toby Eady's greetings and congratulations, not only for surviving but for growing larger. Toby is a London literary agent. He had told her that writers' festivals all over the world are starting to crumble. And I gathered that these failing festivals are not like this one, or like that other one, in that they were started at grassroots level by booklovers and writers and, in fact, although it may seem traitorous to some of you, Murray was one of the original people who gathered together to get the Auckland Writers Festival on the road, until he decided that his loyalties lay with you fellas.

It is inevitable that the character of writers' festivals will change and adapt with changes of technology and aesthetics as the nature of publishing changes, and indeed, to meet what the market demands. I think we must be cautious about accepting what we are told the market wants. There needs to be no compulsion to adopt new, invasive technologies. Let us spend a moment with that adult in 2045, the character we could develop for a novel. Perhaps she is part of a new social elite, a socio-economic group who learned to regulate their online lives and to eschew neurological damage in favour of a pursuit of peace and of the recently rediscovered virtue of privacy.

To conclude, I'd like to read a short excerpt from my new book, *The Writers' Festival*, which I think sums up pretty well why we are here at this moment and this era. Cherish these occasions. Going West is not just a book festival, it's a commons: a place where people can come together to encounter new ideas and ways of thinking; a place where revolutions, big and small can be fomented. So this is just a couple of paragraphs from the very beginning:

> In January he gets on a flight and we let him go. There is no sudden boarding of the plane while it sits still on Chinese soil, no dragging down long corridors to beatings in closed rooms; there will be no gang of thugs to meet him in Taiwan or Hong Kong to administer the punishment he has endured so many times.
>
> He's free. He knows it as he's never let himself know it before. He is as free as the rest of the world will allow him to be. He has received invitations already to speak at literary festivals in the West, in America, in Europe, in Oceania, at those extraordinary occasions when the world's writers in all combinations meet and mingle and talk to enormous audiences, sometimes numbering in their thousands. Where writers take to the stage singly or in groups and are politely questioned about their work. When challenges and queries rise from the floor and are met with good humour from the stage, without fear. One invitation is from a country he has heard very little about, a country so far away that he has never before entertained any notion of it. It is the last country, he understands, ever to be added to the map of the world. The very last. And even there they have writers' festivals.

Thank you.

2016 MAUALAIVAO ALBERT WENDT

Writing from the Edge

Mālō *le soifua. Tēnā koutou, tēnā koutou, tēnā koutou katoa.*
The term 'edge' is multi-edged. Edge is the cutting side of a blade, a line where an object or area begins or ends, the brink, the verge. So for me edge suggests risk, toppling over into a chasm, having to take care. The phrase 'from the edge' suggests moving from that position, from the brink, the outer, towards a less risky position and becoming part of a more acceptable position, a centre. It can also mean toppling over into another edge, another challenging unknown, into new dangerous inspiring territory. The final edge along which we tread every breathing moment of our lives is of course that tightrope. That line between breathing and not breathing, between being and not-being, between consciousness and unconsciousness. When we're young and healthy, that edge seems far away because we're busy being and discovering and creating; we feel youth-proofed against death, there's a future that stretches forever.

One day, according to the Sāmoan Tupuaga, the Genesis, Tagaloaalagi, our Supreme Atua, asked his messenger to go into the forest and cut a branch off the Fue Tagata, the Peopling Vine, and spread it out in the sun in a place on the island of Savai'i. After a while, he asked his messenger to go and see how the Fue was. The messenger returned and told Tagaloaalagi the Fue had turned into ilo, maggots. Tagaloa took the ilo and shaped them into the first human beings and into them he placed the gifts of atamai (intelligence), loto (courage), poto (wit and cunning), masalo (the ability to doubt and question), finagalo (will) and agaga (soul). By the way, the place where the messenger laid the Fue is now known as Malae-la, the Malae-of-the-Sun.

Those marvellous gifts make for contradiction: they make us capable not only of enormous love and creativity, healing and invention, but also of arrogance, cruelty and violence. That contradiction is at the heart of all cultures, philosophies and literatures. Tagaloa's gifts have also made us the most destructive and violent creatures on our beautiful but sad planet. The other basic contradiction is: we can imagine ourselves immortal yet know we have to die. I grew up in the second half of the twentieth century, a time of unprecedented invention in technology, science and the arts, yet also a time of horrific violence and suffering, brutality and injustice. Everywhere today we see as a tragic continuation of that.

I and other writers emerged out of that terrible contradiction, that context and mix, reflecting and contemplating it. We'd just suffered two world wars, and throughout the world, smaller but violent conflicts continued. The development of the atomic bomb and nuclear weapons intensified and threatened a holocaust that will obliterate us. Well over half the planet was colonised by Europe, by the time I came on the scene, Great Britain possessing the largest colonial empire ever seen. And during my lifetime the anti-colonial struggle erupted and reached its fiercest stage. Whole populations were turned into refugees, who created such countries as America. That whole produced an almost overwhelming dread and pessimism in our artists. All the consoling universals were gone, shattered, now the individual self, the I, and the search for that took centre stage. Each artist was seen or saw herself as an outsider at the edge subverting your society, and in doing that, created an individual vocabulary, style and imagery.

I was born and raised in Sāmoa, then known as Western Sāmoa, a colony of New Zealand, into a poor family with a hardworking grandmother and parents who believed that having a good Western education would get us out of poverty. And because we were afakasi (half-caste) we were classified as European so we could enrol in Leifiifi School which was reserved for the children of the Papālagi administrators and other Europeans.

One day during my third year in Leifiifi Primary School, our Papālagi teacher — Miss Bristol, who we all loved — told us during a social studies lesson that Jacob Roggeveen, a Dutch explorer, had discovered Sāmoa in 1722. My imagination immediately conjured forth a vision of his magnificent masted ship breaking through the horizon in a blaze of sun and cloud. I considered this a radical addition to my understanding of our country, knowledge that made me look afresh at everything. And I wanted our grandmother, Mele — at that time the most influential person in my life — to know about it. So I rushed home after school and asked her:

> 'Did you know that a Dutchman by the name of Jacob Roggeveen discovered our country?'
> Patiently, she asked, 'Who told you that?'
> 'Our teacher,' I proudly divulged.
> 'Were we Sāmoans here before the Papālagi came?' she replied, a slow smile on her face.
> 'Yes.'
> 'Was this man Roggeveen a Papālagi?' Her scrutiny was now focused on my face fully, patiently, expectantly. 'Where do Dutch people come from?' She helped me.
> 'Holland,' I replied, with the truth of the matter sliding into my vision and occupying it. 'So he was a Papālagi,' I admitted.
> 'So when you go to school tomorrow, tell your teacher that we discovered our country. Tell her we've been here for at least 3000 years,' she said.

Now I was on fire with pride in my ancestors' achievements, prouder than I'd been about Roggeveen.

I was very fortunate to have had that lesson about decolonising ourselves when I was so young. That set me off on a journey that continues today: of challenging colonial perceptions of us, our histories and our ways of life; of trying to understand how our ancestors viewed themselves, their environment and the cosmos; of trying to comprehend what has happened to us in our intermingling and fusing over the last few centuries. Much of my writing, and the writing of other Pasefika writers, has been about that. Pasefika artists, academics, intellectuals, writers have been at the forefront, at the edge, of our anti-colonial struggles throughout the Pacific and within Aotearoa since the Second World War.

At the age of 13, I sat and won a New Zealand Government scholarship to boarding school in New Plymouth. That changed my life forever. I had never been outside Sāmoa, never been on a ship, never experienced winter or snow, never worn a tie or a long-sleeved shirt or suit or socks and had put shoes on only once. I didn't know how to eat with a knife and fork or dress myself the Papālagi way. Most of what I knew about New Zealand came from the movies, books and my teachers — and my grandmother who'd lived in New Zealand in the 1920s.

I was with six other scholarship students, travelling on the *Matua*. For the six days at sea I was seasick and wanted to suicide. We were distributed to our schools, and on my way to mine I saw Mount Taranaki — a white-topped symmetrical cone, which my travelling companion said was Mount Egmont. And as we moved along, the mountain watched me, steadying my homesickness, wrapping me up in its presence. During my whole time in school there it was present in my vision as a healing, wise, consoling elder. Taranaki has remained one of my ancestral mountains to this day.

For me writing has been and is a very demanding — and mostly enjoyable — activity. Because language is a substitute for experience, trying to explore and use it is like trying to discipline water: it keeps running out of your grasp. Practising your writing teaches you how to see, focus and work, and never being satisfied with what you write and make. Through the practice of writing I've learned to see through the surface faces of reality into its complex depths, that behind all that was, is, and becoming, are profound contradictions and 'truths' about ourselves and reality itself. And if we're fortunate, we catch those fleetingly in the process of writing and trying to see to understand.

My passion for writing and reading really intensified in New Plymouth. My first winter was a mainly miserable one. It was my first winter ever and for a long time I simply couldn't get used to the cold. It settled into my bones and didn't want to leave. Mr Alan Gardiner, our house master, must have sensed that many of us were not settling easily into the cold months. One evening, with the fire blazing in our sitting room, Mr Gardiner came in unexpectedly and told us he wanted to read *Animal Farm*, our prescribed novel, to us. We gathered in front of the fireplace in a semi-circle, with Mr Gardiner in an armchair, and many of us sitting or lying on the carpeted floor and on cushions. He opened the novel and without preliminary remarks, he read out the title, *Animal Farm* by George Orwell. I immediately began to feel I was back in Sāmoa in my grandmother's fale, gathered round her listening to her fāgogo. Then he began to read.

And for the whole of that winter, every Sunday night sang to Mr Gardiner's mesmerising voice as he unfolded the spellbinding satirical and allegorical tale of pigs and other animals and people competing for power, and what that does to them. The rise and establishment of the totalitarian state, the loss of individual freedom and rights, the struggle to restore justice, equality and freedom of expression — they were themes that I would later find myself exploring in my writing. I have never forgotten that winter and how we loved both that tale and its teller — and how we came to our first understanding of power and how it corrupts us.

Since that time, 1953, I have watched and experienced and written about the whole migrant experience of our Pasefika people in Aotearoa and witnessed the transformation of our home islands from colonies into independent countries and what they are now. In that time I've observed and participated in the development of our arts and artists both here and in the Pacific. For me that development has been a vital force in the growth, shaping and survival of our Pasefika communities, in my own development as a writer and thinker, and in how we have influenced and changed the nature of the culture of Aotearoa. Our most obvious contribution to Aotearoa culture is being made through sports. I love sports and our magnificent sports people but I'm not going to talk about them, except to say that our struggle for acceptance even in sports has been an extremely painful one against racism and sexism.

I belong to that group of Pasefika writers and artists who were born in our home countries but who have grown up and lived most of our lives here. Most of our artists are Aotearoa-born. But we all share one thing: we did not come out of a cultureless void. Our parents and grandparents who migrated to Aotearoa brought with them the diversity and complex depths of our ancient island cultures. So we were all born into families and Pasefika communities rich in history, spirituality, art, music, dance and other cultural traditions. And despite the fact that the dominant colonial culture here denigrated our cultures and languages and tried to make us feel ashamed of them, our ways have survived in us and, by shaping who and what we are, have contributed enormously to the ways we make and practice art.

For many of us, our rejection of colonialism, racism and sexism, and our refusal to be colonised, Pākehā-fied, and reject our ways of being, believing and dreaming is at the heart of the art that we do. Our art is our attempt to understand who and what we are, and the marvellous cultures, histories and situations we have come out of. Our art is the search for that and to map and shape the present. All artists everywhere are influenced throughout their lives by everything around them. And our artists, because they have grown up in a society and national culture and tertiary educational institutions that are largely Pākehā, are conversant with Western art and practices and have indigenised roles in their work and, over the last 50 or so years, have produced art that we can call Pasefika, a fusion that is unique to Aotearoa.

Arriving at this fusion has not been an easy or deliberate process. I want to illustrate that by talking about writing and literature because it is the form I know a little about. For me the Tāngata Māori Renaissance, which began to gain momentum after the Second World War and is now for me the most successful anti-colonial indigenous arts movement in the world, was and still is the movement we have learned much from in our political and artistic struggle as a minority group in Aotearoa. So for me the start of what would later be called Pasefika literature and writing by Polynesians (fiction, poetry and drama) in English began in the 1950s and 1960s with the writing of Hone Tuwhare, Jacquie Sturm, Rore Hapipi (Rowley Habib), Harry Dansey, Alistair Te Ariki Campbell, Johnny Frisbie Hebenstreit, John Kneubuhl and Tom Davis, a remarkable pioneer generation who wrote as part of the anti-colonial struggle. (Incidentally, most of the literature about us was, and still is, not by us).

In 1948 Johnny Frisbie and her father published *Miss Ulysses of Puka-Puka*, an autobiography, and in 1960 Tom and Lydia Davis published *Makutu*, perhaps the first novel with a Pacific author. This group went on to publish large bodies of work, poetry, fiction and plays. For me and my generation of Pasefika writers who began to publish in the late 1960s, they became our models, our mentors, our inspiration. Sadly, Hone Tuwhare died in 2006 and Alistair Te Ariki Campbell, Jacquie Sturm and others died a few years on. Those writers had to struggle against the prevailing racism and condescension that plagued even the literati of our country.

As you all know, for any artist, the search for your own voice is difficult enough and takes a lifetime, but it is even more difficult if you're of a minority group trying to do it within a national culture and an international literary culture that enforces monocultural, colonial frameworks on everything. For instance, because that first generation of our writers wrote in English, their work was always evaluated according to rigid standards and criteria determined in England and by the Pākehā literati and academia.

But our writers persisted because they wanted to find their own voice, vision, styles that suited our cultures and subject matter. And they succeeded, and my generation learned from them. And now I can proudly say that in our home countries we've indigenised the novel, drama and so forth, and in Aotearoa we've made them Pasefika and Māori. I take this opportunity to thank that pioneer generation for the rich literature they have bequeathed to us, for the courageous stand they took against racism and colonialism, and for the pathways they forged for us to follow. I will always be grateful to them.

My generation of writers began in the late sixties, and since then other generations of writers, poets, dramatists, novelists and so forth have followed. Our literature continues to invent and define itself, clearing a space for itself in relation to other literature in Aotearoa. It puts us at centre stage, with our accents, dress, good and evil, dreams and visions. Much of it is angry and protesting but it also celebrates what all literatures celebrate: love, sorrow, death, birth, happiness, and through it, language and the gift of speaking. Now the work of our leading writers is influencing the writing of our younger ones. It is also shaping how we see ourselves and our cultures and how we are seen by others and destroying some of the stereotypes and myths created about us by others.

The development of our other arts such as the visual and performing arts has followed a similar pattern, in paths which have been difficult and painful. Now we are flourishing in all the arts, in all the genres from writing and publishing, from music and dance to the tatau and the weaving, to film making and computer art, sculpture, design and fashion. You name it, and we're into it. Perhaps per head of population we now have more artists, and people in the arts, than any other ethnic group in Aotearoa. Yet I am left in a beautiful bewilderment, how have we done this despite the fact that we continue to be the poorest community, suffering the worst statistics in employment, health, housing, and life expectancy and so on? And how have we have done it despite the fact making art is one of the most difficult ways to make a living.

Pasefika literature and writing is no longer at the edge, it is a dynamic strand of our country's literature which in turn is a vital part of the very alive, edgy, varied, vigorous arts of Aotearoa, which I am very proud to be part of. I want to end this 'sermon' with a poem, in memory of Alistair Campbell, Alistair Te Ariki Campbell, one of our finest poets. It's called 'Garden 26' — a very original title. It's a poem taken from the sequence of poems called Ponsonby Poems. There are 40 poems in the sequence and each poem is 14 lines*. This is in memory of Alistair Te Ariki Campbell:

While we were having breakfast this morning
National Radio
announced that Alistair had died after a long
illness
We visited him last year in his house which is
perched above Pukerua Bay
defying the storms as it gazes out at Kapiti Te
Rauparaha's fortress now
bird sanctuary that Alistair loved and turned
into songs of *Sanctuary of Spirits*
Meg had died a few months before so he was
still in mourning
moving gingerly round his house as if even the
air was hurting

He made us tea and wanted to know about
the years we'd spent in Hawai'i
He reciprocated by telling us about Meg's
death and how he missed her
Later he took us into his study and gave us
copies of his collections
to select from for our anthology *Mauri Ola*

As we were leaving he led us into the fierce
wind and his garden at the edge
of the precipice and pulled out three young
aloe vera plants for us to take home
Today despite the winter the plants thrive in
our garden

Thank you very much.

2017 ROD ORAM

Between Here and There

[This address was accompanied by a visual soundscape composed by Celeste Oram]
[Oruruarangi, pūrereuha, chanting, and water sounds]

How silent and peaceful were Waitemata's lovely, sloping shores. The open country stretched away in vast fields of fern, and Nature reigned supreme. We followed a native path, skirting closely, when halfway, a volcanic hill, on summit of which grew one solitary and stately tree. We christened it 'One-Tree Hill', then and there, and to this day it bears that name. We now gently descended towards the shore of a magnificent sheet of water, the harbour of Te Manukau, and away on the West Coast range, we could see the headlands and a peep of the open sea.

[Bird sounds, chainsaws, machine sounds, radio voices, traffic noise, horns, sirens]

On that night, now forty years ago, the large Pakeha population — five all told — slept on the Waitemata's shore for the first time — of Maories I know not how many, but a large number.

And after the passing away of forty more years, who can tell how many Pakehas shall sleep on these shores, but will there then be Maories in number five all told?

… He is enclosed within a limited area, with a seaboard penetrated by innumerable harbours, with a fertile soil, and a climate most genial the world knows, and by its speedy occupation he will be crowded out.

For this land of which I write is destined to be the happy pleasure-ground of all the Great South Lands of the Pacific.

[Water sounds, electronics]

Kei nga Mana Whenua o Tāmaki Makaurau. Tēnā koutou, tēnā koutou, tēnā koutou katoa. Nau mai, piki mai, haere mai. Talofa lava. Mālō e lelei. Bula vinaka. Kia orana. Mālo ni. Namaste. Ni hāo. Hello.

On this night, of all nights, on the bicentenary of Tāmaki Makaurau, the words of John Logan Campbell echo down through our time tunnel of the centuries to haunt us and to taunt us. 'How silent and peaceful were Waitemata's lovely sloping shores. The open country stretched away in vast fields of fern and Nature reigned supreme. On the shores of the wonderful isthmus, which we had walked that day, a future great town must one day rise. Who can tell how many Pakehas are asleep on these shores, but will there then be Maories in number five all told?'

Why did we destroy so much of the beauty of this place? Destroy its very life and spirit? What, then, brought us to our senses? How did we get from there to here? And here to the restoration of life and spirit that we revel in today, but may not be worthy of.

Best I begin at the beginning, on Thursday, April the 30th, 1840. That day, 200 years ago, 4 months and 18 days, was the first day that John Logan Campbell spent on the shores of this isthmus. He and his three Scottish companions, vigorous men, swooned at the beauty of it. They were canny, too. One particular feature caught their fancy, the Remuera ridgeline. Determined to buy some, they sought out Ngāti Whātua leaders. Discovering they were not at home at Ōrākei but rather fishing in the Manukau Harbour, they set off across the isthmus.

They found Kawau, a Ngāti Whātua chief, shark fishing at Mangere. Hearing their Remuera enquiry, he retorted, 'No! Those are my people's best planting grounds. We aren't selling any of it.' Yet he was welcoming to these newcomers. He suggested perhaps, well, his iwi might sell them some less valuable land further up the harbour. The four Scots agreed to look later and set off back across the isthmus to their camp at Ōrākei Bay, as we have now restored its name from that dreadful colonial name of Hobson's Bay.

That evening, though, a dark premonition disturbed Campbell's revelry. He foresaw that Māori would be enclosed within a limited area, and that speedy occupation would crowd them out. Quick as a flash the Europeans descended on this paradise. And yet with extraordinary generosity Ngāti Whātua offered Campbell a 3000-acre arc of waterfront land, which is the heart of our city today. On Friday September the 18th, 1840, 200 years ago today, Governor Hobson planted the Union Jack on the beach, in the lee of the Pākehā-named Britomart Point, and declared this place 'Auckland'.

Three years later, in May, 1844, the collective Waikato iwi organised one of the largest Māori feasts ever held in Aotearoa, to impress the new arrivals with the fecundity of the Waitematā and its shores. It took place between Mount Hobson and Mount St John, in a narrow plane along which today runs Great South Road — populated by car yards, I would hasten to add. The feast attracted some 4000 Māori and most of the then few Pākehā residents. The festivities lasted for a week and large amounts of food and drink were consumed: 11,000 baskets of potatoes, 9000 sharks, 100 pigs, and large amounts of tea, tobacco and sugar. Governor FitzRoy visited the festivities on May 11th, when a haka was performed by 1600 Māori, armed with guns and tomahawks.

Yet, just 15 years later, Ferdinand von Hochstetter visited New Zealand to map its geology. This is how he later described what he saw in Tāmaki Makaurau:

> For the sake of a few serviceable trunks, sometimes whole forests are burnt down and desolated ... The woods are ransacked and ravaged with "fire and sword". During my stay in Auckland, I was able to observe from my windows, during an entire fortnight, dense clouds of smoke whirling up which arose from the enormous destructive conflagration of the woods nearest to town. When the fire had subsided, a large, beautiful tract of forest lay there in ashes, the newspapers giving only this laconic notice: "No damage done to timber wood." That may be, but there will come a time when the question will not be about the timber, but also about the forest!

One of those newspapers, the *Southern Cross*, was owned by Campbell and his business partner, William Brown. In it they advertised their auctions of goods that they imported. Their profit, on British woven woollen blankets for example, ranged from 25 percent to 75 percent, even after all that trouble of bringing them all the way from Britain. Anyway, some of their customers had some money to spend because they were Māori, who Campbell and Brown paid to collect kauri gum. Now, while Campbell was certainly ahead of his time in the market for kauri gum, he failed to make money over several decades of trying, from exporting kauri masts to the British Royal Navy, prefabricated kauri homes to San Francisco, and even produce from his large-scale farm near Whakatāne.

Instead, Campbell made his money on trading land, brewing beer and importing consumer goods, while benefiting from heavy government spending in the new province. Now, if that sounds like Auckland until recent decades, you're right. For the first 180 years after the Treaty of Waitangi, this city, this country, had a simple economic strategy: rip-shit-and-bust. Hey, no problem — if I trash this bit of land or that stretch of water, I'll move on to another.

Our exploitation here and around the country, and in common with people across the planet, peaked in the first two decades of this twenty-first century. From 2000 to 2020 we inflicted on ourselves extremes of wealth, inequality and environmental desecration. We humans were threatening our very existence, even here. Some 30 years ago now it was that Charles Landry, a world-leading writer on creating cities, visited Auckland to see how we stacked up. In his words: 'At best, good city-making leads to the highest achievements of human culture. A cursory glance at the globe reveals the names of cities old and new. Their names resonate as we think simultaneously of their physical presence, their activities, their cultures, their people and their ideas. Our best cities are the most elaborate and sophisticated artefacts humans have conceived, shaped, and made. The worst are forgettable, damaging, destructive — even hellish.'

Well, when Landry visited, we weren't quite hellish. He was impressed by our city's natural setting on these two harbours (and thanks to the creation of Auckland Council, three harbours, when we snaffled part of the lower Kaipara), but he was disturbed by what we were doing to it. He posted unflattering pictures of us on his website. His favourite: the Central Police Station on the corner of Mayoral Drive and Hobson Street; his epithet: 'Early 1970s East European'. Those were very troubling times — I won't dwell on the excruciating details. They are as fresh in my mind and, I would venture, yours, as if it were now.

We had yet to learn, to borrow from Allen Curnow, that there are no more islands to be found, or pleasant planets for that matter. What brought to us our senses? How did we get from there to here? Over the past few months I've wrestled with those questions, hoping to do justice to this oration. This morning I was sitting at home staring glumly at my pages of earnest analysis of ecosystems and planetary boundaries, economics, politics, sociology and psychology and the like. Thankfully though, I was soon relieved of my misery. This being Tāmaki Makaurau's bicentenary birthday, my wife and I, our daughter and her partner, and their kids strolled eagerly down to Okahu Bay, our place of repose and reflection.

We of course stepped around the debris from last night's violent storm. Heavens, that was a doozy, wasn't it? Well, we were eager to see how our regenerating bay had coped with the king tide, pushed high by that howling northeaster — the tail end of which, as we now know, was one of the worst cyclones yet in the Pacific. Some decades back, Ngāti

Whātua, the guardians of the bay, began restoring it. They had lobbied the Council to strip out the sewer pipe under Tāmaki Drive that had cut off the beautiful natural beach from the free-draining land behind. As a result of Tāmaki Drive and that sewer pipe, we had managed to comprehensively stuff up beach and land. Now, though, we all enjoy clear water, verdant sea grasses and rich shellfish beds.

Yup, the beach survived, protected from that storm. And protected from the storm was the Domain behind us and its luxurious native plants and their chortling chorus of native birds. (Sad we can't bring back the huia.) All the waka, tents, stands and other paraphernalia of the party were still standing, if a little dishevelled. And so much to celebrate. Out in Te Kapa Moana, there's kaimoana plenty in the clean, healthy waters. On shore, Tāmaki Makaurau is one of the most delightful, sustainable cities in the world — even Landry would have approved — even though these days almost two and a half million of us call it home.

Here's a quote: 'The city is a fact of nature, like a cave or a run of mackerel or an ant-heap, but is also a conscious work of art, and holds within its communal framework many simpler and more personal forms of art. Mind takes form in the city and, in turn, urban form conditions mind'. So wrote Lewis Mumford, the US social philosopher, way back, 110 years ago, in 1930. Above all, we've started to bring nature back into our city. Oh, not just in nice plantings — that's ridiculous. Our goals are to make the city largely self-sufficient in energy, food, and some other resources; to be an enlivening, inspiring place to live and work. And above all, to restore our relationship with the ecosystem.

There's plenty more to celebrate all around Aotearoa, though we aren't quite a hundred percent predator-free in time for the bicentenary but will soon be, perhaps a few years ahead of that original target of 2050. This morning as I gazed around at the gorgeous regeneration of our bay, our tiny bit of paradise, my eyes dwelt on the far end under Bastion Point and the Ōrākei Marae. My eyes teared up and I didn't know why. Then it all flashed before me. It's a summer's day back in 2020; we're down at the beach. A mutt of a dog, clenching a dead snapper in its mouth, runs out of the surf and up the beach towards a small child. The dog staggers, drops the fish, falls, and writhes on the ground. The child, no more than three or four I reckon, a girl, rushes towards it, drops to the ground, cuddles the dog in her chubby little arms. The dog, slobbering frantically, licks her neck, her cheek, her mouth, then with one last awful spasm, dies. The child howls. The mother pulls her away from the dog. She brings her child up the beach and they sit down near us. Nestled in her mother's lap, the girl quietens and seems to fall asleep. Perhaps 15 or 20 minutes pass, then the girl jerks awake, her little body convulsing. We call an ambulance. Before it arrives, she dies in her mother's arms. News of the tragedy spreads like lightning. First the city is astonished — then it's stunned as news breaks of more deaths of people on local beaches. The nation is shocked. The news whips around the world. What the hell is happening?

Well, it didn't take marine ecologists long to work it out. Curious things had been happening over the previous week — a much-depleted snapper catch, recreational fishers reported. Big areas of eutrophication out in the Gulf, an unheard of event in such strong tidal waters. Then, in the past days, dead fish washing up on beaches.

It turned out that we were the triggers. A few weeks before, a massive storm had knocked out the city's electricity grid. Before an orderly shutdown of the Māngere treatment plant and sewerage network was achieved some back-up generators failed, and then vast quantities of sewage poured into the Waitematā Harbour. We had so abused the ecosystem of the Gulf — its resilience was so depleted — that this very human chain of events caused the Gulf's web of life to collapse. An intense species-jumping deadly toxin new to science was wreaking havoc. The fish, the dog and the girl were just three of its thousands of victims.

The Government faffed around for months with an enquiry, trying its hardest not to apportion blame, not to disturb the settled order. More and more citizens grew angrier and angrier. They realised that dangers that had seemed so far away — big storms, rising seas, environmental degradation, climate change, toxic pollution — were suddenly here. They wanted action now. The Coalition Government fell apart. The snap

General Election was indecisive. Soon, a broad coalition was formed. Its first act was to amend our Bill of Rights to include the right to a healthy environment. About time. Some 180 countries had already elevated the environment to their constitution or bill of rights in the decades before we had stirred our stumps. Two weeks later, all parties in Parliament voted for a climate-change act. This put in the hands of an independent committee of Parliament the power to set carbon-reduction targets and to review government policies and progress towards achieving them.

About bloody time too. The UK had pioneered that in 2008 — by the time we followed them in 2020, some 30 other countries had got there before us. Then we got down to the hard work of getting serious about the ecosystem. As so often happens, we realised pioneers here in Aotearoa had been blazing the trail long before tragedy struck us in 2020: the Land and Water Forum, using collaboration between farmers, recreational users — all stakeholders — to deliver holistic solutions on water quality to the Government of the day. And they did, but the Government didn't have the sense to implement them.

Sea Change for Te Kapa Moana, or the Hauraki Gulf as we called it then, was another collaborative process, culminating in 2016. This time it was a first in the world, to bring terrestrial and marine ecosystems into the same spatial planning process in order to lay out a map for regenerating the Gulf. But the many local governments, and central government, with a say in the Gulf, and all their conflicting agendas, completely dropped the ball. It had sunk without a trace by the middle of 2017. The granting of personhood to Te Urewera and the Whanganui River, not to mention other collaborative arrangements such as with the Waikato River — those too were extraordinary. Those were world leading. To give personhood to a river? But too many people ridiculed those ground-breaking relationships.

Back in the late 2010s, as I remember, the Government had foisted on us a compromised freshwater management regime. It did have one good feature, though. It gave communities the responsibility of trying to set the water quality standards that they wanted. And of course, thanks to the exponential shift in technology, our scientific knowledge was expanding fast, as were the tools we use these days, such as artificial intelligence, drones, monitoring intensely the health of our ecosystem. But it's not all about the technology. These new ways of working enabled citizen science around the country, such as lots of people checking water quality and soil fecundity in tens of thousands of places and giving us powerful, easy ways for people to collaborate — even at vast distances — to debate and decide how we will help our ecosystem regenerate.

And the predator-free campaign fired up peoples and towns and in the country to get involved, to start understanding and appreciating our symbiotic relationship with the ecosystem and to do something about it. We began work on all these things relying on the pockets of good practice in the Resource Management Act's swamp of compromise, while we kept arguing about how we might drain that swamp.

We were still stuck, I think, because we thought we could use all these new devices — science, tools, collaboration — to make rip-shit-and-bust sustainable. But I realised later we were still trying to perfect the wrong thing. We thought we could get so sophisticated at resource management that we could manipulate the ecosystem; we could tell it what to do.

It was only when we realised that our new capability, our sustainable values, and our common causes were at last helping us with our real task — to hear what the ecosystem was telling us to do so *it* and *we* could thrive — that we realised we had to be a humble part of the vastly complex web of life, which is our life support system, things changed. When we realised what kaitiakitanga meant; that we are just a small, dependent part of our ecosystem.

With that insight, we pushed for transformation. People wanted to take responsibility for themselves and their actions and for society. People wanted to seek connection with Nature, which, they sort of suspected, was somewhere deep in their souls.

Today, I marvel at how richly our ecosystem has begun to recover, but it is the *evolution* of the ecosystem. We can never recreate the ecosystem Māori knew before Pākehā arrived. We cannot bring back the huia. Instead, naturally, the ecosystem and the myriad forms of life it supports are adapting to their changed circumstances. We are going somewhere different, but this time, it's healthy.

All we've done — *all* — is to stop trying to bend nature to our will. In return, nature is giving us the greatest gift of all: life itself. And John Logan Campbell?—yes, he too evolved. In the last three decades of his 94-and-a-bit-year life, he achieved a deep communion with this land and water and air and light. He became a creature of it, responding ever more deeply to it. He didn't live to see the renaissance of Māori and the sense of kaitiakitanga they had given us all, but I know he knows.

Twenty-five years ago, in 2015, I read a book that shook me to my core. It was Roy Scranton's *Learning to Die in the Anthropocene: reflections on the end of a civilisation*. Here's a quote:

> The greatest challenge we face is a philosophical one: understanding that this civilisation is already dead. The sooner we confront our situation and realise that there is nothing we can do to save ourselves, the sooner we can get down to the difficult task of adapting, with mortal humility, to the new reality.

For a long time I didn't understand that quote, until the day a dog licked a child and changed the world. But we have barely begun. We still teeter on the edge of ecological apocalypse.

[Waves on the shore, electronics] [Rod Oram closes by quoting the last four stanzas of Allen Curnow's poem 'Landfall in Unknown Seas':]

> But now there are no more islands to be found
> And the eye scans risky horizons of its own
> In unsettled weather, and murmurs of the drowned
>   Haunt their familiar beaches —
> Who navigates us towards what unknown

But not improbable provinces? Who reaches
A future down for us from the high shelf
Of spiritual daring? Not those speeches
      Pinning on the Past like a decoration
For merit that congratulates itself,

O not the self-important celebration
Or most painstaking history, can release
The current of a discoverer's elation
      And silence the voices saying,
'Here is the world's end, where wonders cease.'

Only by a more faithful memory, laying
On him the half-light of a diffident glory,
The sailor lives, and stands beside us, paying
      Out into our time's wave
The stain of blood that writes an island's story.

2018 PAULA MORRIS

Spread the Word

Tēnā koutou, tēnā koutou, tēnā koutou katoa. Ngā mihi nui. Kia koutou katoa. Ko Paula Morris ahau. And I'm going to try and do this without my glasses. I've got them here just in case — just in case sense overwhelms vanity.

I'm very honoured to be giving the keynote address tonight. Within the literary world, we often talk about our delicate ecosystem in New Zealand writing, publishing and bookselling. It's small and beautiful, it's tenacious, but it's threatened, and people like the late Sir Graeme Douglas and his family help us to persist and to thrive. As Mark Easterbrook was saying, the theme of this year's festival is 'Spread the Word' and tonight I'm going to talk a little bit about what that means to me and what it might mean to you.

Spread, I think, is the important notion here. It reminds me of the way we understand whakapapa because all of us, as descendants of other people, have an inheritance. Our ancestors themselves, our tūpuna, and the lines to them are unbroken and there are many lines, like the lines that make up a net. When we think about spreading the word, again we see a net, not a line. We're a community here at Going West, in Titirangi this weekend. We'll take away and interpret what provokes and unsettles us, what resonates and what challenges. We spread these questions and subjects through our own creative work, our conversations, our networks, our families.

Now all of us are taking part in the festival, not simply attending it. You are not a passive audience, are you? And most of the artists participating this weekend will be interviewed or taking part in panel discussions, so anything can happen, anything can arise, anything can be disputed or reconsidered. I'm giving a prepared speech now, but most artists this weekend will not. Festivals may have a formal structure, but they are fluid within these confines. Within we find rivers bursting banks, surging tides, streams popping and gurgling, confluence and divergence, deeper channels, new roots.

Our challenge this weekend is to be open to changes of direction. To go with the flow, if I haven't hammered this metaphor enough. But as you know, I'm not here just to be lyrical. I've been accused of many things in my adult life: of being too emotional; too aggressive; too secretive; too racist. My students regularly accuse me of being too mean. I'm the kind of person who will not let things lie. I wake the sleeping dogs. I'm the writer of letters that point things out. I squabble with people on Twitter, and with colleagues via the University of Auckland email system. At restaurants and cafés I always send back food that isn't hot enough. I have made myself unwelcome at a particular bar that shall not be named, and at a particular lawyer's office on Lincoln Road, and at the St Luke's branch of the ASB (and my sister too).

Why am I telling you this? It's not just to prove that I'm really not secretive. I want you to understand before I launch into my words manifesto that I'm a passionate person of strong views. It means I don't have many friends here, but that's okay. That's why Netflix and Candy Crush were invented. Also, I started Māori weaving last year, which is why I drive around with a large knife in the glovebox of my car, in case I spot any good flax. That's why I carry the knife, really, you don't have to avoid me at supper.

But above else, above all else, I'm a writer, and language is my medium. I care profoundly about it, what it means, what it suggests, how it sounds, how it works together. Without language I can articulate nothing. What I create as a writer, which may be a book, or a story, or this talk, I do word by word. And yet, the work and the play of writing, the business of language and how we deploy it is often devalued in favour of 'the idea'. And when imagination is discussed, it's in terms of ideas and coming up with them, rather than in use of language.

Now creativity, as you know, is an increasingly debased word. It's overused in a business context as something to be bought and sold. 'We have ideas, therefore we are creative — it's all about the *lightbulb* moment. In fact, if you search on the Internet for images of the word 'idea', you'll discover picture after picture of lightbulbs. Now you know not even the lightbulb itself was invented in a lightbulb moment. But still we persist.

Now, a focus on ideas, I think, reinforces the romantic notion of inspiration as the heart of artistry. Creativity has the value, this argument goes, not technique or expertise or insights, not experimentation, not trial and error, not collaboration, not revision. We venerate the idea and those who wave them at us in triumph, proof of their innate creativity and we devalue the next steps of all that it takes to realise or implement or execute or articulate or explore.

I've taught creative writing for 15 years, largely at universities in the US, the UK and New Zealand, as well as for school and community groups all over the world, from Belgium, to China, to Latvia. Now aside from a few unwilling school pupils who'd rather be running wild outside, the majority of participants in my workshops choose to take part. Most like to write. Many think of themselves as writers. In my Masters class at the University of Auckland many of my students are already published. One of them, Amy McDaid, is reading from her novel manuscript here tomorrow morning. (I can see her, and I haven't even got my glasses on.) I really urge you to attend. She won our Sir James Wallace prize last year and her novel is very dark and funny and compelling and a lot of it is set here in West Auckland. Titirangi doesn't come out well, I have to tell you. But when does it?

But, in many other classes and groups all over the world, I experience a resistance to the art and to the act of writing. The most crucial elements of creative writing demand access: access to language and access to the imagination. Without facility of language, the writer is inarticulate, and expression is stunted, derivative, impossible. Without the embrace of imagination, the writer remains on the surface, unable to explore the subconscious darkness. As children when we're running around outside or sequestered in our rooms, or playing bullrush, we understand instinctively the imaginative possibilities of play and the role imagination plays in processing our fears and our questions about the world. But the resistance I described shows up in many creative writing classes — too many — that involve actual writing. Given an exercise prompt, some of the writers will object. Some will sit thinking rather than using their pens, as though they could think their way to good writing. Some will ignore or disobey the prompt, or wander away in their written response, even if a model is given. They will use the time of the exercise to construct an elaborate on-ramp rather than swerve straight on to the road as it demands.

Now prompts and writing exercises, I believe, should be very short and specific, and this makes them difficult — in the same way, I am told, that a crunch or a sit-up can be a small movement that is strenuous and targeted. The first challenges of the creative writer are technical. They begin with words. In the book *Reading Like a Writer*, Francine Prose describes discovering that writing, like reading, was done one word at a time, one punctuation mark at a time. She says, 'It required what a friend calls putting every word on trial for its life, changing an adjective, cutting a phrase, removing a comma, and putting it back in. It's surprising,' she says, 'how easily we lose sight of the fact that words are the raw material out of which literature is crafted.'

How can we articulate what we want to say unless we're vivid and precise with language? How can we convey our vision of the world unless we choose our language with care and imagination? Bland prose that relies on clichés suggests a lazy mind, a lazy writer. Why do we want to write if we don't want to write? Now sometimes people think they want to write, don't they? But they just really want to be or to have been published — ideally a blockbuster that will be made into a movie, and not a New Zealand movie either.

They have a number of ideas and they believe that ideas are the thing, or they have a lot of feelings and they believe feelings are the thing. Creative writing, they think, will allow them to express these ideas and feelings. Not in my classes, okay. They know how to write a sentence they think, or at least a phrase. They wouldn't venture so boldly, I think, into a practical class in visual art or architecture or film making because they're wary of these other technical skills that might be in demand, beyond basic literacy, ideas and feelings.

I don't really believe in ideas, as my students know — not in the context of creative writing. I believe in daydreaming and obsessing and mulling over. I believe in things swirling around in our heads like socks in a tumble dryer, rolling around until one plasters itself against the window. I believe in zoning out, wandering, pilfering, eavesdropping, drifting, spying. I believe in experience and invention, in getting lost and working out the puzzle. I believe in passions and obsessions, dreams and nightmares, shadows across your subconscious. In everything goes, into the tumble dryer of the mind and eventually something coalesces that can be formed into art. We don't need to wait for the lightbulb moment and what that implies, I think, about ideas and inspiration as something external, dangling from the ceiling above us. What we need is already inside us, churning away in the dark. We need to be alert and present in the world, taking everything in, sensory experience in every facet. And then, if we're writers, we need words.

Ideas, I've argued on many occasions to the increasing boredom of people, are the enemy of the creative writer because one of the main issues I face with students of all ages and all contexts is people telling me they get stuck, they run out of steam after a few pages or a few chapters, because they've started with an idea and that's the one thing they don't really need. I always quote the American writer Robert Olen Butler — he exhorts his students to stop thinking. He says, 'please get out of the habit of saying you've got an idea for a story. Art does not come from ideas. Art does not come from the mind. Art comes from the place where you dream. Art comes from your unconscious. It comes from the white-hot centre of you.'

So think about our ideas sizzling within us as the pressure on the page that we don't need to be able to understand or articulate in some kind of statement of intent. Our work is bigger than us and deeper and more intelligent. We don't get the chance to explain it to every reader picking up a book in a shop or a library or browsing online, and this is just as well, is it not, because we would be arguing with readers all the time.

I'd like to return now to the notion of imagination, to reclaim it from the strident battalions of the idea. All of us here this weekend need imagination to engage with the words flowing in the room beyond their literal meaning, to make our own associations and connections and sparks and to continue weaving our larger nets. Imagination in writing is too often defined as making things up: a story; a world; a crazy thing that happens. This is why, perhaps, we put so much emphasis on ideas. I have an idea for a story. Well — great.

Like opinions, ideas abound. I'd like to quote the rap artist, Lady Sovereign: 'Well, everybody's entitled to opinions. I open my mouth and shit, I got millions.' She's an English rapper. Writing is a concrete act, not a theoretical one. It takes time and skill. With more practice we can get better, and this is how exercises, however much aspiring writers resist them, can help. To many creative writing apprentices the techniques of the fiction writer, for example, are still a mystery: conveying three-dimensional characters and moving them around a room, writing plausible dialogue with a dramatic function, exploring all possible aspects of setting, remaining consistent within point of view, working the emotional and dramatic moment — all of these are challenges.

Now if you add the pressure of the idea weighed down by its ostentatious epaulettes of originality and invention, apprentice writers crumble. They prioritise the idea because it seems to speak of voice and vision, but they're unable to realise it so abstractions replace concrete detail and the resulting stories are didactic, derivative or sketchy. This prioritisation of the idea over story skills helps explain the resistance to exercises with tight constraints. Symbols and abstractions feel grand and important. Describing a small rock in the road does not, especially if you're working within a tight word limit. Many apprentice writers rebel against describing a small or ordinary thing because it's boring. How could it help them? They want to write a searing indictment of this, or an emotional dissection of that, not bother with the shape of a rock or the colour of a backpack or the texture of carpet.

The challenge is both beneath them — because they are artists with ideas and feelings, lightbulbs flashing like a halo around their heads — and because it's too difficult. When I taught in Scotland, where it rains constantly, I was working with students on a reduced version of John Gardner's famous exercise: to describe a lake from the point of view of someone who has just committed a murder, without mentioning the murder. So, it's a point of view exercise that asks the writer to locate conflict and atmosphere and reveal point of view through the setting description alone. It's a difficult but very useful exercise, and of course one student was vocal in her criticism. 'We would never do this in a real story,' she complained. And she said this every week about everything I asked her to do. And I would say, 'We don't see tennis players doing sit ups during matches, but it doesn't mean they don't do them during training.'

Now I'm living back in Auckland, my home town. When I'm not working or arguing or lolling around the house watching German supernatural mysteries on TV or slashing at things with knives, I teach creative writing in schools. This is something many artists do to spread the word. How can we excite and stimulate the artists of tomorrow? How can we pass on technical skills? How can we help instil a passion for our materials and their possibilities?

I also feel very strongly that too many of us here like to throw up our hands in despair and demand to know why — without really considering the complexities of why, or having any notion about the context or the steps being taken to address the particular crisis of the day: Why are there not enough Māori or Pasifika or Asian and/or queer voices in our national literature? Why are the evil gatekeepers doing this and not that? Why don't we read our own writers of this or of that? Why aren't our books published in this place or that? Why, why, why?

Well, there are many reasons, starting with colonialism, and those would form the subject of another address entirely. But let me say this: we can't lament that the field is bare when we haven't taken the time to sow the seeds. Since 2015, when I returned to New Zealand, I have visited quite a few schools for ongoing writing projects. Now one-offs are fine, but it's the longer-term relationships that start having impact. My partners in these have been the New Zealand Book Council for the past two years and the Auckland Writers Festival, which is always looking to broaden its reach and make it possible for low-decile schools to get free entry and transport to its school days. It's also keen to encourage and enable keen young writers.

My colleague Selina Tusitala Marsh and I also have direct relationships with a number of schools. When we were growing up she attended Avondale College and Serie Barford and I attended Rutherford College, here in the West. So, we understand the power of getting in front of kids and reminding them that university can be part of their future, that this city belongs to all of us and so do its monuments and institutions. This is what spreading the word means, showing up and reaching out, connecting, and communicating.

Selina, by the way, was head girl of Avondale College 'cos she's a girly swot. I was not head girl of Rutherford. This year I've been working with Rebecca Kunin and the Henderson-Massey Local Board on the Outside the Square project with students at Rutherford and at Henderson High. Two of my former creative writing students — Rachel O'Connor and Ruby Porter — worked with small groups of young writers at these schools over two months. Ruby and Rachel are both very talented writers with novels coming out next year, and they've also been through the austere labour camp that is my approach to pedagogy. The results of the students' work you can see in this little book *Write Here. Write Now!*, launched last weekend in Henderson

Council Chambers. A thousand copies of it are being distributed at public collection points in West Auckland and we have many copies here tonight. So please, pick up one. It's free and it's amazing.

I spoke earlier about the kaupapa of working small, that is writing exercises that have very strict constraints. This may seem counterintuitive when you're trying to encourage young writers. Shouldn't we just want them to write something, anything? Aren't any words better than none? Well, sometimes. But not when we're aiming for writing excellence and to push writers in the one thing they absolutely need — language. I don't want to patronise young writers by deciding in advance how little they can achieve.

So, for this school project we confined ourselves to creative non-fiction, that is true stories that employ the techniques of fiction, like point of view, scene, narrative shape, character, setting, dialogue. What I found with young writers is that they see imagination as something that applies only to fiction. It's about making stuff up, they tell me. This often slows them down as they have to sit waiting for ideas and inspiration. They need to think, which isn't easy when you have me there shouting 'Stop thinking!' at them. The results are often derivative, reflecting the books they read or the games they play, or the movies they see, or they're generic and vague, they're pocked with the black holes of the unimagined.

At another school in a different part of Auckland this year we really stumbled with fiction. When I asked them to describe a fictional city, they all went for very vague sci-fi. This is one of them, and it's not bad:

> Buildings of glass gather around the centre of the city. Skyscrapers tower over shopping centres and apartment blocks. Clipped to every structure is a carbon collector. Streets are lined with fruit trees.

So that's okay, yes? For a 14-year-old. But here's the same writer describing a place she knows. This is her grandmother's home in Fiji:

> Wildflowers grow beside a door, in front of a blue picket fence. Up

roughly-made concrete stairs there's a blood-red terrace with peeling paint. Through the door, handmade from rusting steel rods, rooms are decorated with plastic doilies and dusty furniture. From the kitchen door, a steep slope of spiky grass leads to a field of sugarcane.

There's more precision with detail and more imagination, I'd argue, in the latter. So, for the Henderson and Rutherford sessions we opted to focus on creative non-fiction exercises, like the ones I do with my undergraduates every week, to help develop the elements of storytelling. Writing the truth subverts our understanding of imagination and reclaims it from an association with ideas. We need imagination in how we interrogate ourselves and describe the world. We need imagination to nurture stories, and we can begin with our own sensory experience, the places we navigate every day, the people we recognise, everything both above and below the surfaces of the city.

When apprentice writers are free from the demand to imagine a place or a time or a person, to spirit something unknown out of the whirling cloud of ideas beyond their reach, they can focus on the first steps they need to take as writers, articulating the world they've experienced, without wordiness, without abstraction, and cracking the seal on their memories and imaginations. I'm going to read you a couple of little excerpts from *Write Here*. The first is by Te Ariki Maunsell:

My street is very quiet. You never hear anything but the occasional car and a chirp or two coming from the native trees. But at the end of the road there's a hill and at the top of the hill there's a creaky old bench. From there you can see over the treetops to the sea. There's a salty taste in the air. Every day at 3.50 p.m. on the dot an old man with yellow tinted glasses walks past with his Staffy. We have a little chat, but he never sits.

Here's another excerpt, this one from Miha Kovacevic:

There's a creepy square house on the corner, its windows lined with yellow tinfoil. An old man lives there, though I've never seen him, and we speculate about what dark stuff he gets up to in there. My mother says he's not evil, he's just convinced the British Royal family is targeting him with lasers. When we first moved in here we were told that the neighbours in the house with the huge stone walls were drug lords.

Do you see why I get them to write this stuff? This is Te Ariki Maunsell. I'm going to read you the whole piece, because it's fantastic:

Whenever I see my gran she's either cleaning or cooking. Every day after school she used to stretch this lovely taffy for me. It was chewy and sweet, and then one time I bit into a wedding ring. Her favourite shirt is bright pink, and she's always wearing a grin from ear to ear. Although she's getting old she's still got a straight back. She can talk for hours and she has no patience with stupidity. She's quick as a whip and she doesn't take crap from anyone. One time I came home with the results of a school test. I'd failed and I knew she would be mad. Instead of yelling at me, though, she took me for a drive. We passed some homeless people and she pointed them out to me and said, 'If you don't get good grades, this will be you.'

Last week at the launch I met Te Ariki again and I met his grandmother — she was with him — and from his description I was expecting someone old. Needless to say she was not much older than I am. I think she was 60, maximum. I'm really delighted with the work collected in this little book and the windows it opens into the imaginative and real worlds of our young writers. They laboured away on small exercises about moments, colours, sensory experiences. They dug deep into their own points of view, how they made sense of the world. They were challenged on word choice. They wrote, they rewrote their pieces, they saw how they were cut and edited, and now they're seeing what it's like to have their words published and spread around. Now this is not as sexy as the big idea. Writing a series of short, intense pieces took weeks of work, and demanded trial and error over and over again, rather than a lightbulb moment.

This approach may not feel like creativity because it imposes constraints and asks prose writers, who sometimes resist compression, to consider every word. Students often tell me that they could pack much, much more into their pieces, if only I would double or triple the word count. But no, I'm asking them to be vivid and precise and concrete and to make every word count, to renounce chattiness, to not ramble on, to use imagination to enter a moment, rather than to whirl around it being general and vague and lyrical.

The next step in this programme — the next room, if you like, in my house of pain — is to continue working with some of the young writers from a number of different schools, mainly years nine and ten, who haven't had the joy crushed out of their lives by NCEA. My 1001 Nights Project, which is supported by the Auckland Diversity Fund, asks young writers to rewrite stories from *The Arabian Nights*, like Ali Baba and Aladdin, scene by scene, but to set them in a contemporary Auckland that's recognisable to them — their streets, their neighbours, their lives. This removes the demand of devising plot as the story points are already there. So, they get to do less thinking and more imagining. I've been working on various iterations of this for two years, and it's a challenge for the writers. I should tell you though, that so far Cassim, Ali Baba's wealthy brother, always ends up living in Mission Bay.

When I talk to student writers I say that creative writing is an art, but it's also a discipline. It's play as well, but the notion of creativity does not preclude work and it doesn't mean your first impulse is always right. I was going to quote John McFee, but may I just urge you to read what John McFee has to say on this matter. When I'm writing it demands my full attention, the way my dollhouse once did. I speak as someone who only stopped playing with dolls because I was going to university and I've always regretted that —not going to university but stopping playing with dolls — because once you cross the line from childhood play it's very difficult to go back. You're forced to grow up and become a novelist, which sadly does not include quite so much hair-brushing.

Right now I'm finishing work on a novel called *Yellow Palace.* I have other books available for you to buy of course. It's taken me years to write *Yellow Palace* because I need a lot of time for daydreaming and imagining, for the arguments inside my head, for research, for procrastination, for experimenting and playing around, and also because, like most writers, I also have a day job. I'm writing my novel word by word. I never wait for the arrival from on high of inspiration, or for the flash of a lightbulb moment. The story and the characters who make it are inside me, turning, turning, turning. I have subjects and questions rather than ideas, and I have language.

'The terrible secret about stories,' says the American writer Ben Marcus, 'is that they are made of language, entirely. Nothing else goes into them. Stories are language-made hallucinations. Character is a piece of language, slapped to life by a writer. So are plot and setting and conflict. These are acts of language rubbed over the air to make people appear. The story writer,' he says, 'is an artist of language.'

So, my challenge to you this weekend is to engage with the artistry of language and leave here determined to spread its riches. Buy a book and give it to someone else. Tell other people about something you heard or a discussion that provoked you. Those of you with children in your family, sit them down and ask them to write a vivid, concrete description of an old person in their life, a family member or a neighbour. Not their teachers, I mean someone really old. Look up words together and discuss what they mean. Read aloud together. Teach them the names of places in our city. Explain that there are two harbours, which a startling number of young people do not seem to know and are unable to name.

Interview your old people. Write down your family stories. Embrace te reo and make it part of your everyday life.

Kō te kai o te rangatira he kōrero. Tēnā koutou, tēnā koutou, tēnā koutou katoa.

2019 ELIZABETH KNOX

Cutting Through

Tēnā koutou katoa. It's wonderful to be here; I've been coming to the Going West Festival for ages. Fergus Barrowman and I were thinking about the times we've been here, and we remembered that the first time was 1999. It was about a week and a half after we'd come back from Menton in France — we'd been living there — and it was the most wonderful welcome home, to what is still one of those intimate, smaller New Zealand festivals. I love these festivals. I love Tauranga and Nelson and Mapua and all the little festivals — they've got something special about them. In 1999 Going West must have been going then for about three or four years.

We came with our twitchy seven-year-old. We had bought him a Game Boy, his first virtual drug, as it turned out. He was in this hall as I was trying to speak, and the only way we could keep him quiet was with the Game Boy. He lay under the seats in the hall, which were then school forms, those bent-wood, tubular-steel things, and every so often people in the audience would discover this boy, not only playing with the Game Boy, but using his back legs to scoot himself up and down the rows. Then he'd get into another row and scoot himself along. It was a thing.

I thought, 'Cutting Through', you can do a lot with that, and what I've done is to make a talk of two parts. The first part is the cutting through and the second part is where you find who gets to tell you the story of the cutting through. The story is set in 2006 and mostly in La Rochelle and then on a train back to Paris, where I had what I still consider to be one of the most important conversations of my life. That conversation was with Dylan Horrocks, who is in the room tonight. When I began to think about writing this address, I asked Dylan, 'Do you remember our conversation?' He did remember it, and he remembered where he was at when we had the conversation.

We got together and I wrote down what he said. I had my journal of the time, where I had written what I remembered of the conversation when I got back to Paris and lay in bed and wrote it down. And when we'd had this meeting and Dylan and I were leaving, I said, 'I hope between my memory and my journal and what you've just told me now, I'll be able to put it together,' and he said, 'I'll just make it up.' So, sorry Dylan, in order for this to work, some of it is — mm — stitched. It's a bit of a Frankenstein discussion.

'Tower of the Lantern, Tower of the Chain.' Thirteen years ago, in 2006, I was one of 12 New Zealand writers chosen for Les Belles Étrangères, a festival held every year in November, in which writers from a single country go to France and talk about what they do. All of us had had books published in French. A French film maker came over mid-year and made a documentary about us and there was to be a whole section of a major newspaper devoted to our work.

Several months before we flew to Europe, my extravagantly generous French publishers fled France for Byron Bay. All their stock was pulped before Pierre Fulan, my translator, even knew about it and could secure copies of my book. In short, I went to France with no book in French, with a wonderful full-page review in that national newspaper and no book to sell. Pierre was on the festival committee and did well to get me gigs. I talked in Paris and Lyon, Nevers and Aix-en-Provence; acquitted myself well and sometimes did myself proud. The last place I was scheduled to go was La Rochelle, with Dylan Horrocks. Dylan had talks in two comic shops and we were together at a couple of high schools and, rather strangely, the business school at a university.

We had one public evening event. I was up for all of it: we'd been well looked after; I'd had only good experiences; there were always translators; there were always eager audiences. I did wish I had more French, but I wasn't the only one of us with very little. In social situations I was quite prepared to just listen. I could follow much of the conversation — a great deal went in but very little came out, which is the way my brain has always worked. I was good at paying close attention and being interested.

So, when did it start?

We were in our hotel, sitting at a brass filigree-trimmed table, drinking the local apéritif. I was listening to a conversation about the changes in the character of La Rochelle since the high-speed train was built. More people have retired here, they said, and have weekend homes and there's all the businesses now dedicated to building and maintaining luxury yachts.

I was getting almost all of this but couldn't speak because I had the nouns but not the grammar. Dylan was conversing in hesitant fragments. He'd done French in high school, so he'd been able to read the comics. Somewhere during this introductory and unsettling in-gathering, I began to have the impression that this little group of hosts thought that I wasn't the writer — Dylan was the writer and I was just something they had to take in order to get him.

My book had been pulped. I didn't speak French. I wasn't representative of my country. There were five of us sitting there and I realised the locals were being led by the one who wouldn't look at me, our main host. Let us call him Yves.

The next morning I went out by myself, carrying a book about the town. It was Sunday and everything was closed on the Rue de la Mare. Wet, black silt filled all the pores and wrinkles of the marble paving stones. The creamy stone of the buildings and pavement made the streets look like a channel of old bone. The Atlantic was brown and full against the sea wall and the rampart between the two towers flanking the harbour.

I consulted my book and distinguished the towers by the daylight-dulled lamp burning at the top of one: the Tower of the Lantern, built to guide ships into the port. My book had a diagram of the great winch inside the other tower, the machine that raised the chain, normally resting on the seabed at the opening to the harbour to seal it off from ships: the Tower of the Chain.

There were myriad dull bells of cordage striking the aluminium masts of the yachts in the port; it went on and on like prayer wheels. There was a bronze basket-like sculpture of a globe on the waterfront; it gave off an air of aspiration, not about the journey, but local increase, bringing the bounty home. I turned a page and read that the Palace of Justice was built with money from the sale of slaves. I went up the street to have a look at it.

It was a comparatively low building for one so ornately decorated. Its gargoyles looked avaricious rather than surprised. The sea wind was cold and my hands were numb, so I went into the Galeries Lafayette to look at the clothes: jackets and skirts with appliqué, crusted with sequins and rosettes and bugle beads. They seemed as ugly and opulent as the buildings. I went out again onto cobblestones crusted with dogshit. The whole street seemed somehow hungry and breathing ketones.

At that evening's public performance, I read two excerpts of *Daylight* from the anthology *Les Belles Étrangèrs*, and *Europe* magazine. I read them in English and a translator delivered them in French. Yves was chairing and his first question to me was a statement: 'Let me propose that Martine Raimondi of the first excerpt doesn't seem like a saint, but a very ordinary woman.' I was left defending what I'd done. I said that Martine Raimondi's miracle was in fact another kind of supernatural agency, and was mistaken for a miracle. Martine prayed to God and it could be argued that God sent her a vampire.

Yves gazed at me heavily and didn't even nod. I felt that I was the very ordinary woman being put forward for something unearned. I said that a great deal of the book was about people not having the full picture; that my books aren't holographic — their entireties cannot be deduced from their parts. Later, Yves asked about the passages with Grazide, de

Chambord, Ila, the vampire, her lover, and the young journeyman she brings into the relationship so she won't infect her lover. It's a sickly, sensuous, alienating, scary story.

Yves asked, his face screwed up in an expression of fastidious squeamishness, why I wrote it. It wasn't an interested question. It wasn't puzzlement. It was indignation. I talked about origin stories in vampire tales as being as integral as superhero origin stories and, like superhero origin stories, necessary but not sufficient. I tried to say why it was fiendish, why it was feverish and how it was meant to make readers worry about the principal character, even while he's enjoying himself and thinking he's in control of what's happening to him. Yves cast a look of appeal and complicity at the audience. He watched the translator with an air of dubious disbelief, as if to say, why must anyone be made to repeat these things?

The following day we visited two high schools. The first was within the city limits. Its pupils had elegant uniforms; they were sleek with ski-resort tans. They weren't very interested in us — perhaps their days were a dégustation menu and they were spoiled for choice. The teacher who was translating highly controlled the session, but it was okay; not depressing; not too deflating; just a little blah.

The second school was a long way out among low buildings and fields of glasshouses. We were in the school library. The kids were in mufti; there were two girls in hijabs, whose faces lit up when Dylan mentioned Marjane Satrapi's *Persepolis*.

As we talked, the kids gradually sat up straighter, apart from the four friends lounging at the front who seemed to operate like a row of linked chairs, laughing and tottering back and forth in unison, their hands kept shooting up. The teacher spoke to them in a calm, managing voice. At one point I made these bright-eyed 14-year-old boys laugh, with my mimed description of a plane landing at Wellington airport: seesawing wings, passengers gripping their seats, then wiping their brows, then applauding the pilot. It was a small story I was able to tell, with simple English and acting.

There was a big laugh and a lot of heaving from the front row. The teacher threw one of the boys out. Dylan looked at me, telegraphing, 'How do we argue against this if we don't know what tone to take?' — the teacher's manner was so curt and dictatorial and utterly confident in its authority. We finished up and there was afternoon tea.

The teachers took the time to talk to me; they hadn't seemed at all interested before I spoke. I was sensing by that time that with these hosts I was working against an earlier briefing by Yves. They seemed pleasantly surprised by me.

We were in the staffroom for the better part of an hour. When we left, and our minibus paused for the steel gate to slide open, we spotted on the curb opposite the gate that lively boy. He stood straight and gave us a full-arm wave, a kind of salute. Dylan had said something that encouraged or excited him and I had made him laugh. For a short time, he owned Dylan; he was not exactly dispossessed but wasn't entitled either. He seemed to understand what we had to say about not really being relevant, about being pirates of a sort.

That salute was possibly the loveliest moment in my public life as a writer — the boy who waited for over an hour to show gratitude and respect, that independent soul ejected for being too vulgarly enthusiastic and noisy.

Back at the hotel we met up with Yves again and he asked us what we wanted to do with the few hours before dinner. Dylan said he wanted to browse the comic shops and would go by himself. I said I'd like to buy T-shirts for my husband and son. I asked advice about where to go and Yves chose to interpret that as a sign of my helpless dependence. He insisted on accompanying me.

That afternoon there were rough young men under the arcades near the Galeries Lafayette, a group of them with their family of dogs, including a tired mother dog with one pup: a slit-eyed blonde creature with a long, mean snout, who was lying, sleepy and warm, under a jacket shiny with grime.

When I passed, I stepped out on to the road to avoid the dogs. One young man said in French, 'Well fuck you!' He felt slighted. I was hurrying after Yves, who was trotting ahead of me, his umbrella over his head but partly furled — my guide, but he wasn't really with me. His raised shoulders and brisk walk telegraphed his sense of obligation, of going out of his way to be helpful to an unrewarding charge. I was on the outside, then reproached for wounding the feelings of outsiders. I even liked the look of the dogs, and of them, the young men. I was beginning to feel for all young men — their strength, their lack of confidence in their strength, their struggle for dignity. I detoured the dogs only because I was scared of them. Of course, I must have looked like the property of Yves and his upturned nose because I was being demure — I was being demure to deflect his hostility. I had to make it up to him for something, something essential to me: my prideful expectation that since I was invited, I must be welcome. Since the Lantern in the Tower was lit, the chain must be lying on the sea floor.

That evening Yves and I arrived at the restaurant first. We sat at our table and he kept turning around to watch the door and was as relieved as I was to see Dylan and the other host, Martina, arrive. The wine came; Yves proposed a toast of thanks. He spoke only to Dylan; looked only at Dylan. His body and eyes turned from me, despite Dylan's repeatedly glancing my way in an effort to include me. I felt ill and trembled and just sat there, as speechless as an infant or an idiot.

In my journal I wrote, 'Is this a matter for complaint, or only for characterisation?' The following day Yves arrived at the hotel to drive us to the station. Dylan and I had embarked on a long conversation and had to rush to pack. It was a conversation we continued on the train, about our attitudes to our work and how our decisions to write comics, to write fantasies, seemed sometimes to be taken as a kind of fetishism of independence, an effort to avoid authority, to avoid influence, as in being influenced and being influential. But we were just doing what we could do.

Yves arrived and did his conscientious best, carrying my bag to the car; asking how I slept. At the station he produced his copy of *Hicksville* for Dylan to sign then, as an afterthought, with all the gestures and atmosphere of an afterthought, he called me over to the little bar table to sign my excerpt in the *Belles Étrangères* book, the chapter he had persisted in calling a short story, despite my explanations. I wrote: 'To Yves, thank you for your unstinting support.'

Dylan noticed what I'd written and was amused. I doubted very much that Yves would notice the irony, being so certain that I was a blockheaded little pretender. The train pulled out from under the canopy of the station and gradually picked up speed. We were under a clear sky. There was a rainbow out on the water, behind it a thick blank front of cloud. As we went along the cloud thinned and whitened. There was another rainbow, then clear blue with a radiant haze of moisture in the air, and in the Atlantic two islands visible above the piled brown waves.

Dylan and I were in the quiet carriage with all the knitting women. We watched the scenery until it disappeared above the concrete trench of the railway line. Dylan then said that perhaps Yves was just socially awkward, nervous, staid or shy. I agreed that Yves was clearly a man of propriety, but so much so that his sense of propriety had led him into impropriety. 'Yes, it would be more accurate to thank him for his unstinting *material* support,' Dylan said.

But was it really that bad? I spent the whole time wondering what I'd done wrong and trying to think how to fix it, but I think it was my writing, the rumour of the pulped *Vintner* and its fallen angel, and my *Daylight* extracts. Perhaps he saw it as an attack on his faith? Dylan reminded me how in the documentary I had told a story about my trepidation at seeing a group of nuns in my signing line at the Adelaide Festival, getting closer and closer. And how, when they finally got to me, one said that I'd renewed her faith. When I told the story I laughed. I laughed in amazement — gratitude and amazement. But if Yves saw the documentary, he might have taken my laughter the wrong way. Dylan said that perhaps Yves thought his beliefs couldn't also be my stories; he thought he was someone with strict ideas about where stories belong. I thought that even if Yves hated my writing — or his idea of my writing — a host shouldn't snub a helpless, and dependent guest, dependent for the necessary morale to get up in front of an audience and try to shine.

Dylan said that Yves seemed to have social facility but no warmth. 'I wouldn't really describe him in terms of temperature', I said. Perhaps pH levels, his being acidic. Then, our host disposed of, we picked up where we'd left off at breakfast. Dylan said that on the subject of stories and beliefs he had recently described his creeping feeling of a disenchantment with fiction to an old friend, formerly and for many years, a born-again Christian. His friend said, 'What you're describing is a crisis of faith.'

The crisis seemed to have begun with conversations Dylan had with Geoff Austen, the physicist assigned to him for the *Are Angels OK?* project, a project which matched New Zealand physicists and writers. It wasn't the physics itself that disturbed Dylan's sense of what he was doing, it was the epistemology. 'Physicists describe the world but don't fudge the data', he said, 'there's rigour'. For many years he'd had a quote that was a touchstone to him, Picasso's 'Art is the lie that tells the truth'. Physicists have facts about which they are transparent; they write papers that begin by outlining the limitations of the study, but all fiction creates a model of the world and pretends that it's an accurate model. What do they say to this? Maybe that fiction's subjectivity is a given — limitations of a study can be assumed by the reader. If there's anything missing the reader feels should be there, that's not fudging, that's the flavour of rancid butter in the fudge.

I might have said that, but mostly I evangelised. I recommended reading: 'You say you've lost your faith, but perhaps you've lost appetite.' 'That was true too,' Dylan said, 'I'm not finding that stories are doing for me as an adult what they did for me when I was a very young person. Fiction's goal often declared is to make us feel what it's like to be alive in the world, but none of it feels *of life* to me anymore.' Then he told me a little about his time working for DC Comics, with characters he loved, and how he'd ended up writing what he felt DC wanted him to write, not what he wanted to.

'DC didn't get in my way. I got in my own way. Now when I'm writing, it's with internalised ideas of other people's wishes.' He said that he worried about the responsibilities of art — he didn't trust art; he didn't want to make distinctions anymore between high and low. As a younger man he'd had a kind of cultural cringe about what he loved: fantasy, Dungeons and Dragons. He determined to be serious. 'Okay,' I said, 'maybe part of that is being a bloke — because a male artist has more hope of being taken seriously, sometimes it must feel like there's a duty to try.'

For me, I felt there were far fewer possibilities in what might be seen as serious if I made it — seriousness wasn't something to aim for. It's probably been easier for me to separate my ideas of seriousness from other people's. I'm not trying to be serious, I'm just serious about what I do. Also, I thought, Dylan's dad taught at university and wrote books I'd read and cared about.

My dad's grasp on New Zealand culture was snatched and slippery to begin with, and he never forgot how that felt. He was largely self-educated, starting with the help of the Greytown librarian when he was a thirteen-year-old welfare boy, expelled from school and avoiding borstal by being manpowered to farm work in the Wairarapa.

After the War and the merchant marine he worked part-time towards a degree in English, between the freezing works and being a lab assistant in the Dominion Laboratories and an alpine guide at the Hermitage. He didn't sit his finals because the chief guide wouldn't give him leave to do so. Dad came into New Zealand culture by the tradesman's entrance, as a reporter. Then he was the father of daughters. And what, in the sixties, was one to hope for daughters?

That said, the fullest, truest story of my slow start with seriousness is only partly about gender and class. Mostly it's this: that in my childhood, any hopes Dad had of transmitting his love of literature landed on my older sister Mary, after a Department of Education psychologist, brought in to test her because of her difficulties at school, discovered she was highly intelligent and declared that this was obviously the cause of all her troubles.

An expansion of Mary's educational horizons was recommended. The school's solution was to put her in a model-making class with the boys, but our parents, rather more effectively, began to take her to operas and plays. They gave her art supplies and Dad sat her down now and then for sessions in music appreciation. All the culture in our house, before as environmental as the haze of cigarette smoke suspended below the ceiling, was suddenly directed at just one daughter and, in the eyes of the other two, was clearly remedial.

The attention turned from Sarah and me was freedom to drift into our own interests outside of school and outside of imaginary games, which we were all more serious about than any other thing in our lives. Marbles, trading toy cars, four-square, cowboy hats, hobby-horses and cap-guns, scented rubbers, Bullrush, canoeing, high-jumping, television, old movies, sad ballads, and books of course. Our things were our things and if they were also the things of other kids, they were no more theirs than ours.

I loved Shakespeare, after seeing Lawrence Olivier's *Henry V* at 11. I painted battle scenes with knights and horses, arches and pikemen. I read *Ivanhoe* and made model castles. Sarah drew a long series of cartoons of conversations between *Jaws*' Brody, Quint and Hooper on the not-big-enough boat, the shark often joining in.

In our house, these activities fell under the general description of 'what the kids are doing'. Sarah and I were the kids. We were offered no recommendations; nothing was remedial; no one was holding open a door to a better, higher place. We had no sense of inheriting anything, of being ushered in, or being offered custodianship. So when Dylan said to me that part of the remedy for him for his loss of faith in fiction, and for his deep suspicion of the idea of the responsibilities of art was to stop making distinctions between high and low, it only baffled me.

I got that sensation I get when baffled of someone dabbing with soft fingertips on the skin above my eyebrows. 'People keep finding ways of adjudicating value,' Dylan said, 'so literary fiction has more value than genre fiction.' 'I've been saying for years that literary fiction is also a genre,' I said. 'But I do think it's the genre in which literature is more likely to appear.' 'But what is literature?' said Dylan. 'What lasts,' I said. 'That's the only measure. When we read a new book, we can make bets on it; we can say, this will last. Time proves us right or wrong, and sometimes wrong then right. *Moby Dick* and *Wuthering Heights* were rescued. Georgette Heyer is still in print, so she's literature. She must be. Literature can appear in any genre. But authors with a feeling for what is deep and undecidable more often choose to write literary fiction.'

Dylan at this point must have thought he was having a discussion with someone still mired in concepts of high and low. But in my childhood and teen world of generally benign neglect, I'd had a great freedom of wandering wherever I wanted. No-one ever suggested all this might be mine, I just enjoyed a right of way. I wasn't expected to declare myself or pledge to anything.

'To me,' Dylan said, 'intentions are part of the problem. I don't trust the intentions of art. I don't think any more that art is innately good.' I wondered then whether Dylan was having this crisis of faith because he'd actually had faith, whereas all I'd ever had was enjoyment and a determination to join in with what I enjoyed. He'd been in one place and was now in another and would eventually reach some other place. There was growth and maturity in this progression. I was just wandering through someone else's farmland, across the brook by the stone-slab bridge, then along the edge of the forest, and it wasn't progression. My attitude hadn't changed. And wouldn't change. I wasn't going to drink from the well or pluck the rose or get myself into any trouble. And if nothing belonged to me, maybe I belonged to nothing and that had to be a problem.

'I suppose,' I said to Dylan, 'that what wears me out is always having to explain: why these things and not others. Why vampires? Why angels? Why gollums?' 'Yes,' he said, 'that question: why are you interested in these things? Who could be interested in these things?' I said that I felt I always had to explain why I'd done something and scarcely ever got to talk about what I'd done, the work itself. Again, and again the why, when the why is in the what.

'Why do I need to choose between high and low?' said Dylan. 'It's like having to choose sides or parties, when artists aren't voters among parties. We're mediums among ghosts. I mean, I have friends who love role-playing and fantasy, but not Schubert or Truffaut or Dickens. I have friends who love Goddard and Colin McCahon, but not Barry Linton or Superman.'

I said that one thing I should do is stop telling people that my setting a book in France was an accident. Yes it was, but it was also fate. It wasn't coincidental, isolated or accidental that I sat in that hall, full of bored, rioting eleven-year-olds, wrapt, watching Olivier's *Henry V*. It woke me up: the language, but also the way the story moved from the stage of the Globe Theatre — artifice as artifice — to a sound stage and a column of soldiers marching away into what, only moments before, was a painted flat. That movement from transparent artifice to the deeper artifice of the studio, then to the naturalism of the battle in the open air, then back into the sound stage and fake snow in the wooing scene — all that woke me up.

When I started working on *The Vintner's Luck*, I was one of those unwashed people standing in the pit, where they sometimes have bear fighting when they aren't having plays. I just wanted to be entertained. But to do that I had to build up a world of keenly real artifice. Then I found I'd summoned at some point three dimensions and the open air. *Henry V* is about an English king invading France. I didn't invade — I only didn't ask permission to love. Love doesn't need permission to love.

Dylan said, 'These days when I'm asked "why these things", I try to remember that working backwards from what I've done, I can usually see the necessity. And necessity can look like fate. Also, surely any kind of work can be hospitable, as my former fundamentalist friend would say, "My father's house has many mansions".'

Our conversation was making earthworks in my brain. There was a when: a day in November 2006. There was a where: the train's quiet carriage. There was a who: Dylan, the person I was talking to.

The turning arms of many wind turbines bristled behind the ridges. Beyond the carriage was a conveyor belt of landscape. The knitting women scowled at conversation in the quiet carriage. On the station at Portières a soldier got on, kissing his mother and hoisting his kit bag.

How does anyone lose faith in fiction? Maybe because of too much why and too little where, when and who. That conversation was long, extraordinary and afterwards in my room at the Villa des Artistes in Montparnasse I tried to write down what I could remember of it; what was said and what I thought about in the pauses.

I'd opened a window and couldn't close it. Despite the fierce heat from the radiator, it got cold and my hand holding the pencil was chilled. I made a kind of digest of the conversation, too much of which was our overstatement of our cases.

Dylan hadn't finished thinking through things he at least knew he had to think through, most of which hadn't ever occurred to me because I was pretty much standing on the air like Wile E. Coyote after he's chased the Roadrunner off a cliff.

I'd spent much of the conversation perplexed by Dylan's description of where he was at in his thinking and trying to think of other ways he might be encouraged to see things. But even then, I knew I must be wrong because I'd just had my wrongness rubbed in my face. I guess in the end this is about hospitality; about the experience of being invited but not welcome. Surely no one's existence is an affront. No one's difference insists you change. A bird doesn't want to fly into your house. It wants to fly through your house. No one needs to man the ramparts. The sample of artists trying to con us is statistically minute. A book may mean to take you for a ride. If it does, it's a good one.

Anyway, why this epidemic of doubt, of dubiousness? Why this obsession with credentials? 'Show us that you really are sincere,' is a demand from the same dysfunctional family as 'demonstrate you really are in need' and 'prove that you really were injured'.

The Tower of the Lantern and the Tower of the Chain flanked the entrance to La Rochelle's Vieux-Port. Yves' one kind offering to me was a story. He told me that twice in his life he'd seen the waters of the Vieux-Port frozen and seabirds walking on it. When that happened they raised the chain to break the ice and let the boats in, which is the opposite of its intended use.

Now, 13 years later, still a writer of proper and improper genres, I hope that maybe there is no mechanism of the inhospitable that might not also be used to break the ice.

Thank you. Cheers.

This address will appear as the title essay in a forthcoming collection by Elizabeth Knox, *Tower of the Lantern, Tower of the Chain*.

Postscript

This book was born from a crisis at the crossroads. An entire year almost never happened. We stood in empty rooms. Nobody knew what to do. We just turned on our computers and hoped for the best.

We cancelled our live festival. That hurt, in several ways. First, cancelling just hurts. It's your big thing, and then you're not doing it any more. Second, cancelling hurt some of our corporate partners, and quite frankly things happened faster than we would have liked. And then it hurt still more when we came out of lockdown and people started going out to restaurants, gigs and plays and stuff. And there we were, alone in all the world without a festival to our name.

We thought about bringing it back in some limited capacity. No chance. The big wheel kept on turning and we weren't on it. So it got worse. We looked around at the incredible festivals all over the country — from the biggest stages in the land to the tiniest cafes, to woolsheds, pubs and historic houses — and we realised that what we'd done in the past was just that: done.

And still things got worse. We'd always been super-proud of our programming kaupapa: Aotearoa-exclusive. But with the borders closed there was bugger-all chance of that point of difference remaining. Now, Aotearoa-only is situation-normal. What's the longest-running, dedicated literary festival in Aotearoa to do?

Well, we talked. We got together as-and-when, held a range of hui, and had a bloody big think. What — we asked — was the point? We realised that if we are to make any difference at all, it's not enough to do what we've always done. I mean, we'll always bring people together to talk about books, but we reckon if that's all there is to it, we're doomed. Not just us, but everyone. We're here for the narrative culture of the land. We're here to contribute to that. To explore it, celebrate it and — where possible — create it. Was carrying on with what we had always done the best way to do that?

Besides, what we'd always done was so broad that the word 'literature' hardly contained it. With theatre, music, poetry slams, exhibitions, workshops and something called human libraries (look it up, it's a thing), we felt we were constantly operating beyond the bounds of the textual. That's before we even consider non-Pākeha narratives, in which some of the stories are indistinguishable from lived experience. We knew that, for us, 'literature' went way beyond books, or literacy. For us, literature is about culture, knowledge, transformation. Not so much literacy as *cultural* literacy.

So Going West became a content producer. We know we're here for readers and writers — or, rather, storytellers and listeners. It dawned on us that one of the best things we could do for both those groups was to commission new stories. That puts money in the pockets of artists, and stories in the hearts of the people.

So we thought of podcasts, which Naomi has already covered in her wonderful introduction. We thought of poetry videos, and made a season of them with some of the best poets and filmmakers around. We thought of documentaries about storytellers, and there's a couple of those under way too, and they're wonderful. We thought of lots of new ways of doing our festival that made it new and different — and even Covid-proof — without changing the sense of familiarity and manaaki for which we've become well known and loved.

And, yes, we thought of this book. Twenty-five years of Going West oratorical history. These oratories, as a collection, are like Jorge Luis Borges's idea of the library of Babel, forming the microscopic fibres that connect us as a society, both real and imagined. The range is formidable: from deep analysis and theory to flippant satire and humour, from memoir and anecdote to assertion and — at times — even condemnation. Tracing a network of histories and chronologies, they enrich our collective memory, and illuminate our possible future — or, rather, many possible futures.

In his novel *The House of Strife*, our late friend Maurice Shadbolt put this question in the mouth of an ambitious young writer: 'What are we, if not our stories?' In a sense, Going West perpetually seeks an answer to this rhetorical question. But we do so, safe in the knowledge that it is an endless task. There is no answer, and if there was, it would be: 'Nothing.'

Any other answer is destined to reside perpetually in the future. For now, let's enjoy the crossroads. Let's allow some of the many voices of Aotearoa to keep us company, to reflect us in some way, to shed some light and warmth, and to be our companions on the endless journey to the future.

James Littlewood
Director, Going West
Titirangi, April 2021

The Speakers

NGAHUIA TE AWEKOTUKU is a writer, researcher, and specialist on cultural heritage and contemporary practice. Her works include *E Ngā Uri Whakatupu — Weaving Legacies: Dame Rangimarie Hetet and Diggeress Te Kanawa* (2015), and the short fiction collection *Tahuri: a limited edition* (2017). In 2017 she was made Fellow of the Auckland War Memorial Museum for exemplary scholastic achievement relevant to Museum collections. In 2010 she was appointed Member of the New Zealand Order of Merit for services to Māori culture. She is an Emeritus Professor of the University of Waikato.

DAME CHRISTINE COLE CATLEY was a pioneering journalist, editor, publisher and author. She was friends with the artist Rita Angus, who painted her holding her eldest child. She was the head of New Zealand's first tertiary course in journalism. With her husband Doug she formed Cape Cately publishers. She established the Frank Sargeson Trust, the Sargeson Fellowship, and helped establish the Michael King Writers' Centre. She was awarded the Queen's Service Medal for public services and appointed Distinguished Companion of the New Zealand Order of Merit for services to literature, later redesignated Dame Companion of the New Zealand Order of Merit.

NIGEL COX was an award-winning novelist, essayist, museum professional, bookseller and co-founder of the independent bookshop Unity Books, Auckland. He co-led the project team which created the Jewish Museum Berlin, becoming the museum's Head of Exhibitions and Communications. The author of six novels, including *Tarzan Presley*, he was awarded the Buckland Literary Award in 1988 and the Katherine Mansfield Memorial Fellowship in 1991.

ALLEN CURNOW was a poet, journalist, editor and academic. He is one of New Zealand's most significant literary figures. He published 21 volumes of poetry, seven receiving the New Zealand Book Award for poetry; he received the Commonwealth Poetry Prize in 1988, and in 1989 became only the second poet outside the U.K. to receive the Queen's Gold Medal for poetry. In 1986 he was appointed Commander of the Order of the British Empire for services to literature, and in 1990 was appointed Member of the Order of New Zealand.

PATRICIA GRACE (Ngāti Toa, Ngāti Raukawa, Te Ati Awa) is a novelist, short story writer and children's author. Her first published work, *Waiariki* (1975), was the first published collection of short stories by a female Māori writer. She has won national and international awards including the Neustadt International Prize for Literature, the Prime Minister's Literary Award and received an honorary D.Lit. from the World Indigenous Nations University in 2016. In 1988 she was made Companion of the Queen's Service Order for community service and in 2007 was appointed Distinguished Companion of the New Zealand Order of Merit for services to literature, declining redesignation as Dame Companion following the restoration of titular honours.

CHARLOTTE GRIMSHAW is an award-winning writer and reviewer. Her acclaimed novels *The Night Book* and *Soon* have been adapted into television series. Her novels and short stories have been published in the U.K. and Canada. She received the Montana Book Award for Fiction for *Opportunity* (2007), and the Montana Medal for Fiction or Poetry in 2008.

In 2018 and 2019 she was named Reviewer of the Year at the Voyager Media Awards.

STEPHANIE JOHNSON is a short story writer, novelist, poet, playwright, critic and teacher with numerous publications, plays and radio dramas to her name. She was co-founder of the Auckland Writers Festival. She won the Montana Book Award Deutz Medal for *The Shag Incident* in 2003. In 2000 she was awarded the Katherine Mansfield Fellowship in Menton, France, and in 2001 was made a Literary Fellow at the University of Auckland. In 2019 she was appointed Member of the New Zealand Order of Merit for services to literature.

DAME FIONA KIDMAN has published over 30 books including novels, non-fiction, short stories and poetry. Her novel *This Mortal Boy* won the 2019 Ockham New Zealand Book award and her latest short story compilation *All the Way to Summer* was the 2020 winner of the New Zealand Heritage Prize for Fiction. In 2021 Dame Fiona was the inaugural recipient of the University of Otago Centre for Irish and Scottish Studies Irish Writers Fellowship. She was appointed Officer of the Order of the British Empire in 1998 and in 1988 Dame Companion of the New Zealand Order of Merit, both for services to literature. In 2009 she was made by the French Government Chevalier de l'Ordre des Arts et des Lettres and a Chevalier of the French Legion of Honour.

MICHAEL KING was an author, historian and biographer. He published over 34 books and won more awards for his books, journalism and television work than any other New Zealander. These included the Katherine Mansfield Memorial Fellowship, the Robert Burns Fellowship and the inaugural Prime Ministers Award for Literary Achievement for non-fiction. His last publication *The Penguin History of New Zealand* has sold more than 200,000 copies. In 1988 he was appointed Officer of the Order of the British Empire.

ELIZABETH KNOX has published many novels for adults and teenagers, as well as a trilogy of autobiographical novellas, and a collection of essays. Her works have been published internationally, with the award winning *The Vintner's Luck*, being printed in ten languages and made into a film. She was awarded the New Zealand Order of Merit in 2002 for services to literature, and in 2020 appointed Companion of the New Zealand Order of Merit for literary achievement.

PAULA MORRIS (Ngāti Wai, Ngāti Whātua) is a multi-award-winning novelist, short story writer, essayist and teacher, and the founder of the Academy of New Zealand Literature. She has received numerous residencies and fellowships in New Zealand and internationally. In 2019 she was appointed Member of the New Zealand Order of Merit for services to literature. She is convenor of the Master of Creative Writing programme at the University of Auckland.

BERNARD MAKOARE (Te Uri o Hau, Ngāti Whātua, Te Waiariki, Te Kai Tūtae, Te Rarawa, Ngāpuhi-nui-tonu) is a Northland based artist, traditional carver, designer and cultural consultant, and the Chairperson of Toi Ngāpuhi. He has contributed to and collaborated on works at major institutions in Tāmaki Makaurau including the Auckland Zoo, the Auckland Art Gallery and the Auckland War Memorial Museum.

ROD ORAM is an award-winning business journalist, columnist and writer on economic, political and corporate issues. He writes and speaks about the landscapes of business, economics, innovation, creativity, entrepreneurship and sustainability in Aotearoa and internationally. He is part of the 2014 inaugural cohort of the Edmund Hillary Fellowship, established to create solutions to global problems. He is an Adjunct Professor in Public Policy at AUT.

VINCENT O'SULLIVAN is a poet, novelist, short story writer, playwright and librettist. He is also a distinguished editor, anthologist, essayist, and biographer. He has won premium book awards and numerous fellowships both in New Zealand and internationally. From 2013 to 2015 he served as the New Zealand Poet Laureate. His book *Ralph Hotere: the dark is light enough: a biographical portrait* won the 2021 Ockham General Non-fiction Award. In 2000 he was appointed a Distinguished Companion of the Order of Merit for services to literature.

GEOFF PARK was an ecologist, research scientist and the author of the acclaimed ecological history of New Zealand, *Ngā Uruora: the groves of life: ecology and history in a New Zealand landscape*, which he began researching during his 1986 fellowship at the Stout Research Centre. He was extensively involved in the ecological and conservation communities in New Zealand and was instrumental in protecting the coastal wetland region that is now Punakaiki National Park.

CHRIS PRICE is a poet, editor, essayist, and educator and for a decade the editor of the literary journal *Landfall*. Her inaugural book of poetry, *Husk*, won the Jessie Mackay Best First Book Award for Poetry at the 2002 Montana Book Awards. In 2008 she was the Auckland University Writer in Residence at the Michael King Writers' Centre and awarded the Katherine Mansfield Fellowship in 2011. She teaches at the International Institute of Modern Letters at Victoria University.

DAME ANNE SALMOND is an anthropologist, environmentalist and pre-eminent writer of New Zealand history. In 2013 she was New Zealander of the Year and has won numerous awards in recognition of her works exploring early Māori and Pākehā encounters. In 1990 she was elected a Fellow of the Royal Society of New Zealand, and in 2013 was the first social scientist to be awarded the Rutherford Medal. She was appointed a Commander of the Order of the British Empire for services to literature and the Māori people in 1988, and Dame Commander of the Order of the British Empire in 1995. In 2020 she was appointed to the Order of New Zealand. She is Distinguished Professor of Māori Studies and Anthropology at the University of Auckland.

MAURICE SHADBOLT was a leading New Zealand writer, journalist, playwright and film-director. He was the first full-time New Zealand author to make a living from his writing, and all of his novels and short stories were published internationally. He won every major New Zealand literary prize, some multiple times. In 1989 he was appointed Commander of the Order of the British Empire for services to literature. His home in Titirangi West Auckland, is set to become a writers' residence.

TONY SIMPSON is an award-winning writer and social and cultural historian. He has also had a distinguished career in journalism, editing, television, arts administration, politics and as a strategic planner and policy analyst. His publications explore the diversity of Aotearoa New Zealand's social and political history. He has written on Māori land loss, the Treaty, and extensively on the lives of working-class New Zealanders. In 2005 he was made a Member of the New Zealand Order of Merit in recognition of his services to historical research.

ROBERT SULLIVAN is a poet, academic and editor. He lives in North Otago and belongs to Ngāpuhi, and Kāi Tahu. His seven collections of poetry include *Captain Cook in the Underworld*, *Shout Ha! to the Sky* and the best-selling *Star Waka*. He has co-edited three major anthologies of Pacific and Māori poetry. His Ph.D. thesis *Mana Moana*, examines the work of five indigenous Pacific poets.

TE RADAR (Andrew J. Lumsden) describes himself as a humourist, documentarian and raconteur. He is a panel moderator, an MC and a keynote after-dinner speaker. He has a particular passion for retelling stories from the history of Aotearoa New Zealand. Te Radar has won awards for his television and comedy work.

DAME MARILYN WARING is a public policy academic, an international development consultant, environmentalist, farmer and feminist and is credited as the principal founder of feminist economics. In 1975, at age 23, she was elected New Zealand's youngest Member of Parliament and was one of only four women in the House. In 2020 she was appointed Dame Companion of the New Zealand Order of Merit for services to women and economics. She is a Professor of Public Policy at AUT.

IAN WEDDE is a poet, novelist, critic and art curator, and a former head of art and visual culture at Te Papa Tongarewa. He has been the recipient of over 30 major awards and many fellowships. He served as the New Zealand Poet Laureate from 2011 to 2013 and received the Prime Minister's Award for Literary Achievement for Poetry in 2014. In 2010 he was appointed Officer of the New Zealand Order of Merit for services to art and literature.

PETER WELLS was a writer, filmmaker and an historian. His works were frequently told through the lens of a gay narrator. *Dangerous Desires*, his first short story collection, won the New Zealand Book Award for Fiction and his memoir *Long Loop Home* the 2002 Montana Book Award for Biography. He spearheaded the saving and restoration of Auckland's Civic Theatre and was co-founder of the Auckland Writers Festival. In 2016 he launched New Zealand's first LGBTQI Writers Festival, 'samesame but different'. In 2006 he was appointed Member of the New Zealand Order of Merit for services to literature and film.

MAUALAIVAO ALBERT WENDT is a Samoan poet, novelist, short story writer, teacher and scholar. He wrote the first widely acclaimed Pasefika novel, *Sons for the Return Home* (1973) and is internationally renowned as one of Oceania's most influential writers. He has received numerous awards including the 2012 Prime Minister's Award for Literary Achievement in Fiction. In 2001 he was appointed Companion of the New Zealand Order of Merit, and in 2013, the Order of New Zealand for his services to literature. He is the first person of Pacific ancestry to hold a professorial academic chair in New Zealand and is Emeritus Professor of English at the University of Auckland.

Selected Notes

The edited chapters in this publication are based on the audio recordings in the Going West Books and Writers Festival Archive, which is held at Auckland Libraries/Ngā Pātaka Korero o Tāmaki Makaurau. The collection contains audio and visual material, ephemera and business records, and is searchable on the Auckland Libraries Heritage Collections database, viewing on request. Selected orator's audio recordings are available on both the Auckland Libraries and Going West Festival websites.

The Orators' own works quoted by them in their chapters are listed here, along with selected notes and publication acknowledgements. Some of our orators assigned their talks names different from the festival theme and these are noted here.

1996 Bernard Makoare, Ngahuia te Awekotuku, Robert Sullivan

The 1996 festival theme was 'Breathing Words' and this, the inaugural and keynote session, was titled 'Ngā Kupu Kōrero'.

1996 Ngahuia te Awekotuku

'Purotu' was published in *Below the Surface: words and images in protest at French testing on Moruroa*, edited by Ambury Hall, Vintage, 1995.

'For LMS 145, a bone flute at the British Museum' and 'For one trophy from the Waikato war, now in an unnamed museum' were originally published in *Homeland: new writing from America, the Pacific, and Asia*, edited by F. Stewart; Mānoa 9:1, University of Hawaii Press, 1997, and subsequently in, *Puna Wai Kōrero: an anthology of Māori poetry in English*, edited by Reina Whaitiri and Robert Sullivan, Auckland University Press, 2014.

1996 Robert Sullivan

'A Biography' was published in *Voice Carried My Family*, Auckland University Press, 2005.

'Not the 1990 Poem' was published in *Jazz Waiata*, Auckland University Press, 1990.

'Karakia for Bruce Stewart' and 'Maori are Children of God' were published in *Piki ake!: poems, 1990-92*, Auckland University Press, 1993.

1997 Maurice Shadbolt

The 1997 festival theme was 'Getting A Word In' and this, the key session, was titled 'Telling Stories — Words and Pictures'. Maurice Shadbolt spoke on writing, and Tainui Stephens on filmmaking: a session reliant on film and television clips.

Maurice Shadbolt refers to his books *Season of the Jew*, David Ling, 1987, and *One of Ben's*, David Ling, 1998.

1998 Ian Wedde

*The Foresight Project was a think tank established in 1997 by then Prime Minister Jenny Shipley and Minister of Science and Technology, Maurice Williamson.

**In his subsequent essay 'The Nation's Narratives', published in *Making Ends Meet: essays & talks 1992–2004*, Victoria University Press, 2005; Ian Wedde expanded greatly on his response to the SRAs.

1999 Vincent O'Sullivan

A revised version of 'Exit' was provided by the author for this publication. 'Exit' was originally published in *The Pilate Tapes*, Oxford University Press, 1986.

'Them' and 'Corner' were published in *Selected Poems*, Oxford University Press, 1992.

'Remembering Westmere' was published in *Further Convictions Pending: poems 1998-2008*, Victoria University Press, Wellington, 2009.

Vincent O'Sullivan reads from *Let the River Stand*, Penguin, 1983, and *Believers to the Bright Coast*, Penguin, 1989.

2000 Dame Fiona Kidman

The short story 'A Strange Delight' was reissued as 'Mrs Dixon & Friend' in *The House Within*, Vintage, 1997, available as an eBook, and updated in *All the Way to Summer*, Vintage, 2020. The short story 'A Dangerous Boy', was published in *The House Within*, Vintage, 1997.

'Wakeful Nights' was published in *Wakeful Nights: poems selected and new*, Vintage, 1991.

2001 Michael King

Michael King expanded on the details of the Belgrave family in his subsequent publication *At the Edge of Memory: a family story*, Penguin, 2002.

2002 Dame Marilyn Waring

Dame Marilyn Waring reads from *In the Lifetime of a Goat: writings 1984-2000*, Bridget Williams Books, and she refers to her book *Counting for Nothing: what men value and what women are worth*, Allen and Unwin, 1988.

2003 Geoff Park

The 2003 festival theme was 'Wild New Zealand — Voices from the Landscape'. Geoff Park's talk was identified as 'Writing into the Wild' in the festival programme but was called by him 'Writing into the Bush'.

Within the publication timeframe every effort was made to source the quoted material in this chapter and render it accurately. Some quotes were not able to be traced and so may differ in their arrangement and wording from the source.

Geoff Park reads from *Ngā Uruora: the groves of life: ecology and history in a New Zealand landscape*, Victoria University Press, 1995 and 2003.

The portion of the 1807 Sir Joseph Banks work, 'The Mire Nymph: a poem addressed to the proprietors of the East, West and Wildmore Fens by Martin Mudlark Tide Waiter' was published in *Sir Joseph Banks, 1743-1820*, by Harold B. Carter, British Museum of Natural History, 1988. The original manuscript is held by the Department of Special Collections, Memorial Library, at the University of Wisconsin-Madison. The punctuation and wording used in this publication is that of the original.

James K. Baxter's poem 'Bushed' was published with the kind permission of the Estate of James K. Baxter. It was published in *Collected Poems: James K. Baxter*, Oxford University Press, 1981.

2004 Dame Christine Cole Catley

The Michael King dedication to C.K. Stead appears in Michael King's *Tread Softly for you Tread on my Life: new and collected writings*, Cape Catley, 2001.

The last verse of A.R.D. Fairburn's 'To a Friend in the Wilderness', is published with the kind permission of Dinah Holman. It appeared in A.R.D. Fairburn, *Three Poems: Dominion, The Voyage & To a Friend in the Wilderness*, New Zealand University Press, 1952.

2005 Nigel Cox

The 2005 festival theme was 'Word of Mouth', and the talk was called 'Before I Went Blind'. This address was subsequently published under this title in *Phone Home Berlin: collected non-fiction*, Victoria University Press, 2007.

2006 Patricia Grace

Segments of this talk were not recorded on the night. These portions and notes from the evening have been included in this publication.

Patricia Grace's 'Moon Story' was subsequently published in *Small Holes in the Silence*, Penguin, Oct. 2006.

2007 Tony Simpson

The 2007 festival theme was 'Food for Thought', and his talk was called 'Salt Beef and the Farmer's Ordinary'.

Tony Simpson reads from *A Distant Feast: the origins of New Zealand cuisine*, Godwit, 1999.

2008 Chris Price

The 2008 festival theme was 'The Word Around Us', and the talk was called 'In Trouble with the Truth'.

In 2021, Chris said of her 2008 address: 'A lot of truths and lies have passed under the bridge since this address was written. At the time of writing, I didn't know that I would spend the next twelve years convening the Poetry and Creative Non-fiction MA Workshop at the Institute of Modern Letters. Today I think a little differently about some aspects of this essay — but my unease about our trouble with the truth in real life has only been strengthened.'

2010 Dame Anne Salmond

The 2010 festival theme was 'Right Word, Right Place, Right Time', and the talk was called 'The Joy of Writing'.

Dame Anne Salmond refers in detail to *Hui: a study of Maori ceremonial gatherings*, A.H. & A.W. Reed, 1975; *Amiria: the life story of a Maori woman*, Amiria Stirling as told to Anne Salmond, Reed, 1976; and *Eruera: the teachings of a Maori elder*, Eruera Stirling as told to Anne Salmond, Oxford University Press, 1980.

2011 Allen Curnow

The lines 'Not I, some child, born in a marvellous year, / Will learn the trick of standing upright here', are from Allen Curnow's poem 'The Skeleton of the Great Moa in the Canterbury Museum, Christchurch.'

Allen Curnow's 'Landfall in Unknown Seas' was published in *Allen Curnow: collected poems*, Allen Curnow, edited by Elizabeth Caffin and Terry Sturm, Auckland University Press, 2017.

Permission to reproduce 'Landfall in Unknown Seas' by Allen Curnow, is courtesy of the copyright owner Tim Curnow, Sydney, and Auckland University Press.

2014 Robert Sullivan

The 2014 festival title 'small islands of meaning' is a quote from the 1941 journal of poet Charles Brasch, the first editor of *Landfall* magazine. The full quote is, 'The only way to save oneself alive in the bewildering formlessness of our time is to draw distinctions, to establish small islands of meaning, and there gradually to build up something well-founded and definite that can defy the chaos.'

The poem 'Great Sea', by Charles Brasch is published with the kind permission of the Charles Brasch Literary Executor, Alan Roddick, and is published in *Selected Poems*, Charles Brasch; chosen by Alan Roddick, Otago University Press, 2015.

'Arohanui' was published in *Puna Wai*

Kōrero: an anthology of Māori poetry in English, edited by Reina Whaitiri and Robert Sullivan, Auckland University Press, 2014.

2015 Stephanie Johnson

To date the poetry of Amanda Tauiwi Reinhardt Carlton has not appeared in print.

Stephanie Johnson reads from *The Writers' Festival*, Vintage, 2015.

2016 Maualaivao Albert Wendt

*Due to the length of some lines in the poem 'Garden 26', the words unable to be accommodated across the page appear in a new line below.

The main body of this address is reproduced courtesy of the Pacific Arts Legacy Project and *The Pantograph Punch*. Omitted sections are transcribed from the Going West Festival audio.

'Garden 26' was published in *From Mānoa to a Ponsonby Garden*, Auckland University Press, 2012.

2017 Rod Oram

This address calls on Rod Oram's book *Three Cities: seeking hope in the Anthropocene*, Bridget Williams Books, 2016.

Permission to quote the last four verses of 'Landfall in Unknown Seas' by Allen Curnow, is courtesy of the copyright owner Tim Curnow, Sydney, and Auckland University Press.

Acknowledgements

Publishing is a new venture for the Going West Trust, and we are grateful to Oratia Media for being our partner. It has been a team effort to bring *Voices of Aotearoa* to you, and in record speed, during these Covid-19 times. Gratitude is extended first and foremost to our Aotearoa orators whose words appear on these pages. For their support and encouragement, we would especially like to acknowledge Ngahuia te Awekotuku, Vincent O'Sullivan, Dame Fiona Kidman, Dame Anne Salmond and Stephanie Johnson.

Thank you to Anna Forsyth for her transcription work, and to the Going West festival whānau, Jan Coats, Gary Henderson and Mark Easterbrook, for their initial read, and to Cameron Mason McCurdy for additional transcription.

We acknowledge our funders: Auckland Council's Waitakere Ranges Local Board; The Trust Community Foundation, which continues a fine tradition of supporting cultural, sporting and community services in West Auckland; and Creative New Zealand for agreeing to a turnaround project once it was clear we would not be having a 2020 in-person festival due to a global pandemic.

We are ever grateful to the staff at Auckland Libraries, Research West, particularly Sue Berman, Raewynn Robertson and Brent Giblin. At the Alexander Turnbull Library, thank you kindly to Audrey Waugh and Mary Skarott, and to Lisa Wettleson at the Special Collections, Memorial Library, University of Wisconsin, Madison.

Thank you to: Harriet Allen at Penguin Random House; the publishers and individuals who supplied portraits; the Auckland Art Gallery Toi o Tāmaki, Caroline McBride and Geoffrey Heath; the Gerrard and Marti Friedlander Charitable Trust and Leonard Bell; and The Pantograph Punch.

For their kind permission to reproduce the works of Allen Curnow, Charles Brasch, A.R.D. Fairburn and James K. Baxter, gratitude is extended to Tim Curnow, Alan Roddick, Dinah Holman and Professor Paul Millar.

And thank you always to our loyal Going West audience.

Photograph Credits

Going West Books and Writers Festival Archives, Auckland Libraries | Ngā Pātaka Korero o Tāmaki Makaurau | Research West. Gil Hanly: p. 20 Ngahuia te Awekotuku (2008); p. 86 Michael King (2003); p. 104 Dame Marilyn Waring (2002); p. 156 Nigel Cox (2005); p. 236 Dame Anne Salmond (2010); p. 272 Charlotte Grimshaw (2013); pp. 302, 310 Stephanie Johnson (2015). Liz March: p. 10 Murray Gray and Naomi McCleary (2015); pp. 24, 288 Robert Sullivan (2014); p. 258 Peter Wells (2012); p. 316 Maualaivao Albert Wendt (2016); p. 338 Paula Morris (2018). Ted Scott: p. 16 Bernard Makoare (1997); p. 32 Maurice Shadbolt (1996); p. 252 Allen Curnow (1997). **Marti Friedlander Archive, E.H. McCormick Research Library, Auckland Art Gallery Toi o Tāmaki, on loan from the Gerrard and Marti Friedlander Charitable Trust, 2002. Reproduction courtesy of Gerrard and Marti Friedlander Charitable Trust.** Marti Friedlander: p. 12 Going West Festival Participants at 'Fit to Print' (1999). **Martin and Jenny Cole.** Martin Cole: p. 144 Dame Christine Cole Catley (2007). **Patricia Grace.** Grant Maiden: p. 170 Patricia Grace (2014). **Dame Fiona Kidman.** Robert Cross: p. 72 Dame Fiona Kidman (2018). **Elizabeth Knox.** Ebony Lamb: p. 352 Elizabeth Knox (2019). **Rod Oram.** Oliver Rosser: p. 326 Rod Oram (2017). **Vincent O'Sullivan and Penguin Random House New Zealand.** Photographer and date not supplied: p. 58 Vincent O'Sullivan. **Turi Park.** Turi Park: p. 118 Geoff Park (2008). **Chris Price.** Robert Cross: p. 202 Chris Price (2006). **Te Radar.** Dean O'Gorman: p. 220 Te Radar (2019). **Tony Simpson.** Photographer and date not supplied: p. 184 Tony Simpson. **Ian Wedde.** M.D. Humayunkabir Huron: p. 40 Ian Wedde (2005).

Published by Oratia Books, Oratia Media Ltd, 783 West Coast Road, Oratia, Auckland 0604, New Zealand (www.oratia.co.nz).

Going West Writers Festival

Copyright © 2021 The Going West Trust
Copyright © 2021 Oratia Books (published work)

The copyright holders assert their moral rights in the work.

This book is copyright. Except for the purposes of fair reviewing, no part of this publication may be reproduced or transmitted in any form or by any means, whether electronic, digital or mechanical, including photocopying, recording, any digital or computerised format, or any information storage and retrieval system, including by any means via the Internet, without permission in writing from the publisher. Infringers of copyright render themselves liable to prosecution.

ISBN 978-0-947506-97-1

The publisher acknowledges the generous support of Creative New Zealand for this publication.

Editorial team
Going West: Robyn Mason, Peter McCurdy, James Littlewood
Oratia Books: Carolyn Lagahetau
Designers: Sarah Elworthy, Marigold Janezic

First published 2021
Printed in China